CHERISH

DAVID CASSIDY

A LEGACY OF LOVE

Edited by Louise Poynton

66 I could have been used – I could have been a product they designed – they would have liked to, but didn't. I couldn't have lived like a puppet. I am not manipulated and I run my affairs. I have to work so many hours a day and that's a form of manipulation, but nobody says do this, wear that, don't say this kid....I'm well beyond that **99**

Record Mirror, February 1972

Published in 2020 by
Unicorn, an imprint of
Unicorn Publishing Group
5 Newburgh Street
London
W1F 7RG
www.unicornpublishing.org

ISBN 978-1-912690-80-0

10 9 8 7 6 5 4 3 2 1

Designed by
www.wheeldesign.co.uk

Printed and bound in
Turkey by Jellyfish

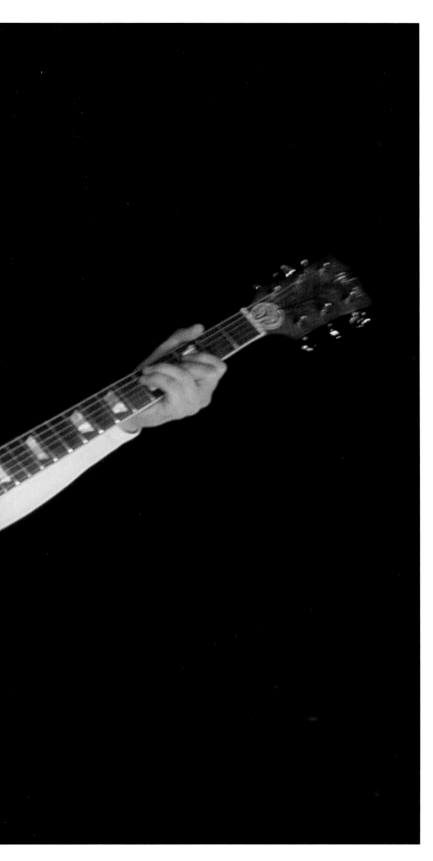

CONTENTS

Front cover: Photo: Henry Diltz/Getty Images
Previous page: Henry Diltz
This page: Photo: Barry Plummer

David Cassidy was a massive part of the 1970s, musically, culturally and emotionally. There was something in his voice, looks and smile. He was so effortlessly a star, a man who captivated a generation, inspired and in many ways, changed everything. His voice was a vocal masterpiece with an unmistakable silky breathy tone that could drip with emotion.

David remains undisputedly one of the greatest male vocalists of all time. He looked beautifully angelic and had a love affair with the camera which caught forever his ethereal beauty, portraying a man who was simultaneously vulnerable, provocative, lustrous and yet palpably real.

David gave more to the 1970s generation of teenagers than can ever be measured. He helped many pre-teens and teenagers find their own identities, uncovering a depth of emotional feeling, unlocking a sense of belonging, of discovery. He was our first real exposure to music, to live concerts, to loving someone. There is something about that connection with our childhood that stays as the years pass.

The stories shared here are a beautiful homage to him remembering the way he made people feel, and how his music as a recording artist and performer was the catalyst for change. He took us to a magical place and belonged to us. He was always there, like a subterranean river. As many admit in these compelling memories, they would never have made it without him. I can't remember a time in my life, just like millions of others, when I wasn't in love with him.

At the height of his fame David was the most popular person on the planet, the highest paid performer with the biggest fan club. His worldwide concerts sold out creating scenes reminiscent of the heyday of The Beatles. His entire persona came at a critical time in many lives, his music more so, inspiring men and women to become musicians, songwriters, actors, and be better people. To someone, somewhere, he was a very significant influence.

These are just some reasons why this book of cherished memories is so important. I first asked fans why he has meant so much before

David announced he was stopping touring. I was overwhelmed at the response which turned into a tsunami of love when he died. Reading these deeply personal stories has been a huge privilege. Visiting many fans to hear their memories and look through memorabilia together has been an emotional journey.

These are the fans' memories which express succinctly how we felt and what he gave us. David lives and breathes across every page with heartfelt emotions in whole epochs. The stories are uplifting, heart-warming and thought-provoking. A tribute to, and representation of, his superstardom, all the lives he touched and how the reverberations of as little as a moment in his presence have been felt for a lifetime.

I was moved to tears reading the unbearable sorrow some went through as teenagers and how David, often unknowingly, helped them cope with life, not just then but many years later. At times I laughed out loud at some of the more amusing memories. I have been deeply moved by the honesty everyone has displayed in opening their hearts about David and their own lives. Some have expressed their feelings in beautiful poetry. He taught us more throughout his life than he could ever have imagined. He often spoke about spreading love and light. There was a considerable amount of love that radiated from and around David during his life, and that will continue forever, proving there is no greater legacy than to love and be loved.

With powerful performances in popular television episodes including *Marcus Welby MD*, *Ironside*, *FBI* and *Bonanza*, David looked poised for a powerful acting career. He auditioned for a new wholesome television sitcom based around a widowed mother and her five children. Cast in *The Partridge Family* as the eldest son, it was a role which projected him into the stratosphere as a teenager's dream.

Taken on as an actor, when it was discovered he could sing, he took over the lead vocals on *The Partridge Family* songs. He often lamented that the role of Keith Partridge, with which he was so closely associated, robbed him of his own identity. His first recording with *The*

Partridge Family, I Think I Love You, remains the purest pop song but no one would ever have guessed the laser beam trajectory of his career, creating a pop phenomenon.

A young man of devastating physical attraction with that quintessential feathered haircut, David's looks may have tended to overshadow his achievements as David Cassidy, of which he seemed most proud. Branching out as a solo performer, giving concerts almost every weekend, live on stage in the 1970s he was a pure rock star, darn good. And he knew it. David's solo work, and especially in the late 1970s, remain some of his most acclaimed work. He continues to arouse curiosity and command attention. It would be interesting to discover what substantial unreleased back catalogue is yet to be heard.

David reinvented himself over the years, appearing in the theatre, on television and in films to considerable acclaim. He was still singing his songs to adoring fans until eight months before his death. We were regularly told he was haunted by his demons, but that never stopped fans from caring over the decades. His health in later years was affected by his long battle with alcohol dependency. David died of organ failure on November 21, 2017. He was 67. A wave of inescapable sadness swept over me. David Cassidy mattered. Very much. The outpouring of grief around the world was like mopping up the ocean with a sponge.

This book is dedicated to everyone who so generously shared their stories. To those whose memories do not appear because there was no room, my deepest thanks to all of you.

To everyone who has shared their memories, including David's friends who worked with him on tour, in the recording studio or in the theatre, and everyone who has spoken with huge respect for him, thank you for being so generous with your time and tributes.

And thank you, David Cassidy. May your legacy shine a light over the world forever.

Louise Poynton, United Kingdom

Photo: Ed Caraeff/Iconic Images

David wows the crowd at the Melbourne Cricket Ground,
March 10, 1974. Photo © Scott Hicks

★ RICHIE FURAY

**Founding member of Buffalo
Springfield, Poco and the
Souther-Hillman-Furay band**

David and I would sit talking, laughing and
crying together in his house. With him I was a
trusted friend, I wasn't someone he needed to
ask: what do you want from me? I would go over
to his house, hang out, we would jam and there
would be no one there, just us. We became good
friends. I always enjoyed his company and liked
him a lot. He felt safe with me at a time when
everybody and his brother were trying to get a
piece of him, the poor guy couldn't go anywhere
in the world. He sang on more than one of my
projects. People look at my career and when they
see David Cassidy listed as a credit on my records,
they wonder....how did that ever happen?

It saddened me to see how life weighed
heavy on him. He did not trust many people.
I allowed him to just be David Cassidy, but I
don't know that he ever reconciled in his own
heart what he accomplished in his life – and
he had every accolade that you could imagine
– or that he fully accepted it deep down.

We met because my wife, Nancy, knew his
housekeeper. We went over to his house one
day and struck up a friendship. He told me how
my bands, Poco and Buffalo Springfield, had
influenced him but after a while we looked at
each other as peers. David would confide in me,
he respected me and what I was doing, and it
was fun. Our time together was about a couple
of years and during that time he was trying to
move away from the teen idol image that had been
created around him. David was a very creative
person but desperately wanted to distance himself
from that image. He wanted to be accepted.

I wanted to give him space and opportunities
to be himself and sing on my projects. He sang
harmonies on a few tracks on my *Dance A Little
Light* album. It would have been nice to have
worked together again. I was trying to build a solo
career at the time, he was doing other things, but

we never spoke about doing something together.

David ran in the line of Frank Sinatra, Elvis
Presley and Ricky Nelson. You can be made to
a certain degree but past that you got to have
something of substance. And David had the
substance. His talent is what carried him – you
could see it. He was an actor, a musician, a singer,
a good-looking kid, but someone other people
could identify with. Here he was on a television
show at a time when people wanted to be in a rock
'n' roll band. I watched Ricky Nelson in *The Ozzie
and Harriet Show* and said I want to do that, so
there are people who were influenced by David.

David actually, to my surprise, credited me
as a co-writer on a song he recorded. He took a
piece of my original song, *For Someone I Love*,
which I recorded with the Souther-Hillman-
Furay Band and put it into a song he wrote,
Love In Bloom. I was very honoured that he felt
so attached to it, and it meant something to
him, but it was a personal song I had written.
Previously, we had both recorded separately
our own version of The Rascals' *Lonely Too
Long*, but never wrote anything together.

I'm sure David had a lot of untapped ideas,
he was a talented guy and very underrated.
From the short time we were together he was
starting to make records that took him away
from the television image, but he was troubled.
The fans would always be there but then there
was the public criticism which comes whenever
you try something new or different. The critics
are not with you because they have already put
you in a box. He was so identified with the
television show he was not allowed to become
who he really was. I think some of that affected
him. I can't even imagine what David must
have gone through – all that he accomplished
and how he was then treated. He was trying to
explain "that person over there is something that
somebody made as me. This is who I really am".

I do wish we had stayed in touch. I couldn't
save him, but I certainly could have been there
to encourage and tell him to just be himself.
I last saw him briefly after a performance in

Joseph and the Amazing Technicolor Dreamcoat in New York in 1983, but it was a fleeting encounter. It left an emptiness in me.

Once our relationship drifted, we didn't see or talk to each other – we moved to Colorado and he was living in California – but I could just sense there was still a struggle going on as if he was asking himself: did I ever accomplish what I felt I wanted to in my life? I don't know that satisfaction ever became a reality in his life. He brought so much happiness to so many people.

David and I did drink a little bit but not to the point where he got to later in life where I believe it was an escape, but how many people do we have to look at and say, this is not an escape it's a dead-end road?

If there had been an opportunity for us to pick up where we left off and share our lives again without any inhibitions, I would have loved to have been there for him. To have been there as the friend to come along and find at that point in time, but we had drifted so far apart I could only read about his life and think despairingly, "oh man, that's my friend I used to hang out with".

When David passed away it was hard for me. There are some people I have been close to. Glenn Frey used to sit on my living room floor in Laurel Canyon and listen to me rehearse Poco. People thought we were the closest of friends, but it wasn't the same connection I had with David. I was there for a time and I hope it was a good time in his life. It was for me.

David at his home in Encino, takes time out from drum practice.
Photo: Ed Caraeff/ Iconic Images

66 DAVID WAS A VERY CREATIVE PERSON....HE WANTED TO BE ACCEPTED. HE WAS A TALENTED GUY AND VERY UNDERRATED 99

NEIL SEDAKA

One of the world's greatest songwriters

I never had the good fortune of meeting David Cassidy, but I was always a fan. He was a charismatic, natural born performer.

David first came to my attention, like he did with many, with the success of *The Partridge Family*. In the pilot episode, one of the songs The Partridges performed was *Let The Good Times In*, a song I had written with Carole Bayer Sager. I was so honored to be part of their history so early on. They would later record an excellent version of *Breaking Up Is Hard To Do*. However, no one can deny just how sensational the record *I Think I Love You* is. The song was everywhere.

At the peak of his success we were living in London and my daughter, Dara, who was a tremendous fan, wanted me to take her to see him in concert. So, I took the family to see him at the infamous White City Stadium show. By the end of the performance, it was complete and total chaos. With the help of security, they escorted us out of the venue and took us to a nearby motel. Little did we know, this is where David was staying. It didn't take long for the fans to find out before they started causing equal commotion at the motel. I could only compare it to the swarms of girls who screamed and chased The Beatles.

David truly deserved all of his success. He solidified his place in music and television history. I'm so sorry to hear that he passed away so young.

RON "BUMBLEFOOT" THAL

Solo artist, producer and former lead guitarist of Guns N' Roses

One of my first glimpses into the music world came from watching David Cassidy on TV in *The Partridge Family*, not long after I began my own songwriting and band experiences at age six. Through decades of twists and turns and the steady patient climb, I'd still draw from my earliest inspirations, never losing the connection to his voice, the songs - many times through the decades to this day I'd be jamming hard rock adaptations of *I Woke Up In Love This Morning* and *I Think I Love You* and others. David Cassidy was a major persona in the journey of musicians in my generation and those before and after, one of the biggest teen idols of our time (who else can say riots broke out after selling out Madison Square Garden in a day?...!). I strongly support any acknowledgment that recognises his musical contributions.

ALAN MERRILL

Songwriter of the first and original 1975 version of *I Love Rock 'n' Roll* with his band, The Arrows

I saw David in concert at Madison Square Garden taking my eight-year-old cousin, Hallie, in 1972. It was a great show. David had the moves and his singing was spot on. Respect!

In 1974 my band, Arrows, had a hit with *A Touch Too Much* which literally fell into our laps. Producer, Mickie Most, offered us the song, written by Mike Chapman and Nicky Chinn, after he had been turned down by David. He was also just saying goodbye to The Partridge Family and had previously turned his nose up at what he called "bubblegum pop". David almost took the bait but then he passed because he doubted its hit potential. My group had only been together a couple of months and this gave us a top 10 hit.

Right: David considered his sell-out concert at Madison Square Garden in 1972 the highlight of his career. *New York Daily News* Archive/ Getty Images

Mum's the word!

Hopalong

PIN-UP PROFILE

DARL DAVID!

A WILD, WILD WELCOME

WHAT a scream! The fans line up to greet the king of crooners. That's him below.

Pictures by Clive Limpkin

Meet the new king of pop

POPMANIA returned to London yesterday because of this man—David Cassidy.

Hysterical scream-agers lined the banks of the Thames as the young heart-throb glided up in his 206-ton luxury yacht.

Two of them even threw themselves into the river in a bid to swim to him.

For Cassidy, pop singer, actor,

TV star and rich man, is the idol who has put the throat gargle back in the bathrooms of the world's teenagers.

Not since those frenzied days of the Monkees and the Beatles has a pop singer evoked such tearful worship.

In America no young bedroom is complete without his picture. And in London yesterday it was obvious that Cassidy fever is now epidemic here.

BYE BYE...

WHAT FUR?

YOUR DAILY MALE
David's heading for top!

THIS is the 22-year-old bed-
room-wall heartthrob of a
million British and American
teenagers.

David Cassidy, with his brown
hair, hazel eyes and winning
smile, looks like the kid next
door.

But he is one of the richest
young superstars. Only Tom
Jones outrivals him.

David, due in Britain any
day for his first tour, lives in
Los Angeles.

Exclusive offer to New Reveille readers

IN FOUR INSTALMENTS

1

DARLIN' DAVID

SUZANNE LAURENCE – AUSTRALIA

My love for David Cassidy started the first time I ever saw his face. It was 1970 and *The Partridge Family* had just started on TV and I was absolutely mesmerized by this beautiful person. I would tape the shows so I could listen to his voice. The sound of his voice on the radio singing his hit song *I Think I Love You* would simply take me to another place than the one I was living in and brighten up my day. Although I didn't know David, those times got me through very lonely days in my youth. I would spend hours in my room listening to my records playing his songs over and over and drawing pictures of him. When I read in a teen magazine that his birthday was the 12th of April the same as mine, I felt a real connection to him.

In 1974 the thrill of my life happened, David was coming to Sydney, for a concert at Randwick Racecourse as part of his world tour. I was so happy, and my two girlfriends bought tickets for us all to go. They knew how much I loved him and encouraged me to do a drawing to welcome him and to hold up in the crowd on the day.

So here it was: Saturday, March 2, it was such a lovely sunny day. We started out very early to make sure that we would be there at the gates when it opened so we could get a good spot close to the front of the stage. As we were waiting a crowd was starting to build, a taxi pulled up with some costumes in the back and a guy got out. One of my friends told me go and ask if he would give my drawing to David which I did. He then asked me if I could help him through the gates with the costumes as the taxi was not allowed to go any further as the stage was still being set up. I was introduced to some of the band and even got a kiss on the cheek from a couple of them. The guy thanked me for helping him and promised me that David would receive my drawing. I remembered the feeling of David bounding onto the stage and seeing him so close up it was such a surreal day for me, I just didn't want it to end. The memory of the day will be with me always.

On the Monday after the concert my mother received a phone call from Harry M. Miller's office [concert promoter] asking me to come down to the office as David had specifically asked that the drawing be returned to me. That he had autographed it was very surreal. I cried to think he had actually looked at it and taken the time to autograph it. I kept reading over and over what he had written and couldn't believe that it had actually been passed on to

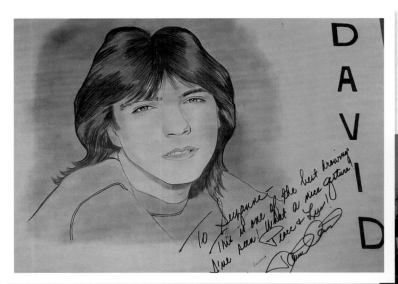

Left: David's personal hand-written message to Suzanne Laurence on her 1974 drawing

Below: Suzanne Laurence's drawing signed by David now displayed in her home

him. I had never felt very important growing up, but this made me feel so special that David had actually taken the time to acknowledge it. David had also left some memorabilia for me to pick up. I read that the day of the concert he didn't want to hang around after to sign any autographs he just wanted to go after it finished, so I feel very blessed that he signed my picture.

The years rolled on, I never forgot that day, and then on November 16, 2002 my daughter surprised me taking me to the Sydney Entertainment Centre to see David once again. I took with me the drawing and was lucky enough to be at the front of the stage. David saw me holding the picture, walked over as he was singing, touched my hand and said softly, "thank you".

A few years ago, I was involved in a really bad car accident and was in hospital for six weeks and off work for a year. I couldn't do very much at all. A friend gave me a book to read that she had found in a little second-hand store, *David Cassidy, My Story*. It took my mind off my pain. Once again, this beautiful man was there

again helping me through another dark time in my life. This is what David has meant to me and how he touched my life. Although I never knew him personally, he was very special to me. The day the world lost David we lost such a beautiful soul. Rest well with the angels, David and know you are loved and missed.

Below: Yasmin Wendling's treasured message from David

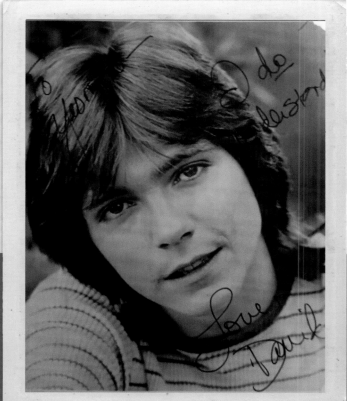

YASMIN WENDLING – UNITED STATES

I was 12 years old and falling madly in love. Like I knew what love was, right? Now, I know it was real, because I still feel the same way about David today. I would never have thought that sitting down and watching the first episode of *The Partridge Family* on September 25, 1970 would shape my whole life. I bought all those teen mags, tore out all the pictures in color and taped them strategically on my bedroom wall. I read every article.

One day in April 1971, I bought a list of addresses and phone numbers of Hollywood celebrities. It had a list of all the studios, producers, etc so I called the first one "Columbia Ranch". A lady answered the phone and I asked for David. Guess what? David came to the phone! Yes, he did. I cried my eyes out, telling him he doesn't understand being 12 years old and living 3,000 miles away that I cannot see him. He was so sweet and kind. He told me, "I do

understand". He asked for my address, but I was so caught up in the conversation I had no idea it was to send me anything.

I called my best friend Frances DePace to tell her. I told everyone. I was so on Cloud Nine. I felt like I was in Heaven. After a week or so, I realized that the majority of my friends were not so excited for me, or at least I didn't feel they were. The next day I received a big manila envelope in the mail. Inside was a black and white photo of DC. He signed it, "To Yasmin, I do understand!"

No one could imagine how fast my heart was beating. I was happy just talking with him. And of course, now I ran all over town showing everyone this autographed picture.

Anna-Maria Ottengren in
her teenage bedroom

ANNA MARIA OTTENGREN – SWEDEN

I was born in 1960 in Sweden. *The Partridge Family* was never shown in my country, so I guess I learned to know David a bit later than the rest of the world. In the summer of 1973, I was traveling to the USA to visit my mother's sister who lived in New York City. I travelled with my grandmother and another of my mother's sisters. It was a wonderful trip in many ways, my first journey abroad and without any parents. I was 13 years old.

We went to a large department store, Macy's, and there he was: the most beautiful boy I had ever seen, hanging on a poster but so alive for me. Long brown hair, deep handsome eyes and that gorgeous smile. I fell in love instantly and did I buy the poster? Oh yes, of course I did!

It was a full-size picture of David from feet to the top of his head. He was wearing a spotted shirt and jeans standing with his arms crossed over his chest and I felt he was smiling just for me. I also watched a couple of episodes of *The Partridge Family* before I went home which gave me more chills, it wasn't just his looks, he could sing too! I went back to the store and bought the *Cherish* album and brought it with me home.

Back in Sweden I start collecting more posters of David and started to dress the walls in my room. I saw him in concert once, in May 1974 in my hometown Gothenburg. Years went by and today, though I am much older, I am still sure that David is the best-looking guy I have ever seen. I still love his songs and I appreciate his voice even more now. Unforgettable memories!

> ## " THERE HE WAS: THE MOST BEAUTIFUL BOY I HAD EVER SEEN "

CONNIE ROSE – UNITED STATES

In 1971, I was 9 years old and living in Los Angeles. One day, I was walking home from school when my friend, Carrie, came running up behind me completely breathless. She told me she had just bought David Cassidy's phone number from a guy hanging outside of our school for $50. I asked her where she got that kind of money. She said that she took it from her mother's wallet earlier that morning. Apparently, this guy was at the school the day before claiming he had David Cassidy's personal phone number. Carrie was a HUGE fan of David's and would do ANYTHING to talk to him. So, taking money from her mom was a risk she was willing to take!

But, now that she actually has the number, she was just too nervous to talk to him, and didn't know what to say. She literally couldn't even pick up the receiver. She asked if I would dial the number, and once I got David on the line then, she would talk to him.

So, a little back story on me….at the time, my fave was Bobby Sherman, and David didn't really do that much for me. I literally had zero trepidation dialling that number. So…..I dialled. It rang, and someone answered asking who I wanted to speak to. In the most mature voice I could muster (remember I'm 9), I said, "David Cassidy, please". This went on a couple more times. People answering, and me saying the same thing. Then, all of the sudden, I heard the nicest male voice say, "Hello." I said, "Yes, I need to speak to David Cassidy". He said, "Speaking." OMG!!!! I nearly dropped the phone!!

I immediately handed the receiver to Carrie. I'm like, IT'S HIM!!! It's David Cassidy! But she couldn't talk to him. She was too nervous and asked me to talk to him. I told him that I thought he had a good voice, and I really liked his hair. I also told him I was a HUGE fan of Bobby Sherman, and it would be really cool if he was on his show. David told me that Bobby was actually going to be on the show in a few weeks and they were going to sing a song. That was actually true, and once I saw that episode, I became a HUGE David Cassidy fan for life!

He did ask me how I came to get his phone number, and I told him what my friend had done. A lot of young girls were making phone calls to that number. David finally wanted to talk to one of us to find out how we got the number. And I was the lucky one he chose! He asked that we destroy the paper with his number and not give it to anyone else. Of course, we did what he asked. We just thought it was the right thing to do. I mean, it was David Cassidy!!! And yeah, I talked to him when I was 9 years old, and he was REALLY nice to me, and I have loved him ever since. I loved when he was on the TV show *Police Story*. Oh, my goodness that was such a great movie and show. He was amazing.

SALLY NEWMAN – UNITED STATES

David came to the opening of a department store, White Front in Bakersfield, California, November 7, 1970. I had just started a scrapbook of him and took it with me to show him. He was just getting popular as *The Partridge Family* had been on a couple months and *I Think I Love You* had just reached number one on the charts. He was truly surprised that anyone would do this for him. After he signed my book, he got up and kissed me on the cheek. I thought I was going to faint! I felt like the luckiest 14-year-old girl in the world! I will never forget that special day as long as I live.

Afterwards, I wrote a tribute to him and

Left: David reads Sally Newman's scrapbook

Below from left: Sally still has the scrapbook David signed

Inside Sally's scrapbook of the day she received a kiss from David

Sally's tribute to David published in *Tiger Beat* magazine

sent it to *Tiger Beat* magazine. I had NO idea they would publish it. I just happened to get the magazine and there it was!

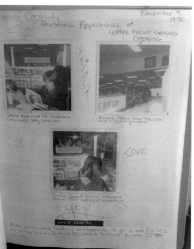

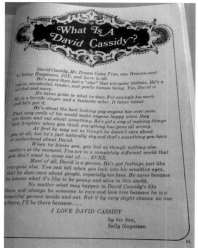

LIZ TILEY – UNITED KINGDOM

When David came to the UK in 1974 on the final leg of his World Tour, I wanted to make something to remind him of our country and see what it was like, as he would not have time to visit everywhere. I came up with the idea of asking other fans to send me postcards of where they lived. My request was published as a letter in *The Official David Cassidy Magazine* and I had a wonderful response with postcards from around the country. I put them in a scrapbook and sent them to him through his fan club. Months later I was shocked to receive a signed photograph in the post "To Liz, Smile!

David Cassidy" and that really made me smile.

When I was 15, I ran a small fan club, the David Cassidy Lovers Club, with a few hundred members. Where did we get all that information from back then? I seem to remember lots of phone calls, the Vice President lived in Wales and the 'helper/typist' in Liverpool. My Mum would type the early newsletters for me.

We ran competitions, collected used stamps for charity, had a penpal file, compiled books for David's birthdays, recorded messages for him on cassette tapes, sent him Christmas cards. I must have sent him something about what I was doing as I received another photo signed: "To Liz and the Club. Happy 1975" I really do cherish them.

I used to chase him round London going from one TV studio/recording studio and radio station to another with other girls. When I read about how he had to hide himself away because we all wanted a bit of him, I did feel I was in some way to blame because he had to live the way he did. It was a really big deal for him to visit the UK as he lived so far away, and the excitement of seeing him was too much.

When David was flying home from one visit out of Heathrow, his plane was parked not far from the Queens Building where thousands of us gathered

Below left: Liz Tiley's cherished possessions include personal messages from David after she sent him a scrapbook of postcards from fans in the UK.

Below right: Liz Tiley, today, with some of her memorabilia

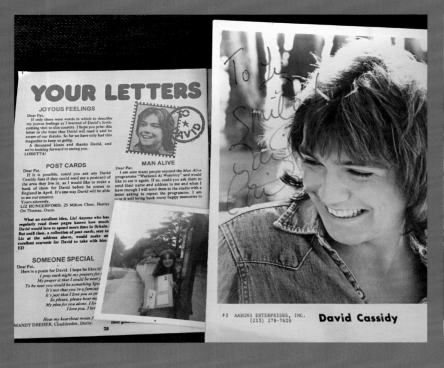

to wave goodbye. Another fan and I found a door out of the building and ran towards the plane. The police stopped us, and I was cautioned. Dad had to come and collect me from the police station.

There was one day in London (1975) when I was with a few other girls at the RCA offices. The security guard said David would be along soon, and we could stay. David was a passenger in the back seat and seemed a bit nervous to see us there but wound the window down and the other girls said they loved his new haircut. He said, "oh thank you".

I had been to one of his Wembley concerts and White City by then, and in 1985 saw him at the Royal Albert Hall. I was lucky enough to see him in *Time* but I didn't see him live again until 2002 making up for the lost years going to concerts across the country every time he visited the UK. I met him at a book signing in Oxford Street which was a really fun day, the fan gathering on the Isle of Wight in 2008 and his Hammersmith

birthday party.

When it was my turn to meet him on the Isle of Wight, I was actually shaking. I had no idea what I was going to talk about. The first thing that came into my head was that I used to work for British Caledonian Airlines in the 1980s. He asked if he was ever on one of my flights. I said, "Sadly no", but it was a talking point. I could not believe I was actually having a conversation with

Top: David shouts it out with a megaphone how much he loves his fans, at Heathrow, 1972. Photo: *Express*/Getty Images
Above: Liz Tiley in 1973

him. I took with me a picture I had taken the year before in concert, and he signed that for me, and I wrote my one and only poem before the trip which summed up how I felt.

We probably never appreciated how great our passion could be. He was so perfect, and I really did love him. That feeling in my stomach when I heard he had died, was simply awful, like losing a very dear member of my family. The love never faded over the years. It was escapism to go to your room and play his music. I find it so sad how things ended up. He made so many of us happy. I look through my memorabilia and I smile. I feel a teenager again.

It almost seems fanatical rather than being a fan when I look back now though. He took over my life for a while, bit over the top? I wouldn't change any of it though, so pleased he was in our lives.

Above: David sent a signed photograph after Liz wrote telling him about the fan club

Right and below: Lovers Club Newsletters sent out to members

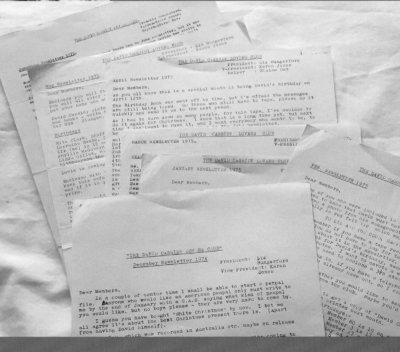

> ❝ I USED TO CHASE HIM ROUND LONDON GOING FROM ONE TV STUDIO/RECORDING STUDIO AND RADIO STATION TO ANOTHER ❞

NANCY KELLYWHITE – CLEVELAND, OHIO

When my girlfriend, Yolanda Martin, first found out that David Cassidy would be in the Christmas parade in downtown Cleveland, Ohio, November 27, 1970, we were so excited. We made plans to get up early, hop on the bus and find out where he was staying. The first hotel we walked in and there he was. We walked over and asked if we could get a picture with him. We were 16, nervous and scared. We could not believe we were standing next to him. It was awesome. He was so handsome and was very nice to us.

When we went to go outside there was a mob of screaming girls. He got into a car and was gone. We ended up going home. It was cold and hard to get past the screaming girls, but we didn't care 'cause we stood next to him.

Left to right: Nancy Kellywhite with David and his co-stars on *The Partridge Family*, Susan Dey and Danny Bonaduce; David captured by Nancy; Yolanda Martin with David, Susan and Danny; David and Yolanda; David and Nancy

SHARON INFANTE – UNITED STATES

I was in third grade and given tickets to go with my family to a David Cassidy concert at the Nassau Coliseum on June 10, 1972. I met two friends waiting in an alcove to go back and meet him. I joined them before there was a rush of photographers and people telling us "let's go and hurry". I went with them not sure if they said to. The next thing I know they knocked on the dressing room door and DC comes out. He was doing lots of funky mouth exercises, what appeared to be mouth warmup stretches and the picture was taken. My two classmates were positioned on either side and I'm next to one of them, David's right hand on my left shoulder. He gave all three of us a kiss on the cheek. I still love the feeling in the gut, heart and mind of this moment.

ROB PREUSS – CANADA

Rob Preuss is a Canadian musician and played keyboards with bands, Spoons and Honeymoon Suite. He was associate musical director of the Broadway production, *Mamma Mia!* He coached Oscar-winning actor, Rami Malek, on his piano work in the Queen biopic *Bohemian Rhapsody*.

The Partridge Family changed my life when I was 5 years old. At the time I hadn't started playing piano, but I think that from watching the show I already began to sense a kind of magic in playing pop music and sharing it with other people. The first episode of *The Partridge Family* aired on September 25, 1970, the day after I turned five. Friday night, my parents, my sister and I would gather in our rec room to watch the show. The musical element of The Partridges was what I really fell in love with, as I was already listening avidly to the Top 40 on our local radio station, CKOC in Hamilton, Ontario. David Cassidy quickly became my idol and hero, along with the rest of his TV family.

One of the first record albums I ever owned as a child was the first Partridge Family record. When I see that first album cover, it transports me back to my very earliest memories of sitting in front of a record player, listening to those songs.

In school, when I was in Grade 1 or 2, on the back of every paper I wrote, I perfected my drawing of *The Partridge Family* performing on stage. I also made little cut out dioramas of the family, which I created inside empty cardboard banker boxes. I made my first scrapbook in the summer of 1971. My cousin Cornelia was visiting from Germany. She was 16 and in love with David. At some point in that summer I 'borrowed' a few of her magazines and cut out all my favourite pictures of David and the Partridges to include in my scrapbook. I also had a huge black and white poster of David on my bedroom wall. I remember feeling so proud that I had a photo of him in my room. It felt like my personal connection to the guy I saw each week on TV.

Many years later, when I was in my early teens, the posters of David hanging on my wall had evolved into posters of Farrah Fawcett, KiSS, Queen and Elton John. I remember taking my David Cassidy poster out of my closet, where it had been rolled up for a few years, and hung it in the garage where school friends and myself threw darts at it. Looking back, I suppose I was trying to destroy my childish musical self in order to discover a new me, trying to grow up and into a more mature musical sensibility, even though I was still only about 12 or 13!

Elton John's song, *I'm Gonna Be A Teenage Idol* was the song that kept running through my head when David died. When I was a kid and discovered Elton, after already loving The Partridge Family, his album, *Don't Shoot Me, I'm Only The Piano Player* was a perfect transition to a new pop world for me and my dreams of playing music. I joined my first rock band when I was 10, and I still think it was possibly because

66 DON'T LET YOUR CHILDHOOD LEAVE YOU, BECAUSE IT NEVER DID 99

David at home. Photo: Roger Morton

of the inspiration I felt from seeing *The Partridge Family* on TV each week, combined with my love of listening to the radio, along with my formal piano lessons which began at age 5.

Many years later when I rediscovered the music I fell in love with in my early childhood, I immediately recognized the deep connection I still had with the sound of The Partridge Family recordings. They were embedded into my memory as precisely as any other early memory. Listening to them, I am instantly transported back to that time when I was hearing things I had never heard before, and they still sound brand new to me.

Our connections to our childhood are stronger than we realize. I love discovering new music too, but our roots really are anchored in our first experiences. For me, I move on and don't look back, but when I do, I realize that these influences have never left me, and as time goes on, I'm happier to welcome them back, like a long-lost friend.

Also, for me, since I keep getting reminded of who I 'was' and what I did, it kind of makes it more exciting to recognize how time moves on, while something essential remains. Same as it ever was. Now I'm reaching far back into my memory banks to understand why I'm so sad about the death of David Cassidy. I think that losing a piece of my childhood makes me want to hold onto it all even tighter, and makes me realize how important it still is, and how it never left. It's right here. I'm still here. That kid.

Don't let your childhood leave you, because it never did.

Above: Rob Preuss' drawing as a 5-year-old of The Partridge Family

Right: The scrapbook he made, aged 5

BERIT LIKA OTTOSEN – DENMARK

I first found David when I saw a poster of a nice-looking guy on a horse, so I had the poster for a while without knowing who he was. At school I did a lot of drawings, and liked to draw from pictures of David. My favourite is the one I did when I was 14, of him with his favourite horse, Apollo: the nice guy on a horse. I am a great lover of music and worked in record stores in Denmark from 1976 to 2000. For my confirmation in 1974 I got a guitar and songbook of *Cherish* and *Rock Me Baby*. *The Partridge Family* was never seen on television in Denmark and I first saw episodes in 2000 when I was diagnosed with breast cancer. I only saw David live once when he gave a fantastic concert in Denmark in 1974.

Left: David by Berit Lika Ottosen

Above: Concert ticket from David's only appearance in Denmark, 1974

NICOLA HILLARY – UNITED KINGDOM

I can't remember exactly how I discovered David as *The Partridge Family* wasn't really well known over here. I think it may have been during a TV interview and I was like "Oh my God who is this fantastic guy?" From this moment on I was love-struck. I immediately bought the vinyl of *Cherish* and joined his fan club. I then tried to find out everything about David. As we lived close to Heathrow at the time, I found out when he was arriving and leaving the country and managed to persuade my dad to take me to the Queens Building a few times. In those days the roof was open to the public and gave a good view of the runways. I just remember being scared at all the pushing as he appeared running on the tarmac and then the deafening noise of all the screaming. It was literally ear-splitting.

I got tickets to the Wembley concert in March 1973 for me and my friend and again the one thing I remember is the hysteria and deafening screams from all the thousands of girls. I don't think we could even hear what David was singing but it really didn't matter as we were in the same realm of the universe as him.

Over the next few years I dreamed and breathed David but by the time he retired I had moved on to real life boyfriends and, when he married Kay, I forgot about him for a bit. I also lost most of my memorabilia over the years which is sad, except for a few treasures which I still have. As an adult I started to appreciate his music again and watched his life evolve with interest. I kind of thought that he would always be around so when I heard that he had dementia it really got to me as my ex-husband had also been diagnosed at the age of 60 so I felt a pull towards David again.

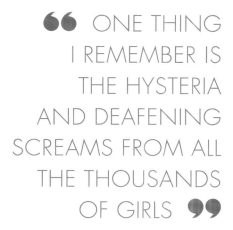

> **ONE THING I REMEMBER IS THE HYSTERIA AND DEAFENING SCREAMS FROM ALL THE THOUSANDS OF GIRLS**

When I learnt of his admittance to hospital with organ failure and subsequent passing I was devastated. I don't think I realised until then just what an impact my feelings for him had meant to me. The feeling that I had actually lost a family member and I still feel close to tears when I realise that he has actually gone forever; the finality of it.

David really helped me in the early 70s as my mother was dying of breast cancer and I was able to channel some of my feelings of grief into loving David. Listening to his beautiful voice and gazing into his beautiful eyes helped me to forget what was happening at home and for this I will always be extremely grateful to him.

Above: Nicola Hillary with her Wembley 1973 concert programme

Right: Nicola would visit Heathrow to see David, here waving to his fans.
Photo: Roger Morton

Opposite: David in concert, 1973.
Photo: Barry Plummer

MICHELLE SABAU – MELBOURNE, AUSTRALIA

The date of Saturday, March 2, 1974, Randwick Racecourse, Sydney, Australia, will forever be burnt into my brain and my heart. I was two months off being 13 years old. Just down the road from where I lived in Paddington, my heart-throb and (in my mind) my future husband, David Cassidy, was performing live in concert. My girlfriend who lived at Bondi Beach and I had saved to buy tickets and we were so excited. I remember exactly what I wore to his concert: a pair of white flairs with a pale pink and white checked smock top.

We were pretty close to the front of the stage and the heat of the sun and excitement was getting to me. People were screaming, pushing and shoving and that, combined with the temperature, had obviously taken its toll on me as I began to feel quite faint. My friend and I started to become separated amidst the crowd of hysterical girls. I remember hearing the MC say into the microphone, "And here he is, the man you've all been waiting for......DAVID CASSIDY".

As the screams intensified, I saw David run out on stage and nearly trip up on the leads.

My head went faint and my body slumped forward. I was 'body surfed' towards the front of the stage where security lifted me up onto the stage. I opened my eyes to see David standing and singing right beside me and I reached out to grab him. In the crowd my girlfriend was looking around for me when she heard David through the mic say "whoooaaa". She looked up to see ME grabbing HIM by his overalls!

I was taken below stage, and attended to by St John's Ambulance staff. They wanted to take me to hospital, but I begged them to let me stay. I heard security several times telling the crowd to back away from the stage as they feared it would collapse.

Due to safety concerns, myself and several other girls were moved to a different area. I was absolutely devastated and crying to see David. Someone came around and said that David would come and visit us after the show, that was all that kept me from breaking free and returning to the concert. Oh wow, the thought of meeting David personally made missing the concert a bit easier to bear.

David didn't come and visit, and I was left feeling absolutely gutted. Not only didn't he visit, I missed the entire show, became separated from my girlfriend, got into trouble for being late home and for being on my own. The next morning to my Dad's horror, he picked up his copy of the *Sydney Morning Herald* only to see me plastered on the front page! He confirmed this by comparing it with the clothes I had worn that were now laying beside my bed, that and confirmation from my friend that she had in fact seen me carried across the stage.

My only wish was to have met David. What a guy.

Michelle made the front page

Left: Michelle Sabau is pulled from the crowd at Randwick Racecourse with David just behind her. From a private collection owned by Jim Salamanis

Below: David on stage at his Sydney concert. From a private collection owned by Jim Salamanis

CYNTHIA THOMAS MILLS – UNITED STATES

I was 7 years old when I fell in love with David Cassidy. I first saw him on *The Partridge Family* on September 25,1970, always thought he was the coolest and like most little girls I would dream of meeting him and marrying him. He was all over my bedroom walls, I loved his eyes, his smile, his shiny silky dark hair, his breathy soft-spoken voice, and his sexy stance when singing and playing his guitar. All those things a little girl can easily fall in love with.

He was a very special part of my childhood, and the day he passed away my childhood went with him. David always made me so happy watching him on *The Partridge Family*. He is my heart, and no one will ever take his place.

The Partridge Family was always a great family night. Every Friday, daddy always made the popcorn and I was always glued to the TV and daddy would always wave his hand in my face to get my attention. My brother always loved making me cry by teasing me saying things like "He can't even sing" or "He looks like a girl" or throwing darts at my pin-ups and posters on my bedroom walls.

I never had the pleasure of meeting him or seeing him live, but I did come close when he came to Detroit, Michigan on June 25,1972. Mommy and Daddy had already made vacation plans to go camping. I remember crying SO hard and begging the whole three-hour drive "Please, I want to see my David Cassidy". They really wanted to take me and felt bad and promised me next time, if and when, he returned. My uncle sat me on his lap and told me that my David Cassidy wouldn't want me to be so upset and he would want me to enjoy my vacation with my family.

I will always LOVE David and I will always do my part to support him in preserving his legacy. He was a great performer/actor and he never received the recognition he deserves.

As an adult it's so heart-warming knowing that the love I saw in his eyes as a little girl was real. David was a loving man with a huge heart and beautiful soul. He never judged others and he always believed in being positive and loving one another, not bickering and always being there for each other. And that's how I will always remember him.

He is always with us. 'Could It Be Forever?' You bet it can. It's never goodbye.

66 HE WAS THE COOLEST AND LIKE MOST LITTLE GIRLS I WOULD DREAM OF MEETING HIM AND MARRYING HIM 99

LISA LONDON – UNITED STATES

When I was 12 years old my father, the celebrated television director Jerry London, directed a number of episodes of *The Partridge Family*. When I found out that my dad was going to direct the show, I was so excited. "Why?" you might ask. Because like every teenage girl in America, I had a huge crush on David Cassidy.

David Cassidy was every teenage girl's dream. He sang, played guitar and he was so "hot". When he would sing, *I Think I Love You*, I would swoon and pretend that he was singing just to me. I had posters of David on my walls in my room and would play his songs over and over. I loved watching the weekly episodes of *The Partridge Family* and couldn't wait for the next episode the following week.

Needless to say, when the opportunity arose to meet David I was so excited, I almost fainted. When I asked my dad if I could come visit him on the set while he was directing, he said, "of course".

My father, who worked with lots of movie stars and Academy Award winners in his career, couldn't believe what

a fan base David had. I mean, his teenage daughter was jumping up and down like a wild person and my dad said, "Lisa, he is an actor playing a role in a television show." Just an actor?! That was the silliest statement ever because David was my generation's Shawn Mendes or Justin Bieber. Fans would come from near and far to see David perform.

When I told my best girlfriends that I was going to the set of *The Partridge Family*, they asked if they could come with me. So, my friends all got to meet David Cassidy, which was probably one of the most exciting days in their teenage lives.

I remember the day we all met David, he was very sweet and charming. He took pictures with us. He chatted briefly and off he went to continue filming the scenes for the day. I remember being so nervous that I was meeting my idol that I didn't say very much.

When the day was over after we got to watch them film the day's scenes, we all went home feeling excited that we had experienced a special moment in time. The memory of us meeting David Cassidy would be imbedded in our souls for the rest of our lives.

Left: Lisa London and her brother Todd sit either side of David, with friends on *The Partridge Family* set. Photo courtesy of Jerry London

In the 1970s when snail mail was the only way to link up with other fans around the world, endless hours would be spent handwriting letters to pen pals – the era's equivalent to Facebook. Lives were enriched by teenagers in a sleepy village exchanging letters with another teen who lived in a vibrant city anywhere from Perth in Australia to California in the United States. In addition to swopping magazines and photographs, fans would also come up with ways to show and share their love for David. These included the formation of fan clubs where booklets of love were sent around the globe among the membership. There was also an International David Cassidy Chain Game which started in Greece. Fans also gathered pictures, letters and poems to send to David in a Book of Love.

Images courtesy of Jim Salamanis

PETER K. ACKERMAN – UNITED STATES

Going to the film studio was always a fun event for me. Whether it was to visit the sets of my dad's, Executive Producer Harry Ackerman, shows *Bewitched* or *The Flying Nun*, or something my mother, actress Elinor Donahue, was on, it was always an event. By the time I reached middle school, around seventh grade, I realized what a treat it was for others who got to join me occasionally.

One of those was my friend, Phil, and on this particular day we went to Paramount where my dad was currently employed. Part of what my dad did there was to oversee certain shows produced by Columbia Television aka Screen Gems. The show he oversaw at the time was *The Partridge Family*.

My Paramount excursions with Phil, Paul, or Mike usually contained the same fun. We would explore the Western part of the lot. Inside the saloon was a giant telephone, made of wood that was used in every, or any, show where the character shrank. The inner area of the saloon was where it was kept. We would also visit the Gun Shop and look at all the weapons available for use on a show or film. And then, of course, we would visit the sets of the shows we watched: *Happy Days* and *The Partridge Family*.

The latter set was one I visited many times. This time with my classmate Phil was a special one. Phil and I watched a scene filmed and while the crew was moving to another set on the stage, and perhaps a bit bored with the repetitive dialogue we suffered watching the same scene filmed over and over, we just hung around in front of an unused set. David Cassidy walked onto it with a guitar and beckoned us over.

"Hi, how are you doing?" he asked.

After introducing ourselves, and mentioning who my father was, David continued strumming his guitar. I think he asked us if we played any instruments; he continued to strum and make small talk with us. He said, "I am working on a song," and he played a little bit of it for us. Sadly, my mind did not trap that moment. I have no idea what song it was, or if it even ever got recorded. Having been on a lot of sets I knew to be careful about approaching working folk, including the actors, and this was the first time where one invited me into his moment.

Later in life I went into the administrative side of various television shows, before becoming an ordained priest in the Episcopal Church. Yet, I always have that memory of him. A guy so comfortable in his skin, and stardom, that he was okay inviting a couple of 12-year olds over to talk and listen to his work.

When he tragically died, I felt a deeper connection with him than ever before. I became sober a few years before his demise and understand what a struggle he faced in life. Hopefully his soul soars in a place buoyed by the goodness he brought to those around him. That includes two young pre-teens for whom David invited to hang with him.

66 HE SAID, "I AM WORKING ON A SONG," AND HE PLAYED A LITTLE BIT OF IT FOR US **99**

DON KRISCHANO – UNITED STATES

I met David back in the summer of 1974. I had run away from home with not much knowledge of what was ahead of me. I drove from Seattle to LA straight through for 24 hours. I hit the exit to Hollywood and found a Holiday Inn on Hollywood Blvd to rest my weary body. I walked into my room and crashed on the bed without even taking my clothes off.

Next morning, I went to look for the person I was due to meet, but turned out he left LA before I got there, but I hooked up with another guy. He did not know me but let me sleep in his studio apartment in Pacific Palisades. I soon found myself work, a job in the valley at Chicago Pizza Works where I met a guy who just happened to live across the road from me at my new apartment and was often in teen magazines *16* and *Tiger Beat*. He knew David through the magazine shoots he did, and one night we got talking.

He called David and we went over the following afternoon to his place which was in the hills. It was gated and he had his metal trash cans out at the bottom of the gate with "DC" spray painted in red on them. I didn't want to be one of those "autograph" fans and tried to just keep things on a cool level to not make him feel uncomfortable. He played his guitar, we had tea, and all just hung out. It was a really nice time.

David liked me, I think, because I didn't treat him like an idol so to speak, and I like to think he respected that. I left my number not expecting anything, but he called me.

I went over one afternoon and he wanted to eat so we went for lunch to the Hamburger Hamlet on Sunset. He didn't want to drive his Vette so asked if we could drive my 74 Pinto. It was his idea, as he didn't think people would think twice looking at my car............he was right, but people did try and approach him at the burger joint.

He was a great guy, I felt sorry for him not being able to live a normal life.

Don Krischano
October 4 1958 – May 11 2019

> **DAVID LIKED ME, I THINK, BECAUSE I DIDN'T TREAT HIM LIKE AN IDOL SO TO SPEAK**

MARTHA KELLEY MANKO – UNITED STATES

David's death left a hole in our hearts. When I heard the bad news it not only broke my heart once but twice because I had pictures of David in concert at the CYC in Scranton, Pennsylvania (1972). They were thrown out by my family when my father passed away in 2014.

It ripped my heart to pieces but that won't stop the wonderful times that I had enjoying his music, kissing his poster and album covers and watching *The Partridge Family*, which I still do today. It keeps me smiling. Our local newspaper covered his concert. It makes me cry just looking at things like that, but I will never forget you David. You are in my heart and in my soul. No one and nothing can take the memories that I have in my head and my heart. Tangible things can be replaced, but the feelings and love that I felt growing up as a teenager in the 70s for David, will never go away. Thank you, David for you were a part of my life growing up and I will never forget you as long as I live. Thank you for being you.

LORETTA UEBEL –
UNITED STATES

I don't recall what I was doing the first time I heard David sing, but I remember it stopped me in my tracks. I'd had four years of vocal training in school and knew a great voice when I heard it. I was a naïve 14-year-old, but I saw kindness and inner beauty in his lovely hazel eyes. I was very drawn to that because I needed more of both in my life for so many reasons. I have a physical disability which, ironically, hindered me more socially than it did physically. My peers seemed to take delight in teasing me. I was taught to ignore them and pity their ignorance rather than feel sorry for myself. Ignoring them worked, but it made for a lonely existence.

In that spring of 1970, my youngest brother was born. I had already been doing most of the household chores for at least a year, so it was a given that I would take care of the baby and my 6-year-old brother when my mom returned to work. In hindsight that's a great deal of responsibility for a 13-year-old to bear.

No wonder I took such joy in listening to David sing, watching him on TV and looking at pictures of him. His voice comforted me and made doing my work so much easier. I saw him as a true friend who would never turn on me. He was always my safe place in a tumultuous world.

I saved my money and asked mom to go buy me a ticket for David's concert at the Cincinnati Gardens in 1971. When she managed to get me a coveted floor seat I was absolutely thrilled.

Being at the concert was very exciting, but I couldn't understand why almost everyone chose to scream instead of listen. I couldn't see much of David because everyone kept standing on their chairs. At the end of each song David would patiently and politely ask them to sit down, saying, "I really, really don't want anyone to get hurt". This would help for a few moments, but soon he'd have to start pleading again. I saw that he was a sensitive person trying to deal with the concert madness as best he could.

I knew I was pushing my luck when I asked her to drive me all the way to Columbus to see

David at the State Fair in 1972. When she said that she couldn't really afford to take us I wasn't surprised. I was very upset, but the fact that the concert was on September 4 is what saved the day for me. My birthday is September 10, mom changed her mind and decided to make

Above: David in playful mood.
Photo: Ed Caraeff/Iconic Images

❝ I SAW HIM AS A TRUE FRIEND WHO WOULD NEVER TURN ON ME. HE WAS ALWAYS MY SAFE PLACE IN A TUMULTUOUS WORLD ❞

that concert my birthday present. It's still one of the best gifts I've ever received. I also had my cassette recorder with me so I could listen to the concert afterwards. Many years later the audio was converted to digital, posted on You Tube and in 2017 used by Left/Right Productions in a documentary on David they were making for A&E.

There are many things I wish I had been able to tell David. That he was wonderfully talented in so many ways. That I appreciate how much he loved his fans and worked so hard for us throughout his life; that from the beginning I knew he was much, much more than a mere "teen idol" with a pretty face; how incredibly fortunate I feel to have been on this earth at the same time as he.

Most of all, I wish I could tell him how outstanding he was at bringing light and joy into my life, especially when I needed it so much. I'll always love him unconditionally.

YASMIN WENDLING – UNITED STATES

I don't have a clue as to how, but, I got the phone number of David's mother, Evelyn Ward. I called and actually spoke with her a few times. She was absolutely lovely and a very proud mother for sure. I was so young, I had no clue as to why I would bother this wonderful lady. She knew exactly what to say to calm me down and was very comforting. And I don't remember how many times I spoke with her. I would think that if I got her number, then others did too. Why she didn't change her number to an unlisted number, I'll never know.

NANCY SIEGEL KULAK – UNITED STATES

I knew nothing about *The Partridge Family* or David Cassidy when a mutual friend of my mom and Shirley Jones made it possible for me to visit the set. I was a huge fan of Shirley's and was so excited to meet, get to know her and find out what an amazing person she is. At the end of the day during which I met David, she thought her son, Shaun, and I would make great friends and we did. We were almost always together every day or on the phone for hours. I really treasured our friendship. Friends would go crazy when she came over to collect Shaun in her Station Wagon yelling: "Wow! Look, it's Mrs Partridge!"

I spent many days at the family home in California. Shirley would be singing, Jack humming or whistling a song while Shaun would just jam on the drums or keyboard while I was doing my homework. Jack took Shaun and I to the set when he was filming for an episode of *Alias Smith and Jones*. It was such a great time. David would stop by on days I was there. I had given David an 11 x 13 photo before to sign for me and he couldn't find it. Shirley said David asked if I had another photo as he lost the first. Then, before I gave Shirley a new photo, David said he found the first one which he asked if he could keep. He signed my photo and wrote: "I'm so sorry about the other pictures – hope this will do".

Left: Nancy Siegel Kulak with David standing by The Partridge Family bus

★ LANE BRADBURY

Legendary Broadway actress, Lane Bradbury, was the first actress to play Dainty June in the original Broadway production of *Gypsy* alongside Ethel Merman. She also starred alongside Bette Davis in *Night of the Iguana*. Early on in her illustrious career, Lane was in *The Partridge Family* episode Love At First Slight in which "Keith" is being followed by girls, which he is unhappy about, and dealing with fame.

Share David's Kisses!

NOT TOO LONG AGO a pretty and gifted young actress—Lane Bradbury—was asked to do a guest role in one of *The Partridge Family* segments. When she showed up for rehearsal, little did she dream that she was going to be kissed by the one and only David Cassidy! On this page, take a look at lucky Lane and see how it was when she got kissed by David. And then—on the next page —it's your turn!! So watch how David does it, and then—*from your point of view*—how it would be done if David kissed you!!

David and Lane pucker up for a rehearsal of their famous kiss.

Well, Lane might not close her eyes when she gets kissed—but David sure closes his!

I went into this little sitcom which was one of the first episodes they filmed for a television series which turned out to be a huge success around the world. For my role I'm not supposed to like Keith, he doesn't mean anything to me. Some other little girl was in love with him and he wasn't paying any attention to her. My character, Janet, was one girl who did not recognise him, became the apple of his eye at that moment but she wasn't interested in him. I enjoyed the scenes we did together and probably still have the script buried somewhere.

About a month before *The Partridge Family* offer I had a major operation to try and get pregnant. I told no one except my best friend. I didn't want people to worry "oh she's not pregnant yet" so when I got the part of Janet what was happening in my private life was the foremost thing in my mind.

I had appeared in other television series, but I don't remember reading for this part. It was given to me and I accepted roles because I was an actress. I remember I wore my own wardrobe for *The Partridge Family* episode because I thought it was adorable, and they liked it. I was only on the set for three, maybe four days, and had no idea who David was at that stage, and that worked well for the role I was playing. This was very early on in the first season. He was very nice, and I would have loved to have worked with him again in the future. David certainly had a screen presence *au monde*. I look back at those few days with fondness. It was an enjoyable time.

During the few days I was on the set, one of the teen magazines which plastered David's face across the covers, wanted to do a photo shoot about what it was like to kiss David. It was a rather bizarre request, but it would have helped to sell magazines I suppose. They just turned up on the set and inbetween takes we posed for what turned out to be a two-page piece with me the envy of all those young girls…..it was all in a day's work.

And here's how it is from your point of view!!

"You mean, you're shy? Well, that's all right! I'm kind of shy myself!"

Do you mind if I kiss you just once—pretty please?"

"O.K., look pretty and pucker up—please."

"Aaaah—that wasn't so bad, was it? Hmmmm—maybe I could have another kiss?"

Lane Bradbury was asked to do a photo shoot with David for *16 Magazine*. This appeared in their March 1971 edition

ELZA CHANTLER – AUSTRALIA

I never met or heard David Cassidy live, sadly enough… however I grew up in a place in Africa called Rhodesia. Most of my life growing up in that country we experienced a Bush War, from July 1964 to 1979. We had what they called the Unilateral Declaration of Independence (UDI) declared on 11 November 1965; this meant that Rhodesia, a British territory in southern Africa, now regarded itself as an independent sovereign state. My whole family, parents and brothers and sister were all called up to join the forces for their two-year call-up. They each had a pattern, they would be six weeks out fighting on the border and two weeks home for rest and recuperation. They each left at different times so often I would be home alone, as I was the youngest.

As the result of UDI and the war, we were very cut off from the rest of the world, sometimes we'd joke and say we were 10 years behind time. In 1970 David Cassidy started with *The Partridge Family*, but we only got to see it a couple of years later, in comparison to the rest of the world.

Many a night when I was home alone, I would watch David Cassidy in *The Partridge Family* and enter into my fantasy world. However, my world was different from other young girls. While they dreamed of being his girlfriend and marrying him, I dreamed that *The Partridge Family* was actually my family. Those nights sitting there watching that half hour show I would go so deeply into the show, some nights I could swear it was real.

He was like a big brother to me. They all cared so much for each other and showed so much love. It brought me great comfort to pretend they were my family than for me as a young teenager to actually look at my family, I didn't even know where they were, or even if they were still alive! Wow! that thought used to terrify me, I stayed in *The Partridge Family* dream as long as I could.

So, David Cassidy helped me, somehow through very dark times of my childhood where fear was a natural thing, to know what was right and wrong as a teenager, how to treat people, how to behave, in fact, most of my life values! As a family, they were so safe and kind and they gave me great comfort. I wanted to walk like them, talk like them, look like them, it brought me so much comfort, to have them as my invisible family. I would put my tape recorder close to the speaker of the television and record the show, this way I could play their "home sounds" any time. No one will ever know how much peace they brought into my heart. How they helped me with "normal" in life.

As the years went on, and the war ended, I got older, got married, became a mother and forgot all about *The Partridge Family*, until I heard the news of David Cassidy's death. All my memories, good and bad, came flooding back. I was sitting in a dentist's chair when I saw it announced on the news. The volume was down so I wasn't sure what was happening.

As soon as I got home, I went into Google to check. I listened to his music on YouTube, was able to watch some of *The Partridge Family* episodes, I read stories, looked up everything I could find about him and his life, bought and read one of his books. I saved so many pictures of him, 70s, 80s and 90s era mostly, I was not fond of his look much after that, his magic to me was gone, he was just a guy singing with a guitar.

It was a very strange emotion I felt that day, the feeling of losing a brother I'd never met, but had loved dearly, oh so dearly. I was terribly sad, I cried so much, for months, I was angry, that he died so lost, lonely and sad. The more I saw him the more I loved him, the sadder I felt. Such a vicious cycle. I realized a number of things during that time, life is serious and truly short, live every day to the maximum! Love unconditionally, say what you feel, and think about what you say. Think of tomorrow, take ownership of your life and live healthily.

So now, these are all the soft and fluffy things I thought about, however, the two big things that stuck in my mind, and made a difference, was the alcohol and music. I, like David Cassidy, drank alcohol, for me like there was no tomorrow, it didn't ever cross my mind how it affects you later in life. After seeing how it destroyed him, his life, his family, everything, it really made me scared. Seriously, and almost immediately I stopped drinking totally because I don't want my life to end that way. I don't want to become this sad and lonely old woman.

The second point: music, my whole life, and perhaps it was an escape, I don't know, anyway, I have loved music. I was a dancer, it's one of the many things I did at school. I also wanted to be a singer when I was young, used to sing my heart out over records, but because of the situation in the country, there was just no way I could go any further with that dream.

I had also always wanted to learn to play the piano. So, I thought, I'm going to follow this passion. I decided to buy a guitar, it was cheaper than a piano and I loved the way David Cassidy played. I wanted to sound like him. I bought my guitar and signed up for lessons and you know playing my guitar brings me so much joy.

Every day, I must confess, since he passed, I listen to his music. I listen when I shower in the mornings, during the day when I'm cleaning my place, hanging up the washing and of course when I'm driving in my car. The only singer I can listen to still since he passed is David Cassidy. His voice is so beautiful, and I just love his songs, especially his last work, *Songs My Father Taught Me*.

So strange, even in death he brings comfort to me, once again on a daily basis. He is in my heart, my life and shares every day with me.

One of Elza Chantler's drawings of David

66 PEOPLE COME UP TO ME AND SAY – AND IT IS SO WONDERFUL – 'CAN I TELL YOU SOMETHING…. YOU HAVE MEANT MORE TO ME THAN ANYBODY IN MY LIFE, IN MY GROWING UP'. I GET THAT. IT JUST MAKES IT ALL WORTHWHILE 99

David speaking in 1985

CLEA MYLONAS – UNITED KINGDOM

I am a David Cassidy SUPERFAN.......there I said it, still am and I miss him. I was one of the super lucky ones to meet David in April 1975. I still wake up these days and can't believe I met him. I say lucky, but now older and wiser I believe that luck had nothing to do with it. From the very first time I saw him on TV 2/3 years earlier in *The Partridge Family* it was as they say "love at first sight". I was obsessed. I bought everything with his face on and written about him. I was determined I was going to meet him whatever it took. I've had some wonderful imaginations of our meeting and wild dreams of how I would make things happen.

Obviously, I did not know how, or where to begin but the imagination and determination was so strong that I guess I attracted every opportunity that came my way to try and get close to him. It nearly happened a couple of times before it actually did. *Fab 208* magazine ran a competition a couple of years previous, and I came so close, finishing second to another fan who later became a friend.

When I went to see him in concert in 1974 in London, in the programme was an advert for another competition that I participated in to raise money for a children's charity. It seemed like months later, but only several weeks, I had the call that I won. I was so excited that my whole body was aching, and my heart was really thumping with the adrenalin and smiling to myself that I DID IT. It was an agonising five months before I was due to fly out to Los Angeles.

Fast forward: RCA studios, Thursday, the evening of April 3: Finally here sitting in a corridor lobby waiting, then I saw him with a couple of other people coming up the corridor with his best friend, Sam. I felt butterflies, shyness, excitement, my mind went blank, my mouth dry, and in some ways I wanted to flee. I was not ready, and yet I was excited at the same time. He looked exactly the same as the photos, on TV, his gorgeous face, quite petite looking for a man/boy who was coming up to 25 in a few days. Sexy looking of the times, those jeans and famous patchwork looking shirt that really clung to him, and when he stretched his arms the buttonholes gaped and showed his body.

I had brought a present for David wrapped in a guitar case. As he reached us he said: "Look, we've got a hired group here tonight", before leading us into the recording studio where I helped him open the present, a mirror, the standard size of a guitar with painted strings, and handed him a birthday card. "That's really nice," he said. I had carved a message on the back of the mirror, and he laughed reading: "You cannot play it, but you'll put a good show on it". He seemed really pleased with it and the card.

Watching him at work with Bruce Johnston, who was really lovely and producing his album with him, my mind was all over the place. I was awe struck I was so close to him like this in this time of the universe....him and me, and nobody would ever be able to change this time between us. It was definitely one of the happiest times of my life.

We were sitting and laughing, and he was looking at me, when I opened my autograph book for him to sign and a $10 bill fell to the floor, "You're rich", he said. I cannot believe the excitement and emotions that go through your body, all I can say is "electric", and when he kissed me on the lips before we said

Above: Clea Mylonas when she met David

Below: The competition advert Clea entered

'Meet David Cassidy in California' Competition

Jet flight to a Dream-of-a-Lifetime

WIN A FANTASTIC ONCE-IN-A-LIFETIME CHANCE TO MEET THE FAMOUS DAVID CASSIDY. THE WINNER WILL BE FLOWN FREE (Together with Parent./Guardian) FOR A FANTASTIC THRILL-PACKED ALL EXPENSES-PAID STAY IN HOLLYWOOD INCLUDING A VISIT TO THE STUDIOS AND DISNEYLAND

*Although the winner will be accompanied on the trip by a responsible adult should she/he so agree the age of 15 yrs. & over if successful winner will be able to make the arrangements. The winner to be U.K.

DOZENS OF FAB DISCS BY TOP RECORDING ARTISTS TO BE WON

DAVID CASSIDY BADGE AND SPECIAL 'THANK YOU' MESSAGE FROM DAVID TO ALL THOSE RAISING £2.00 OR OVER

DAVID'S COMPETITION TO RAISE MONEY TO HELP PHYSICALLY HANDICAPPED AND DEPRIVED CHILDREN

Send for competition form NOW!
Write to David Cassidy competition
72 Westfields Avenue London SW13 0AU
(enclosing Stamped/Addressed envelope)
or Telephone 01-878 4366 (24 hour answering service)

How the winner will be decided
Points will be awarded on the basis of number of correctly answered questions and the amount of sponsorship money raised and given to the charity.

THIS COMPETITION CLOSES ON THURS. 31st OCT. 1974
(Applications to take part will be accepted up to Thurs. 24th Oct. 1974)

In aid of THE FRIENDS OF THE CHILDREN SOCIETY
(Registered Charity)

A PROMOTIONAL FUND RAISING EVENT DEVISED & PRODUCED FOR 'THE FRIENDS OF THE CHILDREN SOCIETY' BY PORTER + POCOCK ASSOCIATES LTD

goodbye.....well it made all the waiting worth it. He was so gentle. To think that at that particular time, and who knows if he ever remembered me, he knew my name and my existence and that has been good enough for me.

I know I felt incredibly sad and empty for the rest of the trip as we didn't have that much time with him at all. The feeling was like the title of the album he was recording *The Higher They Climb.....The Harder They Fall*. It fitted my mood entirely. The excitement was unbearable, the adrenalin rush was thumping in my chest. Then the sadness afterwards was just draining the life out of me.

My dream did come true, and I believe I will see him again.

Left: Letter asking Clea to supply a photograph for David

EAMON CATAQUIZ – UNITED STATES

In October 1970, my family relocated from Japan back to California because of my father's job with the military. We were staying with some friends and on a Friday night the kids were excited to watch the ABC TV line-up consisting of *The Brady Bunch, Nanny and the Professor* and a show they were all giddy about called *The Partridge Family*. Being 6 years old at the time, I had no idea what *The Partridge Family* was about, but I was immediately hooked seeing this musical group singing. Never mind the plot, it was the music that stuck with me. Through *Tiger Beat* magazine and my older sisters reading the articles to me, I learned that they were not really a real family. What a shock to my 6-year-old heart.

Going back to school, I thought I was so cool in the first grade because I was a fully-fledged member of The Partridge Family Fan Club. My father had sent in the coupon and the $2.50 membership for me. My first Partridge Family album was *Up To Date*. I didn't know about the first album because their picture wasn't on it. We were at the Base Exchange where military families shop and my mother said I could choose an album for being good, so as soon as I saw The Partridge Family smiling up at me on that blue album I asked my Mom for it and she laughed and said "Ok, but are you sure you wouldn't rather have 'The Grass Roots'. "No Mom", I said, by then all that hard rock stuff I liked in Japan was a passing fancy; I became a "bubble gummer".

I did see David Cassidy in 1971 when I was 7 years old as my uncle who was visiting from England took me. Then again when I was 10 in 1974 at White City in England. It was hot, crowded and what I saw after the concert shook me up. Seeing girls being treated for injuries, some fainted and bloodied, crying, etc. scared me senseless.

In 1990 I did finally meet David Cassidy at Tower Records

66 I WAS IMMEDIATELY HOOKED SEEING THIS MUSICAL GROUP SINGING 99

when he was doing a meet and greet for his comeback album of that year. I took time off work, however it was a good thing my boss, a Navy Captain, drove me to the store. When it came to my turn to meet David, I just about froze and said: "da da da". I was tongue-tied and there I was being so cool about it a few hours prior. My boss had to speak for me and handed him my *Cherish* album to sign. David was so gracious. He just laughed, smiled, spoke with me, what he said I couldn't tell you as I was in shock, except I know he said hello and my name and within five or six minutes it was over. I wish we had cell phones back then so I could have had a picture of my dumb frozen self.

David passed away a few months before my surgery for cancer. That alone was pretty devastating but with his death I felt my world had crushed. The music of The Partridge Family and David Cassidy as a solo act has helped me a lot during my therapy along with other artists including David's brother Shaun.

I would just like to say: Thank you to David Cassidy for being an integral part of my life.

BARBARA SMALL – UNITED KINGDOM

Watching *The Partridge Family* on television, and buying the records, is what led me to love David and wanting to see him in concert. Buying *I Think I Love You* started my journey with David. I went to see David on March 17, 1973 at the Empire Pool, Wembley. I was 14 years old. My friend Anne and myself were at the 4pm concert. We sat in the middle of the auditorium, downstairs on the end of the aisle. When David came on stage, I remember standing in the aisle screaming with my hands waving in the air, the atmosphere was incredible. I could not hear David for the screaming. After the concert, once outside, everyone rushed to a 6ft high fence and we shook it so much it gave way. It was such an amazing experience.

ANN KING – DAVID CASSIDY FAN SINCE 1971

David was performing at the Garden State Arts Center in August, 1971. I called to find out if his concert was going ahead as he had cancelled other shows having had his gall bladder removed. Two days before the concert I called again telling them I was a cousin planning a surprise party on the Friday for him along with his Mom. They told me he was flying in on Saturday morning the day of the show and read the telegram his manager sent stating the airline and the flight number.

My sister came with me and we casually waited. At first, I didn't see him, but just then I saw a guitar case appear out of the door of the plane, then David with his manager. As he walked into the waiting area at Newark International, I went up to him and said, "Hello, welcome back to NJ". He seemed to be half asleep when I was talking to him as he wasn't answering me. I patted him on his shoulder and said, "David, I'm talking to you". He apologized for not responding and went on to explain he didn't get much sleep on the plane and was still tired.

I asked him if I could have my picture taken with him as well as an autograph and he said sure. I told him I had tickets to see him later that day at the Arts Center and he said that was nice. We talked and I walked with him and his manager to where you would rent a car. I did something I thought I would never do – I handed David my car keys and told him, he and his manager could use my car for the weekend. He asked me what was the catch? – I told him I come with the car. Either his manager could drive, or he could. With my car keys in his hand he told his manager, but came back and said, "Thank you but I already got a car".

At the Garden State Arts Center my girlfriend and I had seats in the balcony. David came out in his white jumpsuit, singing Summer Days. After one more song David asked everyone if they would keep quiet as he wanted to say something. You could hear a pin drop. He said he was greeted by a few fans at the airport that morning and was told they would be at the show. He asked wherever we were to please stand up. I felt so embarrassed not expecting him to say that. When I stood up, he said thank you for being there.

I worked for the probation department in Essex County. My work took me to the Prosecutors Record Room where I became friends with someone whose sister owned a hair salon that Evelyn Ward (David's mom) went to on occasion just up the street from where she lived in West Orange.

A friend of mine was getting married so I called the salon, asked to speak with Joanne and made an appointment, during which David's name came up. She asked if I would like to meet Evelyn, if she would allow us to visit for a short time. She called her, told her about me and we went over to her house.

Evelyn opened the front door, showed us into the front sitting room where she had a piano, and asked me some questions. She said that the next time David was visiting she would call me, and I could come over to visit. She gave me her phone number and I could call her if I wanted to, which I did from time to time. I only met David's grandfather once, when I dropped a gift off for David.

In early 1974, I was over a friend's house visiting and I had a feeling something was terribly wrong. I called David's mom and her sister answered. When I asked if I could speak with Evelyn, she told me she was not available as she buried her father that day and David was with her. I gave her my sincere condolences and to please pass the information to Evelyn and David.

She said she would have Evelyn call me in about a week, which she did but I wasn't home at the time. My mother told me she called, had said David was still at the house and would like me to come over to visit. I was sooooooo mad at myself, but I didn't know he was still there, and she was going to call me. I sent Evelyn and David a sympathy card. She replied with a thank you note.

PHILIPPA KENNEDY – UNITED KINGDOM

I remember that I was a little cynical when I was sent to interview David and wasn't really a fan as such. However, I was fascinated by the excitement he generated and found him a thoroughly nice young man, really cool, polite and pleasant and not at all full of himself. I think he was a little overwhelmed by the attention he was receiving in the UK. The words 'I melted' were very much an afterthought and not in the original copy that I sent to the newspaper. The reason I added them was that I left the interview with a very pleasant impression of a nice young man. I knew his fans would want to see his bedroom and he was fine about it when I asked him. Nowadays you wouldn't get anywhere near that kind of access. Stars are surrounded by PRs and managers and you just can't get close.

Right: Philippa Kennedy's memorable interview in 1973

"I THINK I LOVE YOU"

Above: The bubblegum card which won Sarah Robinson's heart

Below: Boat trip tickets to get close to David on the River Thames, 1972

Fans storm the BBC in London, Sarah circled in the crowd

Opposite: Photo: Barry Plummer

SARAH ROBINSON – UNITED KINGDOM

The first time I saw anything of David was on a bubblegum card an American friend gave me sometime in 1970. David was unheard of in the UK at that time. The card had a picture of him on one side along with his name, and on the other, the lyrics to *I Think I Love You*. I took one look at that card and I was smitten. I had no idea who he was, knew nothing of *The Partridge Family*, all I knew was his name. None of my classmates were at all interested, so I pinned it on the notice board nearest my desk and gazed longingly at it. About six months later *The Partridge Family* aired in the UK and then my classmates started eyeing up my bubblegum card with envy. It was removed and taken home to safety.

I remember vividly the excitement of his first visit to the UK and I was at Heathrow airport, along with THOUSANDS of fans, to see him arrive. I don't think I'd ever experienced anything like it in my life. I was literally crushed against the balcony and I remember being hit in the face by an instamatic camera. It was pandemonium, but I've never been so excited in all my life.

On that visit he stayed at The Dorchester Hotel in Mayfair. I went up to stand outside for hours to try to get a glimpse of him. I don't know what came over me, but we managed to get down to the hotel's underground car park and saw him in those famous furry boots being whisked away.

The hotel did not know what hit them so on another trip they put him on a boat, the *Ocean Sabre* on the River Thames. That caused us (my friend Nicole and I) a headache or two trying to figure out how on earth we could possibly get close to him. We were the first to have the bright idea of getting on a pleasure boat cruise down the Thames. We chatted up the captain, told him we wanted to get close, and why. He laughed and said he'd see what he could do, but said he'd probably only be able to slow down a little at best.

That first pass by on the pleasure cruiser, David had come up on board to wave to the hundreds of girls on the shore who were screaming his name. He had his back to us and was waving to them. Our captain was brilliant, he got as close as he was able and slowed as much as he felt he could. Nicole and I screamed 'DAVID WE LOVE YOU!!!' as loud as we possibly could. We couldn't believe it when he turned his back on the shore and waved to us on the pleasure boat shouting out 'I love you too!!' Oh, it was amazing! I can't tell you how exciting it was. After that those pleasure boat trips were absolutely loaded with DC fans, but Nicole and I were the first.

We saw Ed Stewart or 'Stewpot' as he was known, arrive to interview him for BBC Radio One. Although he was safe from fans on the boat, they did have to bring him ashore, and we were lucky enough on a couple of occasions to guess correctly where they would land him, so we did manage to get quite close to him – but never close enough.

Being seasoned fans and having a fair idea of how things worked when he was in the building, if there were too many girls at an entrance he might come out of, we would run round the corner and SCREAM…sure enough a stampede would follow, at which point we would hot foot it back to where we had been.

We also tried to start a UK fan club with some girls we'd met from Rotherhyde, South London. We really tried to do it properly. I got my dad to cut a stencil of his name and tried making ribbons with his name stencilled on. We worked quite hard on it but never met with any encouragement and it fizzled out.

The first concert he did in London was at Wembley Empire Pool in 1973. He wore his white suit which had a sunshine on the bum. The night before David's concert – Friday March 16 – my sister and I spent the evening pampering ourselves. I'd had a Mary Quant herbal vapouriser and face pack and brush dried my hair. I wrote in my diary:

Diary entry 1973

"The next morning [Saturday March 17] we got up at 6.30am to get ready and listened to the radio to make sure he was going to do a Radio One interview – he was, so we went up and saw him at Broadcasting House, very closely infact. He was only 6 feet away and stood there for about one minute.

Later at the concert I wrote: "I spent £1.80 on souvenirs. The concert was fantastic and he wore a white skin tight suit and had a little sunshine on his bum. He played guitar, sang, played the drums and the piano. He's really talented and is fantastic at singing live. He threw flowers into the audience and he kept pointing to certain parts of the hall. He wiggled his bum the whole time. It was great."

During David's first UK trip I wrote a letter to him, persuading someone to pass it on to him. I was absolutely over the moon when I received a letter back on Partridge Family Fan Club paper. It was typed but signed by David. Years later – 1995 – I showed it to him when I met him outside the stage door in Oxford where he was starring in *Blood Brothers*. After the show my husband and I went to the stage door and waited. When he emerged I could not believe it….I really couldn't believe I was actually that close to a man I'd 'loved' for 25 years. I showed him the letter I received in 1972. He was amazed that I had it and signed for me a second time.

I was so nervous and realised I hadn't a clue what to say to him, so I said the most unoriginal thing ever – "I've waited 25 years for this moment". He was absolutely lovely to us…he didn't rush us or anything. David looked at other items I brought along, signed what I asked, we took pictures and he was just lovely. My husband shook his hand and then we left.

I was six months pregnant at the time, but I was practically floating down the road I was on SUCH a high! I felt someone come alongside me and slip his arm around my waist. I thought it was my husband and I turned to say to him "WOW wasn't that AMAZING!" but it wasn't my husband, it was

DAVID CASSIDY! He had walked up to me while I was walking down a street in Oxford, slipped his arm around my waist and said, 'Thank you SO much for coming, it means such a lot'. He smiled at me, then my husband, and walked off alone into the night. I think my jaw was on the floor. We couldn't believe it.

I've stood outside every TV studio, radio station, airport etc. I even climbed scaffolding once. I saw David in concert many times and also when he was in *Time*. But meeting him that night was one of the best moments of my life. He was a beautiful looking man and I had 144 pictures of that beautiful face on my bedroom walls. I used to fall asleep listening to his music. No one had, or has since, a voice quite like his. The whole memory of David and his songs brings with it mixed emotions for me. I was painfully shy when I was young. I wasn't one of the popular girls. I was very lonely actually. I found being that age very difficult and felt that I didn't really fit in. Yes, I had a couple of good friends, and the fact that a couple of them loved David as much as I did brought us closer together. So being a devoted David fan really helped me through quite a lonely and difficult time, but also hearing some

THE OFFICIAL

PARTRIDGE FAMILY FAN CLUB

58 Parker Street, London, WC2B 5QB   Fan Club Secretary : Susie Miller

February 1972

Dear Sarah,

It was great of you to write to me, particularly after what happened at the airport, but as you can guess the officials did not give me much time to do anything. I hope soon to return to the U.K. with the rest of the gang and do some concerts here and meet my fans.

Bye for now,

Love,

P.S.   I have my fingers crossed for your exams.

of those songs now it does bring back some of those sad lonely feelings I felt at the time and also how desperately I wanted to meet him.

Every time I saw him perform – right up to the Hammersmith Apollo concerts in more recent years, I am 15 all over again. Isn't it funny how music has that ability to transport you to another time or another place?

How tragic that in the end, a man who brought so much happiness to so many people never succeeded in finding it for himself.

THE HIGHER THEY CLIMB ALBUM COVER

I had no idea I was on the cover of David's album, *The Higher They Climb*. It was only when I was looking at the cover – my husband lent me the album soon after we met in 1979 – that it dawned on me I knew where the photo was taken. I recognised Nicole's distinctive coloured trousers and dark hair, my coat and long blonde hair. The photo was taken from the balcony of what used to be London Weekend Television. My dad worked there at the time and security was so tight when David was visiting even he had trouble getting to areas of the building that day.

Above: David was an exceptional pianist. Photo: Barry Plummer

Left: Sarah Robinson finally meets David in 1995 after a performance of *Blood Brothers* in Oxford

WENDY READDY – UNITED KINGDOM

The Partridge Family aired for the first time on UK TV. That was the day I fell in love for the first time. I could not stop thinking about him and wanting to know more. My whole life changed, and so it did for many other young girls too. I used to hop on a bus with my best friend, Mandy, and go to Woolwich with my pocket money all of which was £1.50 and buy all the magazines with him in. I particularly loved *Jackie* and *Fabulous 208*. The Dream Come True page was brilliant. I wrote to them many times wanting to meet David. But my wish never did come true.

BUT then it was announced that David was coming to London to do concerts. I was running around my lounge screaming, "I have to get tickets. I must do this", like some crazy person. My friend and I had very good seats. We attended the Saturday afternoon show. I wore a black satin jacket and covered it with badges and stickers of David. They showed clips of the concerts on the TV over the weekend and I saw a clip of myself. I was by the fence with other fans and some started to climb the wire fence. I looked terrified.

Compere, David Hamilton, came on the stage, and we had to spell out DAVID CASSIDY. I actually think I went into some kind of trance. Then the most amazing thing happened. David was singing, but he started to pull four tassels off his costume. He threw them out in the crowd. To my amazement I caught one. I was being jumped on, screamed at as many fans were trying to pull it off me but there was no way I was going to let this go.

Once the concert was finished and we were outside I waited until no one could see. Then I opened my hand. After holding it tight for so long it was difficult because my fingers had got stuck, and there it was this beautiful leather studded tassel that once was attached to the man I was in love with. I couldn't wait to get to a phone box to tell my parents.

We got a train back to Belvedere where we were to meet my parents at the working men's club. It was there that a young girl had also been to the concert and heard that I had caught the tassel. Her father came over to my father and asked if I would sell it. He offered me £500, which back in the 70s was a hell of a lot of money. But of course, there was no way I was ever going to sell my tassel to anyone.

The other concert I particularly love was at the Royal Albert Hall [1985]. I was pregnant with my daughter at the time. Again, once he came on stage and all us girls now older women with families and husbands were going crazy. In the second half women were moving to the front of the stage. So even though I was pregnant I managed to climb my way through and on the video of this concert my sister appears near the front.

What fantastic memories of a man I loved all my life and will continue to do so.

Thank you, David for being you.

Below right: Wendy Readdy with the tassel she caught

Below: The missing tassels, one of which Wendy Readdy caught, at Wembley Empire Pool. Photo: Barry Plummer

ALAIN M. BERGERON – CANADA

'm not afraid to say out loud or to write, that David Cassidy was one of the most important people in my life. His music and his great talent were very helpful to help me go through my painful teen and young adult years. He was my hero, the big brother I never had, the one I could look up to. He made me smile when times were really difficult for me and my family. I must point out some things to put all of this in perspective. I grew up in Victoriaville in Quebec, a French province in Canada with a father who was very ill. From his late thirties to the end – he died in his mid-60s in 1988 – he suffered a blood disease that was incurable at the time.

To make a long and painful story short, the doctors had literally cut him to pieces so he could stop feeling the horrible pain. He had more than 30 surgeries over the years. He lost a leg in 1969 and the other in 1973. The disease later attacked his fingers and his arms. When he passed away, he had just three fingers left. Now, you must understand that seeing my father, who I loved dearly and whom I admired for his inspiring courage, in so much pain was terrible for the sensible young man I was.

That's where David Cassidy comes in with *The Partridge Family*. The show wasn't broadcast in French and my English was not very good. But it's a vivid memory for me while looking at what was on television that I stopped on Channel 6 (CBC Radio-Canada – English). And I felt what I still consider today as a *coup de foudre*! Nothing less than that.

The Partridge Family singing *Rainmaker*. WOW! What was going on in my mind? To this day, I still remember the lights, the velvet costumes, the scene, the song. Each time I hear *Rainmaker*, it brings me back to 1972 when I was 14. (In fact, as I'm writing this – and believe me, it's not easy – I'm listening to the *Sound Magazine* album).

Something was happening in my life. I never forget how I felt, seeing David Cassidy for the first time. I still get very emotional just thinking about it, even in my 60s. David Cassidy brought music and light in my life when clouds seemed to hang permanently over our house. I bought all his records (solo and group) and followed him at a distance, reading all about him and his career. Hey! I wanted to be David Cassidy! He was a role model for me. I even bought a guitar, started singing and writing songs.

Nevertheless, I realized, even today, how talented this young guy was. When he emerged as Keith with *The Partridge Family*, he was my daughter's age! How could such a young artist be prepared for such an international sudden career and popularity?

It was a very sad moment for me when the PF ended. But I watched reruns with the same pleasure and continued to follow DC through his solo years. All the while, my dad still went to the hospital and I found comfort while listening to David's music (and PF). It helped me keep my mental health. His songs brought me joy when I REALLY needed it. I'm sure it prevented me from going mad over my father's destiny.

I met David Cassidy once, in 1990, at Toronto, for the release of his Enigma album. There must have been hundreds of fans like me, eager to meet him at this little club. Just saying "Hi! I drove eight hours to meet you", was enough for me (remember that my English is all but fluid). I did not want to tell him my whole story – too many people around. Looking back, I should have written a letter to explain the importance he had in my life and to thank him (I'm in tears writing that).

When David died in November 2017, I wept like a baby as I realized I have lost my idol, my big brother, the man who had such a positive and warm impact in my life. I was like a zombie for two or three days, crying whenever I thought of him. I couldn't help thinking that DC would never know how much I owe him.

My modest contribution to this book is my personal way to say to him, even though he's no longer with us: Thank you so much, dear David. Merci!

> **DAVID CASSIDY BROUGHT MUSIC AND LIGHT IN MY LIFE WHEN CLOUDS SEEMED TO HANG PERMANENTLY OVER OUR HOUSE**

JULIE RICHARDS – AUSTRALIA

Newspaper cutting re
forthcoming documentary
Julie Richards appeared in

From 1973 until 1975 I was president of the Australian David Cassidy Fan Club, with the full support of Phonogram Records. Harry M. Miller was responsible for bringing David to Australia in 1974 and their publicist, Patti Mostyn, asked me on one of my visits to the record company offices to get the club newsletters printed, if I'd like to appear in David's upcoming Australia TV Special, *David Cassidy: To Australia With Love.*

He arrived on February 28 and was whisked away to a press conference which my friends and I were allowed to attend. We squeezed our way to the front. The big moment arrived when David, our idol of TV and all those records was right there in front of us, with the most gorgeous smile and sparkling, friendly eyes. We were captivated. Towards the end, Patti introduced us. David was so friendly and genuinely pleased to see us. I gave him a book made up from poems, letters and drawings fans had sent in.

A taxi came to collect us for a longer meeting with David which was filmed by Channel 7 for the Special. He came into the room and I'm sure all three of us screamed inside. He was even more handsome than before, wearing a colourful cotton shirt which he had worn on a Partridge Family episode and blue jeans. Those eyes, that smile! Those memories are so special. David's voice was so warm, and he was trying to make us laugh because we were so nervous. We gave David presents but he couldn't stay long because he had another plane to catch. He finished off by telling us to take care, and was again gone.

His concert on March 2 at Randwick was an awfully hot day, no seating in front of the stage or any shelter from those merciless rays beating down. I was standing maybe 10 rows back and David's entrance was the start of non-stop screaming and pushing. Everyone just wanted to get up front. I can still remember my tired legs from hours of standing on my tiptoes to see over the waving arms.

I next met David at his press reception at the Boulevarde Hotel during his second visit to Sydney in October 1974. A lot of people were speechless when he turned up for the press: David's lovely long locks were replaced by a short cut and he was wearing glasses. What a transformation. I didn't like it at first but soon changed my mind. He still had a good sense of humour and those same sparkling eyes and warm smile. I spoke with him and had a lovely photo taken together.

ANNA CANAZZA – AUSTRALIA

On March 10 on a hot Sunday afternoon he took over the Melbourne Cricket Ground. I was 9 in 74 and there was no way I was going to be able to attend the concert but my aunt and friend did. Upon their return home they told me of the stifling heat, lack of water available, hysterical girls, ambulances and being hit in the back of the head with flying missiles of full soft drink cans.

David had everyone screaming with hands held high reaching towards their idol. The rickety thrown-together stage was dubious, and the show stopped and started as his team tried to convince the crowd to back up. It all sounded incredible to me at 9. I did manage to attend one concert in 2002 in Melbourne and got upfront so did get to see him perform some of his hits which I am grateful for.

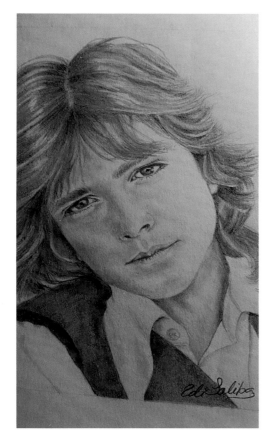

EDI SALIBA – AUSTRALIA

David by Edi Saliba

It was 1974 and I was 12 years old. I had just received my tickets in the mail for my first concert for David Cassidy. You couldn't imagine my joy. Now all I had to do was wait, and wait, and wait for what seemed an eternity. Only four very long weeks to go. I knew that ahead of me were many sleepless nights.

Finally March 10 came around; the concert was at 2pm at the Melbourne Cricket Ground (MCG). I think I was up and ready to leave by 6am. We finally made our way in, but unfortunately by this time only the lawn section was available. So, there we stood, way back to the right of the stage, but very happy with the view. The stadium was full to capacity by this time (it was estimated that the crowd reached well over 70,000 that day). The weather had already reached a sweltering 30 plus degrees Celsius (over 90 Fahrenheit) by now, and with only a hat for shelter I was wondering if I would last the day.

The announcer approached the microphone and before he could get a word out there were screams of anticipation and rushing to the front of the stage. There were fears it would collapse. And finally........he said......"Okay everyone, now give me a D..."as we spelt his name. The crescendo of screams reached another level, and that's when David ran on stage with so much energy. I was in awe and in love with this gorgeous young man; he was definitely my first crush. There was no denying David's stage presence. Not forgetting to mention his smooth breathy voice.

His 1974 concert will forever be etched in my memory. David did return to Australia again in 2002. It was a brilliant show, a very polished performer by now when compared to his first concert here in '74. But for me that will be the David I will always remember; he was at his ultimate peak.

I wandered into his orbit and fell forever into his gravity that day.

Edi La Rosa Saliba

IAN "MOLLY" MELDRUM – AUSTRALIA

There were never any airs and graces with David. He was always very down to earth, easy to get along with and a really, really, nice person considering he was such a big star. I first met him in the United States and swam in his pool a year before he came to Australia on his World Tour. I toured with him across the country. He captivated everyone and loved Australia, even our Vegemite which I was responsible for introducing him to.

We would walk around the famous shopping area Chapel Street in Melbourne. I took him to pat and hold kangaroos and koalas, he was a good friend and fun company. David was also very supportive and helpful to me when I was working as a record producer. He would come up to the studio and surprise everyone, but also help me out with suggestions for some of the songs I was producing.

David had a mass appeal and that coupled with being a great singer and all-round nice bloke make him a great person. In more private moments he wanted to be respected and more recognised as the outstandingly talented singer he was. He was a dear friend.

Ian is Australia's most iconic music journalist, record producer and entrepreneur.

REIKO YUKAWA – MUSIC CRITIC AND LYRICIST – JAPAN

I interviewed David in 1974 and got the impression he was a very polite and nice person. He was very smart and quick-witted. I introduced him in Japanese to my listeners on the radio station where I had my program, All American Top 40, and asked him: "Do you understand what I am talking about?" He replied, smiling, "No, I don't at all". I asked him to say hello to his listeners. Laughing he said, "Hello to my listeners," adding, "it's nice to be here".

David was destined to become a teen idol because he was very good looking, but he got sick and tired of that image. He already made it clear that he was getting tired of being a teen idol when he came to Japan. It was hard for him to have been labelled with that, which was a tragic destiny in some ways. I think he struggled.

When I heard his covers of many songs I was surprised, but I think that showed the direction his music was maybe heading. In 1975, David released his album, *The Higher They Climb*, which he produced with Bruce Johnston of the Beach Boys. One track, *I Write the Songs*, was released as a single but Barry Manilow ended up with the bigger hit. David was out of luck in some ways.

Reiko was a Japanese DJ for "All American Top 40" of Casey Kasem between 1972 – 1986 in Japan.

SANDRA – AUSTRALIA

I saw David in concert in Sydney in 1974. I was so excited. When David appeared, he was wearing white overalls with embroidery on the legs and a red T shirt. I remember his first words on stage were "This is our first show". Girls were screaming and fainting near the stage and being carried off. I never screamed, I wanted to hear that fabulous voice. The stage started collapsing and several times David said to the crowd "push back". Thankfully the stage remained intact. This concert was shown on TV here a few weeks later. David also appeared on our Logie Awards and had a holiday while he was here.

I'd love to pay tribute to David Cassidy who I have loved since 1971 for his immense talents – he was multi-talented and did it all – singing, stage performances, acting and for his kindness and charity work and for the wonderful man that he was which cannot be overstated. I've never loved any other entertainer the way I have loved him. I think he was the most beautiful and genuine man both inside and out and he gave his all to his fans. He was an important part of my life, particularly in my teenage years. Sadly, I never had the opportunity to meet him, one of my great disappointments.

I still feel his loss so very deeply. There will never be another David Cassidy and he will never be forgotten. I feel so privileged to have lived during his lifetime and to be one of his many devoted fans. I will love and miss him always.

Opposite page: All images of David in Australia from a private collection owned by Jim Salamanis

SCOTT HICKS – AUSTRALIA

Film director Scott Hicks is best known as director and screenwriter of *Shine* and the Oscar-winning biopic of pianist David Helfgott. In 1974 he was following David on tour for a local newspaper in Australia. On March 12, many fans without tickets for David's concert at Memorial Drive, Adelaide, were left outside the venue screaming for their idol. Scott went down to see them and capture their emotions. When one of his photographs resurfaced more than 30 years later it led to a remarkable reunion between two of the fans who had been there that night.

Sandy O'Keefe captured by Scott Hicks to the right, covering her mouth while her friend, Cindy, has her arms stretched out. Photos and contact strip opposite © Scott Hicks

I don't know if you've ever seen anyone in the grip of a real hysteria. This was my first time, and it was extraordinary to see how the girls had undergone a full-on metabolic change – their breathing as rapid as a small and very frightened animal, sweating, involuntarily mumbling – with all the appearance of a high fever and delirium tremens combined.

I was struck by the young fans eager for a glimpse of him they could only hear on stage. They varied from quiet patience to love-struck desperation. One girl in particular fascinated me. Though she never laid eyes on David, she spent the entire evening, her arms outstretched through the black cast iron gates of Memorial Drive, in a state of genuine anguish, real tears rolling down her cheeks. As Sam Hyman, David's long-time friend

and room-mate, remarked to me later: "How can anyone maintain such a pitch of emotional intensity for so long?"

At the show's end, David swiftly left the stage. The first limousine departed, passing the excluded girls. Some reacted with joy, but the particular girl I'd been watching reached a climax of desperation with both arms thrust through the railings towards her passing idol. The irony is that the occupant of that lead vehicle was in fact a decoy – David's double, in this case a girl with a towel over her head – so the young fan's final emotional pitch was unknowingly discharged to a doppelgänger. David himself was on the floor of the van which followed behind.

I discovered the negatives from that night, while compiling an exhibition and made a public appeal to trace the fans.

SAFETY FILM   KODAK TRI X PAN FILM

→16   →16A   →17   →17A   →18   →18A   →19   →19A

SANDY O'KEEFFE – AUSTRALIA

My friend Cindy and I were huge David Cassidy fans in our early teens, playing our vinyl records on a little record player in our rooms, posters on the walls dreaming of the day we could see and hear him live. That day arrived but I still can't believe my mother allowed me to go as we were only 15 years old. He had two concerts in Adelaide: one at the Oval we attended and the other we listened and screamed outside the venue where the photograph was taken and years later in 2015, appeared in our local newspaper.

Cindy is the one with outstretched arms and I am to the right with my hands covering my mouth. We had no recollection of a photographer present as we were too engrossed in the concert. We stood outside the hotel David was staying in hoping to catch a glimpse. Unfortunately, we did not have cameras or obviously mobile phones to record those days and memories. Now 45 years later the memories wean a little, but thanks to Scott Hicks we both have a lasting recollection.

It was quite by accident that I read the article regarding the photo and when taking a closer look realised we were both in the photograph. It was a wonderful memory and turn back in time. Scott gave me two copies of the photograph and it was then that I had some detective work to do in locating my long-lost friend to present her with her copy. I had tried social media avenues to no avail. Then I appealed to her whereabouts via our weekend newspaper asking if anyone knew where she lived. Her brother's friend saw the post and she rang me immediately. We have reunited in person since, we live 2,700 km apart and hadn't seen each other for 36 years. She was thrilled with her photo and we are in touch regularly.

SCOTT HICKS

On October 25, 1974, David returned to Melbourne as a guest presenter of the TV Week King of Pop Awards. I happened to be in Melbourne at the time, and late that evening I called into the International hotel where I imagined guests might be staying. I asked for Henry Diltz at the desk, on the off-chance that he might be there. Henry had accompanied David on his tour earlier in the year. We'd got on well together – initially he was quite flattered to be recognised as I recall. Anyhow, he was there, they put me through, and Henry invited me up to catch up. I went up to the room, Henry ushered me in, and to my surprise there was David Cassidy lounging on the bed. I sat next to him and remember thinking at the time what would any of those teen girls I'd seen on the tour make of this moment with their idol! We drank some champagne and relaxed watching a delayed TV broadcast of the awards ceremony.

SCOTT HICKS

This was at the Melbourne Cricket Ground (MCG – biggest stadium in Australia) on Sunday, March 10, 1974. I found among my notes from that day that these police were actually forcibly dragging her to the exit, and she was struggling and throwing herself on the ground screaming "Don't throw me out I've been waiting for years to see him". When I asked the police what they were doing, they responded "Trying to calm her down". According to my notes, I took the photo to "warn them" (!), which might account for the glance at me from the officer with his hand on her.

Left: Two Victoria police officers comfort a young fan

Opposite page: David dazzling in his white tux at the piano when he played at the Memorial Drive, Adelaide on March 12, 1974

Below: The scenes at the MCG on March 10, 1974 with girls climbing on stage to get close to David. All photos © Scott Hicks

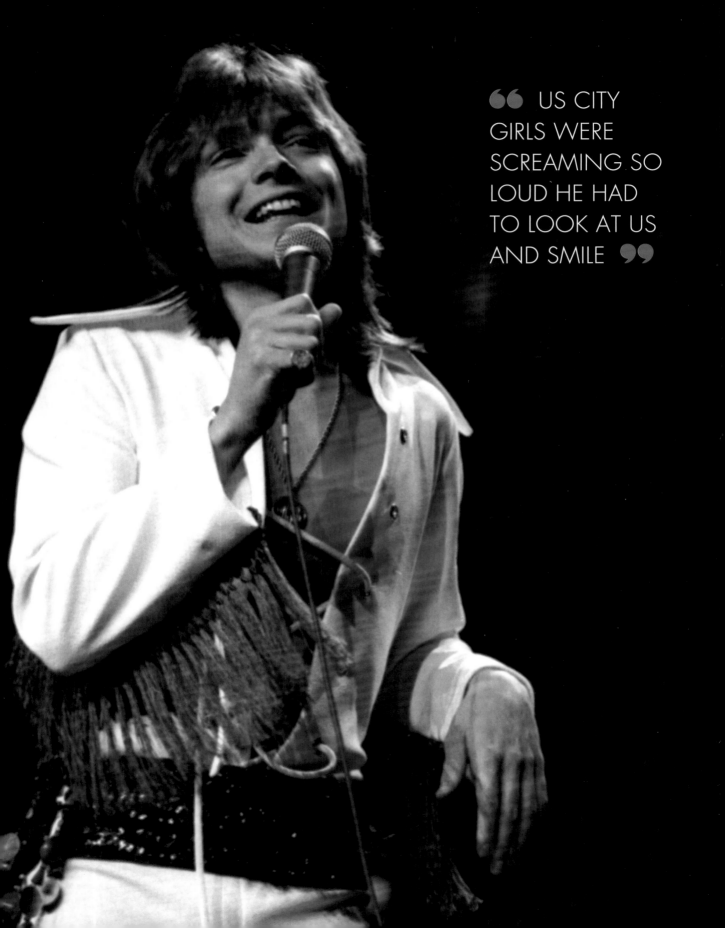

US CITY GIRLS WERE SCREAMING SO LOUD HE HAD TO LOOK AT US AND SMILE

YASMIN WENDLING – UNITED STATES

David was at the very top of his form when he played Madison Square Garden in 1972 to more than 21,000 fans. He mentioned this concert as one of the best, since his family including his grandfather were in the audience. Cathy DePace, sister of my best friend, Frances, worked at MSG and we were joined by Fran's sister Marianne and Linda DeJesus. I only took a picture of a poster on the wall of the escalator going to our seats. I bought a tape recorder with me to get it on tape and recently got it transferred to CD.

In his white jumpsuit he sang song after song and I knew sadly it would come to an end. I started moving down towards the stage, got to the right side and just stood there watching. He sang his last words and practically flew off the left side of the stage. I walked to the back of the stage and saw him running towards the limo. I felt like the only person there as I saw the limo pull up and him jumping in. In that moment he turned to me and smiled, and I smiled back. I was so happy he smiled at me. I was done!

In the summer I saw David twice in concert in a two-week period. First at the Nassau Coliseum in Long Island, which was just as exciting as Madison Square Garden, and then at the Garden State Performing Arts Centre in Holmdel, New Jersey. We earned extra monies by doing odd jobs around the neighborhood so we could go to New Jersey. This was so intimate compared to the other concerts. We had pretty good seats and could see him so clearly as he jumped and slid across the stage. Us city girls were screaming so loud he had to look at us and smile.

Not sure how many songs he sang before Linda passed out. Me and Fran looked at each other and didn't know what to do. We were screaming for help and yet no one thought anything was wrong. They did place her on a stretcher and when we knew she was going to be OK, Fran and I went back to the concert. As we sat back down in our seats, DC noticed that we had come back and gave us a really big smile.

Above: Madison Square Garden ticket

Yasmin Wendling's outfit worn to Madison Square Garden concert

Left: Young fans are mesmerised by David on stage at Madison Square Garden

Opposite page: David, aged 21, at his peak rocks Madison Square Garden

Photos: *New York Daily News* Archive/Getty Images

Above: David standing by his car captured by Yasmin

Opposite: Bar of soap taken from the bathroom

• I had been working at a coffee shop and saved up $127, which was only enough to get me from New York to California where I was determined to find David. My father's brother lived in the Los Angeles area, so I stayed there for the two weeks in August 1973 I had planned. Now understand, that my parents had really no clue as to why I wanted to go to Los Angeles or what I was up to!

The next day I went into a laundromat and met a lady who was also from New York. She lived right across the street. I explained to her why I was there. She smiled. This city girl was now on a quest to meet David Cassidy. I called the bus lines and planned my route. It took approximately two and a half hours to get to Burbank where I discovered I was not the only one there, other girls like me stood at the gate waiting for him to drive in or out. Not that day.

The next day I met a girl as crazy as me and suggested we climb through the window in the bathroom that they allowed us girls to use at the gate. So, there we were sneaking out of the back of the building, grabbing a bar of soap as we did. We climbed, scrambled, tiptoed and crawled. We got to a barbed wire fence, climbed and jumped over the other side. The

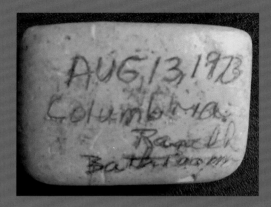

other girl cut herself and was bleeding badly. We saw someone coming. I told her she'd be okay, and I ran. I kept going until I ran right into David's BMW, his name was on the wooden stand marking his parking spot. I just stood there and couldn't move. I heard someone coming. It was David. He looked at me with that smile that has melted so many hearts, and I have no memory as to what I said. I did take a picture of him leaning on his car, before security arrived. David assured me they were not going to arrest me, but they did. I was handcuffed, put in the backseat of a patrol car like a criminal and taken to the Burbank police department. Since I was a minor, they had to call my parents. I was in a cell way down the hall and I heard my mother screaming on the phone.

ANDREW WESTERN – PASTEL ARTIST, UNITED KINGDOM

I am a deep trance medium and often feel a spiritual presence when I work. Painting David is no exception. I felt him around me, and his personality when I was painting him.

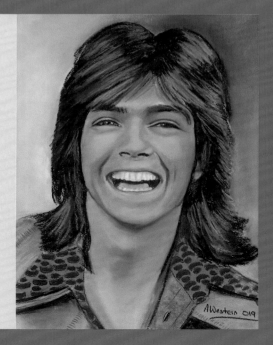

Wanda McCarthy with some memorabilia

WANDA MCCARTHY – UNITED STATES

David has always been a special part of my life. Many people who know me don't know that because it's been private for me up until now. My home life was difficult to say the least. My father drank and there was lots of angry shouting and ranting. There were tears and times I wished I could just run away and disappear, but I couldn't because I was too little to do those things. My escape was David. I could go into my room and listen to David and shut out whatever else was going on around me. I would watch *The Partridge Family* and wish I could be their neighbor so that I could go over to their house and hang out to get away from my house. David was a lifesaver for me in so many ways. I know he saved my sanity back then.

When he came on the screen I was mesmerized. He didn't look like the boys at school. He was beautiful. He had the shiniest brown hair and the most beautiful eyes that I had ever seen on any person. His voice when he spoke was beautiful too. I could not take my eyes off of him. I was head over heels in love. My mama called it David Cassidy Fever.

Watching *The Partridge Family* had become a Friday night ritual for me and my friends. One night my little friend Donna called me. Her mama had just bought her a whole pot of love beads and elastic string. We made chokers and ate popcorn, watched the episode where Laurie gets braces, and fought over which one of us David would marry.

I had met a boy at school named Jerry. He and I got along quite well. He also stayed with my babysitter over the summer and after school. Jerry was no David Cassidy but he was fun and he played guitar. After school at the sitter, he had told me that I was the grooviest girl he knew because I would play war with him and died better than anyone else he knew. Jerry also liked *The Partridge Family*, in particular Susan Dey.

The next day, I walked up to Jerry and not knowing exactly what such a relationship might entail, I said that I thought he should be my boyfriend. And he said okay. We spent the summer playing Partridge Family. I was Laurie, Jerry was Keith, my friend Mary Ann was Tracey, my little brother was Danny, and we had other kids from the neighborhood fill in for the other family members. We would put the 8 tracks in and we would pretend to play the instruments and lip synch. We got really good at lip synching *I Think I Love You*.

David was always a ray of sunshine in a dark place. I will always love him, and never forget him.

SCOTT KALCHERT – UNITED STATES

There I was, a 5-year-old boy minding my own business, playing with children's toys, listening to children's records etc when one day I heard the most incredible sound I ever heard: David's voice on the radio. My mother heard me singing along with *I Think I Love You* the very first time I heard it and rushed out to buy the 45. Then after wearing that record out *The Partridge Family* came on TV and changed my life forever. I was obsessed.

I received every album for holiday and birthdays. When I was 7 years old my dad surprised the family with front row center seat tickets to see him in concert at Blossom Music Center in Cleveland. I was mesmerized. I couldn't believe that I was sitting just feet away from the person I admired so much. David was my hero and I wanted to be just like him. My parents bought me a plastic David Cassidy guitar for my birthday. I played, or thought I was playing, along with his records day and night. My parents later bought me a really nice guitar and I was on my way to emulating David and his music. I stayed true to him. I even sang the PF songs as solos in my high school choir concerts.

Sitting here now in my early 50s I remain loyal and a true fan. I still play his music, listen to it loud and proud and he is still my hero. The devastation I feel over David's death is heart-wrenching, but all the other fans out there have comforted me. David will live on through every one of us that love him and his music and will be remembered and cherished forever. God bless you, David.

> **❝ I COULDN'T BELIEVE THAT I WAS SITTING JUST A FEW FEET AWAY FROM THE PERSON I ADMIRED SO MUCH ❞**

JAC – AUSTRALIA

Once upon a time back in a simpler era that was undoubtedly the best decade to be a teenager, the best music, the funky fashions, both hot on the heels of the psychedelic 60s, a gorgeous young man with a voice to match, took over the world. Or so it seemed at the time: David Cassidy, the love of my teenage life.

Melbourne 1974 and Cassidymania hit like a tornado. I was 13 and a half, and not allowed to go to the concert. Two of my school friends came back to my home to share the experience. I can still remember them; arms flailing, lost voices, but still managing to tell me everything that happened and even more amazing – me, understanding every word.

We used to save our pocket money then head down to the newsagent to buy the latest teen magazines. But you know there is always one girl that likes to give you a hard time and this one brought a copy of the *Rolling Stone* issue to school to gloat that Mr Clean Cut wasn't so very after all. I refused to look at the cover simply walking away and categorically stating that wasn't "my" David. Of course, many years later I was delighted to get a copy of the very same cover. Who knew, right?

On my 16th birthday we moved, and I came home from school and all my David stuff was gone. My mother decided I was too old for that stuff. I still have the first record I bought, *I Think I Love You*. On my 42nd birthday, my friend Jim got tickets to a night time show called *Rove Live* and after 28 odd years I got that EP signed along with a copy of *Old Trick New Dog*. I was finally in the same room and seated only a few rows from the front.

Let's head back to around February/March 1990, the local TV station was running the final syndication of *The Partridge Family*. I had two small children so I taped the show every day. While I was cooking dinner, I would put it on for them. The show hadn't lost its charm.

My friend and I started wondering what David was up to, no internet, no social media in the day. She called his most current record label but was told he was no longer with them, but when she contacted another they were so stunned to get a long distance call from Australia they sent a promotional pack including his latest album titled *David Cassidy*. We hadn't heard any new material for years. I popped it on the CD player, we listened to it together over the phone and I made her a cassette copy. It was a priceless possession for both of us.

In the package they sent us was also a list of David Cassidy fan clubs. One night we got a call from a Melbourne guy called Jim who only lived 15 minutes from me. We met up and have been friends ever since. He gave me some doubles of items he had, that I once had. I put a poster up in my daughter's room of "Keith Partridge" as she knew him. One day mum came to visit and I asked my daughter to take her grandmother down to her room and show her what was on her wall. All I could hear was "Oh my God not him again!"

I feel sorry for the generations of kids who followed us that didn't experience what we did. Sure, they had their own stars, but no-one like David, no-one even close. But then again the 70s were the best time to be a teenager.

SANDRA ALAN-LEE aka SANDY SERRANO / SANDY ALAN – UNITED STATES

I was a young actress and got a call from my agent to read for a pilot at David Gerber Productions/ Columbia Pictures called *Man Undercover*, a cop show and my role was the wife of an officer.

I had no idea at the time it was as David Cassidy's wife in the show. My name was called, and I walked in and to my left was David sitting on a couch with the warmest smile, simply saying, "Hi, nice to meet you", as he handed me my sides (script pages) to read.

Of course, I was dying inside and praying I would be able to calmly read with him, especially since I had to sit right next to him and stare into those beautiful kind eyes. He was totally disarming and put me right at ease. We ran through lines a few times, hugged and off I went. A short while later I got a call to be on his show

but not as his wife but as his partner's wife. The guy that played my husband was a very well-known child actor, Phillip Brown. I had a couple of scenes with David. One was in the first five minutes and at the very end of episode three, "Cage of Steel".

Once on set he always made me feel comfortable and had no problem running through lines for the last scene we had together. So easy going, he made sure everyone was happy and acted like any other crew member, not the star of the show.

Working with David was one of my favorite times filming in my acting career. Unfortunately, after the show, we never stayed in touch, but I always cherished those moments, thinking OMG I worked with and was kissed by David Cassidy!!!

DAVID HAMILTON

David Hamilton – Radio DJ and presenter who spent a lot of time with David on his 1973 tour of Europe and the United Kingdom.

I first met David when I "scooped" everyone else on radio having him as a guest on my BBC show in September 1972. We hit it off straight away. David Bridger, who was very much his minder and very close to David, was the plugger for Bell Records, his recording label at the time. We played football together in the Showbiz XI and it was probably through him that I was asked to compere David's shows at Belle Vue in Manchester and Wembley's Empire Pool on his 1973 tour. I think David wanted someone on board he liked.

There was always a great deal of excitement at Broadcasting House when David was going to be on the air, and he was on Radio One a lot especially with my good friend, Ed Stewart on Junior Choice. We generated a tremendous amount of excitement in the build-up whenever he was coming to the studio. Loads of fans would turn up, listen outside on their trannies and catch glimpses of him through the studio windows.

During his 1972 visit David had to stay on the *Ocean Sabre*, a yacht moored on the River Thames as no hotels would have him. They were not prepared to take the risk of being invaded by teeny-bopper fans who had stayed outside The Dorchester Hotel throughout his earlier visit that year bringing Park Lane to a standstill. I was his guest aboard the *Ocean Sabre*, and as we were chatting on the deck, girls who had lined the banks of the Thames dived into the water to try and swim to reach him. They were rescued by a police launch but it was clear David needed this level of security to guard him from his fans. They would have torn him apart.

He could not go anywhere. While he was in England, David would have liked to have had a normal life: see the country, go horse riding and relax before his shows. He was an example of how stardom can be too big, you become such a big star you become a prisoner, and he was.

I joined the 1973 tour in Belgium ahead of the UK leg. I saw what he meant about the pressures. While his entourage sat down to a dinner of steak and salad in the restaurant at the five-star hotel where they were staying, David ate his meal locked away in his room.

In more private moments he would tell me he had absolutely no social life at all. "In Hamburg, I've been out and enjoyed fresh air for exactly one hour. I managed to slip out of my hotel, hop into a car for a drive into the country," he once explained to me. "While in England I was hoping to see some of the countryside, but I know there's no way. These

David Cassidy was a guest on David Hamilton's radio show, September 1972. Show producer Paul Williams joins in the conversation as they read cards and messages from fans who gathered outside. Photo courtesy of David Hamilton's private collection

are the pressures of the pop star. I have to spend the whole time locked away. But while people want you, you have got to see that you don't let them down".

It's an interesting phenomenon when you think that it's men who are usually regarded as the aggressive sex and yet in teenage girls this was their first awakening of being attracted to the opposite sex. And somebody like David, who was a really handsome man, would be their absolute dream. The bloke at home is the spotty teenager who is likely to ask them for a dance or ask them out, but here is someone beyond their wildest dreams who fills their fantasy. David was constantly running and hiding from his fans for his own safety. He would disguise himself in a long, tatty coat, pull a cap down over his face, wear glasses and avoid the fans to get into venues unnoticed as he did in Antwerp.

Fans would rush outside after concerts hoping to catch a glimpse of him. A large black limousine – known as the Decoy Car – would slide up near the stage door. Fans would rush towards it expecting it to be for David who is instead bundled into a

smaller, less conspicuous saloon car, arriving at another door, dive into the back and lie flat on the floor. The planned manoeuvre never failed.

The first night we played Belle Vue in Manchester, I was grabbed by the mob when we left the venue half an hour after the show. The fans did not believe David had left and in the short distance I had to walk to the car one girl got hold of my tie, pulled it tighter and tighter trying to take it as a souvenir. I thought she was going to strangle me. The chauffeur pinched her

The emotion seeing David in front of you at Wembley. Photo: @RichardImageArtPhotography

> 66 FOR THE TALENT HE HAD, THE BIG STAR THAT HE WAS, I THOUGHT HE WAS NEVER REALLY AS HAPPY AS HE SHOULD HAVE BEEN. SOMEONE AS NICE AS THAT SHOULD HAVE BEEN A LOT HAPPIER 99

arm and she let go but it was a frightening moment.

On stage David was fascinating, giving an act in a white skin-tight jump-suit with multi-coloured embroidery and an equally dazzling belt, which was calculated to wring the last drop of hysteria from a mainly teenage audience. He loved his fans, but he hated the screaming when he was on stage because he had a very good singing voice and he wanted them to hear him sing. He put cotton wool in his ears so he couldn't hear the girls screaming and then, unfortunately, he couldn't hear the band.

But after the show it was a lonely life. He was a very nice guy to spend time with, but he was troubled, and I felt a sadness with that whole way of life as perhaps it wasn't what he wanted it to be. He was really an actor who could sing, was certainly one of the all-time great pop stars, but probably a lot more than that with everything else he did. He was a thorough professional in every way, always very courteous and pleasant.

I was very, very sad when I heard he had died at 67, so very young. I think he was a reluctant

Badges, rosettes, posters and unconditional love for David at Wembley. Photo: @RichardImageArt Photography

teen idol, something he was pushed into and really wanted to be recognised more as an actor or a rock musician. For the talent he had, the big star that he was, I thought he was never really as happy as he should have been. Someone as nice as that should have been a lot happier.

Back in 1973 I remember thinking David was looking forward to the days when he could entertain a more adult, and in many ways, a more demanding audience playing cabaret at London's Talk of the Town and The Sands in Las Vegas, developing as a strong film actor, and having time to do the things he really loved.

66 HE WAS A VERY NICE GUY TO SPEND TIME WITH, BUT HE WAS TROUBLED 99

Photos: Barry Plummer

JUDITH WILLS – UNITED KINGDOM

Judith Wills was working as a reporter for UK teen magazine, *Fabulous 208*, when David made his first visit to the country in February 1972. She spent most of the week with him as she had also been commissioned by US magazine, *STAR*, to be their UK correspondent for the visit. In her book, *Keith Moon Stole My Lipstick*, Judith recalled that week.

By the time he arrived – on February 7 (a fact recorded in big letters in my diary, almost as if I was impressed by this myself) – he was the biggest star, in teenybopper terms, that the UK had ever seen. The crowds at Heathrow and the hysterical fans who followed him round everywhere that week proved it. I firmly believe that if you want to be a teen idol, you can get a long, long way on great hair, a wide smile and a good set of teeth.

On the 8th there was a bus organised to take David and selected press, me included, round all the tourist spots of London for photo opportunities – but sadly we only got as far as Buckingham Palace and had to pack it in because the weather was

Below: Erna Haagsma, centre, with two of her Transavia colleagues

DAVID IN EUROPE 1973

David's first British concerts in March 1973 were all sell-outs. An estimated figure in excess of 70,000 people saw his 10 concerts which had a top price of £2 a ticket. The dates included four at Belle Vue, Manchester and six at Wembley's Empire Pool (opposite Wembley Stadium) where he set a new record: the first artist to sell out six consecutive shows over three days.

Costs for the European tour, which took in Belgium, Germany and Holland were in the region of £12,000 with a Caravelle plane belonging to Transavia of Holland chartered by Bell Records for £7,000. The name DAVID CASSIDY was carried down the side of the aircraft along with the Bell record label logo.

The touring party was 30-strong, with musicians and management including Tony Barrow, whose PR company was hired for the tour. He had worked with The Beatles in the 1960s and coined the phrase "The

Fab Four". He looked after the press corp who travelled with David and his team. In an interview in *Record Mirror* following the tour, he reflected on the way fans reacted to seeing David: "I haven't seen anything like it since Beatles' days and the Press we got on tour was staggering."

Airport security was tight everywhere. It was announced David would be landing in Holland at Rotterdam, but he arrived in fact at Schipol in Amsterdam in an attempt to avoid too many fans. It didn't work. Cassidymania was unstoppable. In scenes repeated everywhere, fans were there to welcome him with scarves, banners, screams, tears and hysteria.

"We had to be careful flying into Luton," Barrow admitted at the time. "It was a weekday for one thing, and not a school holiday, and we were aware it could be dangerous for the kids if they all surged forward to meet Cassidy. We were also aware that the exact airport location could have been leaked out. So many people knew about it – my office, Bell and the newspapers. But in the event, it was a well-kept secret and everything went according to our plans."

Erna Haagsma was one of the stewardesses tasked with looking after David and his entourage on board the tour aircraft. "I was awfully proud and excited to be chosen to accompany David on his 1973 European tour," she reflected. "I really liked

dire and David didn't want to get wet and cold.

On Thursday 10th I had my proper private interview with him at the Dorchester in his suite and had to shove hundreds of girls, who were crowding the outside, out of the way in order to get there. Even after all these years on *Fab* I still found this something of a buzz. I guess it made me feel glamorous, that old stardust rubbing off on little old me again. The fact that they all hated me for going to the one place they wanted to go – David Cassidy's bedroom – kind of didn't matter.

In truth, David Cassidy was quite unexceptional in every way, as far as I could tell, except that he had quite heavy pancake make-up on, which, in those days, wasn't the norm apart from glam rockers on stage. This was, I daresay, an attempt to mask the spots which had broken out on his face due, no doubt, to the stress of the tour.

The famous smile didn't show itself a lot except when the photographer, David Porter, turned his camera on him; he was a bit grumpy and a bit taking himself seriously, and while he wasn't the worst person I've ever interviewed he was not easy.

Judith's first report about David in *FAB 208* magazine, February 1971.

him, and he seemed a very nice and modest person.

"Girls were screaming loud and he was their hero or idol. I thought that maybe it was too much for David to be worshipped like this. He was far too young when he passed away. God wanted him to have a long life. It was good that he used his talent to give so much pleasure to so many. I hope David is 'home' and that someday we will meet again."

Planning for the tour had started in 1972. At the time, David's manager, Ruth Aarons, recalled: "David came to London after a skiing holiday in Europe and from the fan reaction at that time we knew he had a big following in Britain." They returned to the capital later in the year to plan the tour, David staying on a yacht on the River Thames after hotels refused to take him following the chaos he caused back in February. Thousands of fans brought the roads around the Dorchester Hotel to a standstill waiting outside the hotel to catch a glimpse of him and chasing him round London.

Barrow insisted his job was to make "as much noise as possible" about the tour throughout the world. The media interest was intense. "The travelling Press party was my idea – something we always did during Beatles' tours – although that was

a last-minute arrangement once it had been decided not to take any of the equipment in the aircraft."

All stage equipment was left in the States due to the cost of shipping it across to Europe, where road crews were hired for the 16-day visit. "There would not have been any room for the equipment and the Press. Cassidy's management thought it strange that the English Press party should want to speak to him," Barrow said at the time. "It should have been obvious that they would want to speak to Cassidy. We sorted the whole thing and the tour was a success."

Security was handled by Artists Services, formed by Don Murfet and Jerry Slater in the late sixties. They looked after all safety matters, investigating potential security issues.

Below: David with his tour party

David on his first visit to London in February 1972. Photos: Barry Plummer

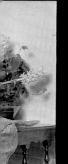

GAIL MERCER
– NEW ZEALAND

I was a shy girl in my first year of high school when I wandered into class one day to see all my friends in a circle buzzing about this gorgeous boy in this magazine. I wasn't your typical scatty 13-year-old, I was very mature and older than my years. My dad had died when I was 11 and I think as a result I grew up quickly. I went over to see who they were looking at and there on the page was a photo of the most beautiful boy/man I had ever seen!!! The man staring back at me took my breath away. I started buying magazines, and his records like my life depended on it. I was a self-confessed David Cassidy fan.

Two years later, January 13, 1974 started out like any ordinary Sunday in our sleepy little city of Dunedin in the lower South Island of New Zealand. I read in our local paper that David was coming to New Zealand performing at Eden Park in Auckland for one night only on February 26. The promoters were really good sending me parcels of promotional material: large black and white photos and stickers advertising his concert, and a huge poster which has become one of my most prized possessions. The promoter was Harry M. Miller and the lady I was writing to all the time was called Priscilla Edbrooke.

Elton John was to perform two days after David in Auckland. I liked Elton but not in the same way I LOVED David, but I bought tickets to David's show and Elton's. My mother was seeing a man called Jim and he had family in Auckland. He arranged for them to put me up for a week and their house was a 20-minute walk from Eden Park. Perfect! Because I had only little over a month to plan for this trip my funds were not going to allow for a return plane ticket. If I had been 14 or under the ticket would have been only $42 but because I was classed as an adult the ticket price was $92.

My babysitting jobs and part time café work were not going to cover this. I had paid nearly $10 for my two tickets. The only way I was going to be able to afford to go was as my sister. She was 13 years old, so I booked my ticket under her name. I felt like a criminal handing over my ticket in my sister's name. I was quite small for my age, very skinny and nobody paid any attention.

I had a week before David arrived so popped in to see the promoters almost daily. I got to meet Priscilla, and she was very nice. I think it must have been her who gave my name to a journalist, but I will never be sure how the next part of my adventure came about.

The following Friday a journalist (Dave Wheeler) from the *Sunday Star Times* came to see me. It had been arranged that I was to be the first New Zealand fan to meet David. I would get on the bus with the rest of his entourage at the airport. Later at an undisclosed hotel he would transfer from the bus to a car which would take him into the city.

Later that day I went to Dave's office to arrange the final details. David, his band, manager and friends were all arriving in Auckland and I was getting the chance to meet them all. It became obvious there was not going to be enough room. Plan B was for me to meet them at the hotel in the lounge for breakfast. Unfortunately, things didn't go to plan as David had endured a long-haul flight from LA and when he stepped off the coach, one of the promoters told me David wasn't feeling well and thought he was coming down with something.

I briefly met him, gave him a huge hug, handed him a letter and some photos I wanted him to have. His only words to me were: "don't come too close I think I have cholera". He asked me my name and if he should open the letter now. I said no, so he took it from me, shook my hand and got in the car. When I look back now at the photos that I took of David that day I realise he wasn't well. He looks tired and worn out. I don't

> ## ❝ I WILL NEVER FORGET THE IMPORTANCE OF HIM IN MY LIFE… HE WILL HOLD A SPECIAL PART OF MY HEART FOREVER ❞

Above: Gail Mercer captures David as he arrives in New Zealand, 1974

think he would have realised that me meeting him that day was one of the highlights of my life.

That night I was on the national news. They said this 15-year-old girl had hitchhiked 800 miles to see her idol. I didn't want to contradict their story as I didn't want the airline to find out I was travelling under my sister's identity. I might not get home.

As soon as I was dropped back into town by the reporter, I made my way to the Hotel Intercontinental where David was staying on the 11th floor. I waited outside for about an hour and later was joined by more fans. Two reporters came up and asked us questions about our vigil. The next day there was a photo in the paper of us standing outside the hotel looking up at his hotel room.

Me and another girl, Janine, decided we would try to get in to see him. Yes, looking through adult eyes now I feel bad about that, the poor man was sleeping off a bad bout of jetlag and possibly getting the flu. But we knew these chances we were taking were once in a lifetime, so we tried to get in to see him. It didn't work.

We went up to chat to the guard outside his door, when two of his entourage walked down the hall. One was Dave Kemper his drummer and the other, Jim the stage manager. We ended up showing them around town, they bought us chips, told me I had been really lucky to meet David as he wasn't feeling well at all, and promised to tell David about us when they saw him.

The concert was being transferred from Eden Park to the Auckland Town Hall and there was now going to be TWO concerts so I swapped my Elton John ticket for a 5.30pm concert of David's.

The next few days were spent outside the hotel David-spotting as more fans joined us. Janine and I saw Jim loading instruments into a truck. When we asked what was happening, he said they were heading to the town hall for a rehearsal, and if we were really good, we could come along. It was a hot day and the guys sent us out to get ice for their drinks. After waiting for hours, David arrived and looked fantastic. Unfortunately, we were spotted and booted out by Don [Murfet] who was head of security.

Lovely Dave told us to sneak up to the gallery and watch from there. We were up there a long time before David finally spotted us and asked who are those girls up there. Don came up and

chucked us out again. We found a way to the back of the stage and watched from there. I wrote in my diary that night that David seemed quite small, like about 5ft 6 or 7 and we discovered that he smoked a cigar.

We returned to watch more rehearsals the following day. Everyone had given up trying to get rid of us, allowing us to hide backstage in the curtains watching him. I think it was the fact that I foolishly took a photo with my flash that got us chucked out again.

A highlight of the concert was when Elton John appeared in the final half hour and they sang a medley of old rock 'n' roll songs together. I think I felt a bit flat after the show. I had expected so much more from him. Now as I look back, I realise that he was totally exhausted and that he hadn't had much more to give.

In 2002 I joined Jade Tan, who had started a website a few years earlier, David Cassidy Downunder, at one of his concerts in Melbourne. David looked so healthy and happy and he was so different to the last time I had seen him perform. He looked like he was glad to be there. His voice had matured and so had he. He was grateful to his fans for sticking by him and that came through in his performance.

I wasn't to meet up again with David until 2007 when Jade put my name forward for a show they were making in New Zealand called *Whatever Happened To...?* David came on and I remember rushing him just like I was 15 again and accidentally knocked his face trying to get a hug from him. Of course, he didn't remember me from 1974 but it was nice to meet him again.

I thank David for what he gave to me and millions of his fans. He helped me through some very

Newspaper cutting as fans gathered outside the hotel

Below: Gail stole the headlines as the first fan to greet David when he arrived in New Zealand

troubled times, and I will never forget the importance of him in my life. I thank him, too, for the friendships I have made because of him.

One of the tunes I want played at my funeral is one of his songs, *I'll Never Stop Loving You*. It sums up my feelings. I will never stop loving him, and because he is gone doesn't change anything. He will hold a special part of my heart forever.

ROBIN NASH AND ANN MANN

In the UK, Top of the Pops was the weekly chart-based music show on the BBC. Each weekly programme consisted of performances from some of that week's best-selling artists. Along with The Osmonds, David was banned from performing on the show after fans posed a security risk.

The late Robin Nash, who was the show's producer from 1973 until 1981, recalled in an interview in *Record Mirror* in 1974 how tight security had to be if they wanted David on the show.

Ann Mann, who worked as a production assistant on Top of the Pops from 1970 to 1974, also remembers her encounters with David. Here are their memories including when David appeared on the programme's 500th edition in 1973.

ROBIN NASH

"The Osmonds and David Cassidy are now banned from the TV centre through no fault of their own. If we want them on the show, we have to go outside to film them. Last time David was over [October 1973] we had to go out to the airport to film him in an aircraft hangar.

That was a weird day because somehow or another his suit had got lost on the way and he had absolutely nothing to wear. One of his entourage was sent out to buy another one. The one he came back with was white as requested alright, but it was also about five sizes too big. Poor David did the show with pins all over him in a haphazard tailoring job.

It all went OK in the end though, but it was kind of weird filming in secret – and believe me there was absolute secrecy. Virtually nobody was told. It was a bit like working for the French Resistance. It's a shame we have to go to all these extremes but it's definitely necessary now."

ANN MANN

"The first time he was on the show he seemed very aloof and unsure of himself. He seemed to expect everything to be done for him and, to be quite honest, he was rather difficult. That was the time we had him on signing autographs and talking to Tony Blackburn.

The next time he was on, we filmed him on the river [Thames] and he was still a bit like a spoilt kid, but you could sense that he was improving and gaining more confidence. That was a bit frightening because all these girls were throwing themselves into the river and trying to swim out to the boat. How none of them was drowned I will never know!

But the last time he was on, when we went out to the airport, he was just great and a real gentleman. You could tell that he'd finally come to terms with himself and he couldn't have been more courteous or amiable. He thought the whole bit about the suit disappearing was very funny and gave a great show even if he did have pins sticking into him. I don't think any of us really blame him for the times before. The pressure he was under in those early days must have been tremendous."

IAN EDWARDS – UNITED KINGDOM

I was a 21-year-old recording engineer working at Radio Luxembourg and we had celebrities coming through the studio all the time so to a certain extent it was a bit routine. In pre-internet days if an artist wanted to promote their record/book/film they had to tour the radio and TV stations and there was only Radio Luxembourg that wasn't a BBC station, so we had pretty much everybody who was anybody passing through our doors. If they weren't in for an interview they were there to voice commercials or record song demos.

The day David Cassidy visited was exceptional in that I don't remember another occasion when we had to defend the building from screaming fans. I was ensconced in the studio waiting for David to arrive. The fans were all at the front of the building in Hertford Street screaming their hearts out and, although I could hear it but didn't see it, David made an appearance on the balcony, much to the fans' delight. He was then whisked through the control room, where I was sat at the mixing desk, into the studio where I think he was interviewed by Ken Evans, the programme

director at the time.

I seem to remember an entourage of four or five people, more than usual for this kind of thing. The studio had a back door into Shepherd's Mews. At the end of the interview David was escorted out through the back door and driven away past a few fans who had taken the chance that he would leave that way.

My impression is that he was very affable and approachable and thoroughly enjoying the attention, but more than that I don't recall. I wasn't personally a fan (wrong gender really) but he was a big star at the time and it was quite an occasion.

NICOLA ELDON – UNITED KINGDOM

In 1976 I was living and working in London, having left school earlier that year. Through various contacts and friends who lived in Luxembourg we knew that David was flying out there for interviews. We managed to get hold of his itinerary and booked the same flight out from London.

When we got on the very small plane you can imagine how excited we were. David asked us to join him in the seats next to him. We chatted and he asked where we were staying. Our friends out there had said they would sort out something for us, so we told him we didn't know until we got there. He insisted we stayed at the same hotel as him. He gave us his lovely suite room and paid the bill.

At the hotel he spent time with me and my two friends chatting and taking photos. Of course, he

then had interviews at the radio station and other things organised for him. I subsequently returned to Luxembourg, living with my friends Kate and Chris (station manager and DJ at Radio Luxembourg). I was there for about six months looking after their young daughter.

Years later in 1991 I was on holiday in Florida with my own young daughter visiting MGM studios as it was then and by pure coincidence David was there to do his handprints and a question and answer on stage.

Above: David walks onto the balcony on one of his visits to Radio Luxembourg's London offices. Photo from a private collection owned by Jim Salamanis

Below: Nicola Eldon, far left, and friends with David in Luxembourg

JUDY ARONSON KAAN – UNITED STATES

Our story all started with a simple phone call. I was 15 and a half, and my friend Debbie Warner Gualtier two years younger. We were very giddy and nervous to make this call to David's beautiful mother, Evelyn, who graciously answered. She was very warm and pleasant. We talked for a while and she invited both of us over for lunch to her house in West Orange, New Jersey.

We lived in the same small hometown, and she was ready for us when we arrived. Conversation went so smoothly like we knew each other forever and our nervousness disappeared immediately. She talked about her dad who we briefly met who lived with her, and shared some stories about David. We made plans again to see her and told her that we were going with Debbie's mom and her little sister to the concert in March at Madison Square Garden.

I believe we saw her again right before the concert and another time in June. On one of our visits with Evelyn, Debbie thought that David was there. Many years later we read that he used to stay and hide away, I guess from the craziness he just wanted to relax away from it all. The time before the concert, myself, Debbie and another friend Sandy presented her with a scrapbook that I made. We also brought an early birthday gift for David of jade cufflinks.

When we arrived at Madison Square Garden, our seats were in the nosebleed section. Being daring as I was, I told Debbie there was no way I was sitting there. These days you never would have been able to do what I did. We walked down to the floor seats and saw two empty seats in the 10th row. We sat there and it also happened to be the same row Evelyn was in.

Years later, I was living in Encino, California, and met David at a play he was performing. He was so touched when I gave him the picture of his mom

and his grandfather, Fred, who he was so close to.

I was very blessed to go to many concerts including, of course, MSG, Nassau Coliseum, Atlantic City, NJ and a small venue called the Paper Playhouse in NJ back in the 90s. Ironically, I lived in West Orange, NJ, growing up, moved to Encino when I went to college and moved with my husband to South Florida. Unfortunately my husband passed three years later but he also loved David's music.

I will always remember and never forget David and his beautiful mother. I learned guitar because of David. But more importantly, he brought together two friends who are now lifelong friends forever.

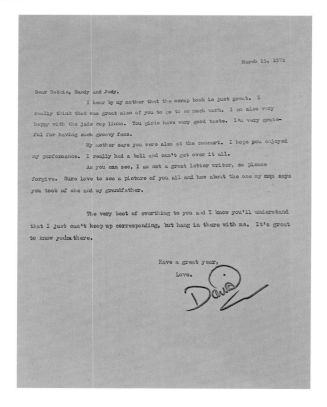

Right: Letter from David, courtesy of Judy Aronson Kaan and Debbie Warner Gualtier

Opposite page: Photos: Barry Plummer

BONNIE STRIPE – UNITED KINGDOM

I really fell into the abyss never to climb out again thankfully when I heard David sing on the radio and saw him on Top of the Pops. A state of adoration had begun. I would wash my hair before The Partridge Family show came on and of course he couldn't see me but that's no reason not to look one's best. He may have been in the UK on a secret visit and maybe knock on the door as a surprise. Oh, how lovely to be young and full of outrageous expectation.

I collected everything I could find with regard to David and my mother relented and allowed me to put his posters on my walls. She hung sheets up to protect the wallpaper and gave me pins to pin them to the sheets. I collected the monthly David Cassidy Magazine and scoured the teenage magazines of the day for anything David related. I still have a lot of the posters, magazines and my fan club membership packs and a box crammed full of newspapers or magazines, even if the name David was in print. Safe to say my world mostly evolved around everything David.

When David came here to tour in Scotland, there was no way I was going to be able to go, so I continued to wash my hair before the show and promised myself I would see him one day, all would be well, after all then I would be of an age to marry. The young girl who fell in love with David was about to be dealt a crushing blow. I was living and working in London when I passed a newspaper advertising board outside Victoria train station in 1977. I read the bold type as I stood in front of it for quite a while. I was aware of people bumping me as I was clearly in the way and a few grumbled at me to get out of the way. I still stood there.

Then tears tracked down my face. No sound emerged and a young girl who appeared to be the same age as me around 18 asked if she could help me, looked down to see what I was looking at and burst into tears. The pair of us had just read that David had married. We moved to the side aware we were causing a problem and stood holding onto each other for a few minutes silently crying. I have no idea who the girl was or anything about her, but she was there just when I needed her and hopefully if she was a fan then I helped her too.

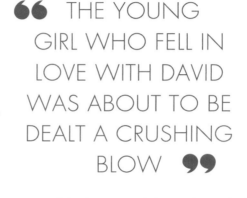

> 66 THE YOUNG GIRL WHO FELL IN LOVE WITH DAVID WAS ABOUT TO BE DEALT A CRUSHING BLOW 99

I first saw David in the flesh when he was in the UK in a production of the musical Time in the 80s almost 10 years after the Victoria Station shock. When David came out I swear I stopped breathing. Then the tears, oh for goodness sake this is what you have been waiting for. David breathing the same air as you and you're crying. I left a teddy bear, some flowers and a card for David at the box office.

My daughters grew up and the youngest in her twenties came with me to my first David Cassidy concert in Brighton. He held my hand whilst singing How Can I Be Sure.

At one Hammersmith concert, David said to the audience that he probably wouldn't be back. The lady behind me was inconsolable. I sat with her for a bit and talked to her saying that I was certain it wouldn't be forever. Again, no idea who this lady was but hopefully I was there for her and this is what David's fans are all about.

In 2017 things changed for all time. David had had troubles before, but he was clearly in trouble now and looking very unwell. The days before David's death were truly horrible and being in the UK the time difference from America was an extra difficulty. There we all were in the world praying for David, even I'm sure as if we'd never prayed

Evening Standard headline announcing his marriage which broke Bonnie Stripe's heart

before. It was not to be, and we all lost David that awful November day. Tears again, but this time they were tears of bitter anger, sorrow and desperation. The tears that flow now are of love and gratefulness of a love that I was privileged to have and will always have.

In the weeks that followed I took a rose for myself and my David Cassidy "sister" – she knows who she is – to a place we both know and left it there in remembrance of David.

What David meant to me is impossible to communicate but I know I am not alone in this and the friends I have made because of David understand completely.

Below: David would sit on the edge of the stage, as here at Wembley, while he sang I Am A Clown. Photos: @RichardImageArtPhotography

THIS WEEK – TV SPECIAL

Current affairs programme THIS WEEK broke new ground in March 1973 when reporter, Peter Taylor, and a film crew were given exclusive access to David during his record-breaking six shows at Wembley's Empire Pool. The Thames TV broadcast – Weekend at Wembley – featured concert footage, observations of fan worship capturing the excitement around his visit, plus conversations with David and his fans. Peter Taylor and his crew share their memories.

Peter Bluff: Our boss on *This Week*, John Edwards, in the weekly Thursday meeting announced that although there was a scheduled film/programme for the following week he would be open to other suggestions. "What's the most important thing happening this/next week?" he asked. Peter Denton bravely said: "David Cassidy at Wembley." There was much giggling. Edwards, surprisingly, wanted to hear more. Denton (a fan) explained.

Jonathan Dimbleby [reporter and presenter] was outraged at the suggestion, then after a 'show of hands' agreeing it was a good idea, Edwards quickly declared it a GO project. Edwards brushed the outrage aside and assigned Peter Taylor, Peter Denton, and me to make it happen. Jonathan continued his outrage, simply and perhaps rightly because *This Week* was always a serious vehicle, and this idea was off centre. But very much a decision of our great leader, John Edwards, who we all referred to as "Big E".

This is my most vivid memory: On the day, and on the ground at Wembley, in addition to other devices it was decided we needed to engineer a meeting between Cassidy and some of his fans. Tricky 'cause there were thousands and such a device might have been dangerous. I took on that bizarre task. It involved wandering around mixing with fans, mostly girls/young women. I remember asking dumb questions like, "How would you like to meet David?", "What would you say to him?" and other similar embarrassing and dumb-sounding questions. I then told them to "follow me!!!"

I remember there being several, but eventually 3, 4 or 5 made it upstairs into the hotel. Somehow it worked with much giggling. This was in fact a minor part of the film. Taylor and Denton were the chief movers. That it worked is due to them. Jonathan, appropriately, continued to be outraged. I suppose Edwards' decision to do the programme was the kind of breakthrough decision that only John would or could have made.

Peter Taylor: Weekend at Wembley brought THIS WEEK its biggest audience ever – and certainly the biggest audience I've ever had. I was saddened to hear of David's untimely death. I have no record of the girls' names, but I will never forget their reaction. I do remember being in the back of his getaway van and stopping at a random house to see if David could use the bathroom. The occupants couldn't believe it.

Peter Denton: After John Edwards, gave it the go-ahead, on Thursday, March 15 I met Ruth Aarons, David Cassidy's manager, at the Berkeley Hotel in London to discuss the shape of the proposed programme.

The following day at 6.30pm we met Cassidy himself at the Empire Pool, Wembley, where he was appearing, basically to make him aware of what we'd be doing and where we'd be during his performance later that evening. After he came off stage at around 10.30pm, his minders wrapped him in blankets so as not to lose body heat and spirited him away in a medium-sized furniture van containing an armchair (for him) and a Thames TV film crew. We piled in with him, but the fans caught wind of what was going on and started hammering on the sides of the van; rocking it, as well. Inside, it was unnerving and incredibly noisy. The fans had also discovered where he was staying, the hotel was under siege, and there was no question of going there.

We eventually ended up at a place called Horsenden Hill near Perivale, not that far from

Wembley. The place was deserted, so the back of the van was opened and Cassidy plus film crew came out for fresh air on a cold, crisp night. We all stood around for a while, and the whole thing was so bizarre that I simply have no recollection of what happened after that, or where we (and especially he) eventually ended up. It would have been way after midnight, and I was probably too zonked – I don't even have any idea how I got home that night!

As I remember it, the girls were in a long queue waiting for admission to the Empire Pool – and quite understandably, they didn't want to give up their places. But we had a brilliant ace in the pack; Ruth Aarons had given us a dozen or so premium seats close to the stage, so we were able to offer these in return for their participation. Their parents would certainly have been around as well, because we would have needed their permission for their kids to appear. But I have no recollection of the adults.

Two groups of girls were interviewed, and both used in the programme. One of the groups which included a girl called Tina and another named Theresa gave a typical response to meeting their idol, screaming when he walked into a small room in the nearby hotel where he was staying, to surprise them. We later filmed the girls (already thrilled out of their minds at meeting their idol) at the concert, and everyone was happy. The girls were terrific, the sequence was shot in one take with a hand-held camera and the girls' response was entirely spontaneous.

On Tuesday the 20th, Peter Taylor filmed a long, in-depth interview with Cassidy at the Churchill Hotel in London. We were with him from midday to around 2.30pm. And that was it....and at 8.30pm on Thursday the 22nd, we were on air. It was bang on in terms of reporting a news phenomenon that week.

A couple of observations about the experience. First – remember the whole programme was shot on film – not video (which was in its infancy). The camera was heavy and cumbersome and the film magazine which sat on top of the camera had to be changed every 10 minutes – which meant we could only film in segments. Not only that, but the sound recorder was also less than compact, and the reel-to-reel tape had to be synched with the film camera.

Second – throughout filming, David Cassidy himself couldn't have been more co-operative or courteous. He did everything we asked him to, even agreeing (much against his will) to wear the same

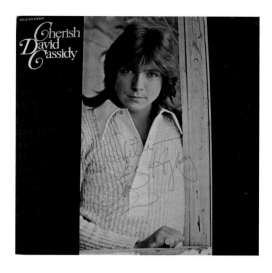

Peter Denton's *Cherish* album which David signed

sweat-drenched black sequinned costume for two consecutive performances for filming co-ordination. Bear in mind that this was a pop megastar, at the time one of the most famous people on the planet with a huge global following. No tantrums. No hissy fits. We filmed at his 8pm performance on Friday the 16th, and his midday, 4pm and 8pm shows on Saturday. I do have an LP which he signed for me after the shoot. Now, of course, it's a much cherished (pun intended!) possession.

For the few days we were with him, he was charm personified – and that, I think, is why all of us who worked on that edition of *This Week* were so genuinely sad when we heard of his death more than 40 years later.

Some 12 years after 'Weekend at Wembley', he appeared on the West End stage in *Time*, a musical fantasy, at the Dominion Theatre. I took Kier, my young godson (12 years old, I think), to see the show, and I wrote a brief letter to Cassidy which I left at the stage door. After the show, the doorman said: "Mr Cassidy wants to see you", and we were ushered along corridors to his sumptuous dressing room. He appeared, freshly showered, and made a huge fuss of Kier and treated him like royalty, as if he were the only person in the world who mattered.

David Cassidy was a delight, and I've never forgotten him for that. Nor has Kier – who, now in his 40s, still talks about that encounter.

This Week – *Programme Producer: John Edwards. Director: David Gill. Reporter: Peter Taylor. Researchers: Peter Denton, Peter Bluff. Transmission on the ITV Network: Thursday March 22 1973.*

KEVIN BARTHOLOMEW – LIFELONG SUPERFAN, NEWCASTLE UPON TYNE, UNITED KINGDOM

David was a huge influence on my life, 100 per cent. There was a wide range of music I enjoyed but for sheer talent and fortitude, David Cassidy was my Elvis. He was the personification of charisma. Cut me in half and there is David Cassidy like a stick of rock – he is part of me. I would never say I fell in love with him, but I did idolise him.

I learnt to play the guitar because of *The Partridge Family* and David. On learning that David's own musical favourites included B.B. King, Jimi Hendrix, The Beatles and a whole raft of 1960s pop acts, it encouraged me to explore. I did try to write a few songs and David's songwriting was my influence there. I copied everything about him – his hair, his clothes. I would have loved his teeth too!

Every shirt I had, had to be a copy of a David shirt. The shagstyle haircut gave me an identity as a teenager. Prior to that there was no eye candy. All of a sudden, I felt comfortable in my skin, having a hairstyle like David, wanting to be like him, it made me feel I had found myself as a teenager, taking pride in my appearance. No one had a greater impact than David. He never left my consciousness. It was

Kevin Bartholomew (right) wanted to be like David and recreated a rooftop pose

the lifestyle, he was the fabric that has become part of my own fabric. It's interwoven.

I really did love his self-compositions on Partridge Family albums, and they made most of the impact on me. In 1975 I read that the BBC were going to make a show with him to showcase his musical range and that was what I was looking forward to the most. I really wanted to see him just sitting there, playing the piano demonstrating his creativity and talent.

He was far more talented than anyone gave him credit for – he could play the drums, piano, guitar – his live drum solos were incredible. David is certainly one of the most under-rated singers of his generation. When he recorded *The Higher They Climb* he had arrived in terms of what I was waiting to hear. I love the grittiness of his cover of the Beach Boys' *Darlin'* and then switching to his breathless kind of whisper romantic songs. I love the control he had on his voice. I regard his live version of the Beatles' *Please Please Me* as far superior than their original.

I could see the conflict his music created within him. As soon as he embraced some of the heavier tracks, that was the David I longed to see and hear. *Rock Me Baby* was a revelation for me. I remember watching the documentary Weekend at Wembley in 1973 – he spoke about having to live up to the image sold to the teenage magazines and you could sense his frustration at not being allowed to be the rock star he clearly longed to be.

David was far more than just a teen idol, he was in reality the quintessential rock star. He could have been a younger Mick Jagger and he would have been incredible. If he had worked with David Bowie, I have no doubt that would have changed the direction of his music career and elevated it to another level. It is what we would have liked, a bit of the real David we really wanted to see. His RCA albums, especially *Home Is Where The Heart Is*, was so, so good, I had been waiting for that music from him.

The first time I went to London in 1976 I went round all my David Cassidy sites. I got the tube to White City which was like a shrine for me even though I had never been to the 1974 concert. I went to the Dorchester Hotel where he stayed in 1972, and to Parker Street to find the fan club office address. I was devastated to discover it was just an office block.

I have revaluated many things and I am sure David did the same. I thought that maybe he should have taken a different direction with his music to become more credible with the music press. We all see him differently. I totally embraced David Cassidy. His life must have been difficult at times and it is summed up in *I Am A Clown*. It's really Pagliacci. You achieve the American Dream and there is nothing inside the box.

When he was starring in *Time* in London I went to the first and last nights. The last night was on his birthday and that is etched in my memory now. David was amazing as he was every time I saw him including *Blood Brothers* and his Romance tour in 1985. There were many conversations I imagined we could have had. I always saw him in the role of John Paul Getty III, something which was spoken about some years ago but never materialised. It would have been one of many powerful acting roles which would have put him up there with the best. It would have brought to the surface the skill he had, his understanding of the art and demonstrated his acting. As an example, it is testament to his skill as an actor that people actually believed a 23-year-old was a 17-year-old.

I always wanted to say to him: This is the impact you had on me. It was his music and charisma for me. He had so much more within him we never saw. His influence and impact on my life was just massive. David helped me to personally develop a similar style, shape my own image and expand my appreciation of other music artists. I always wanted to just let him know how much I appreciated that.

Below: A security guard tries helplessly to try and stop fans from screaming. Photo: @ RichardImageArtPhotography

Opposite page: In concert 1973. Photo: Barry Plummer

This page: Pop star David Cassidy was mobbed by about 50 fans when he arrived at London's Heathrow Airport on June 21, 1975 for a private visit. The girls became hysterical when airport officials were seen trying to smuggle him away, and the experience proved too much for some of them, collapsing in tears. Photo from editor's private collection

BARBARA BALDUCCI – UNITED STATES

was 15 years old when I first saw David Cassidy at Madison Square Garden on March 11, 1972. According to David, it was one of his most memorable concerts, as it was mine. He was truly extraordinary. In my opinion he was never given the merit he so truly deserved. His striking good looks might have just overshadowed his talent in the eyes of the TV and music industries as well as with some of his fans. I was in awe of this man each time I saw him, but at 14 began my David Cassidy era which unbeknownst to him or to me, would be much more than an era as this man affected much of my life in many different ways.

PRESS CONFERENCE

Above right: Photo from Barbara Balducci's scrapbook

Above: Barbara meets David in 1993

Below: Signed photo taken at Special Olympics

I was approximately 12 years old when my grammar school class visited NBC studios in New York. I knew on that day that I wanted to be in broadcasting, and at the age of 18 I became a full-time-employee of ABC-TV in New York City. Why ABC? My favorite shows were being broadcasted by ABC and most especially *The Partridge Family*.

On June 17, 1974 I started my first day in the Broadcast Operations & Engineering Dept and was an employee for only one month when David appeared on *Good Night America*, a talk show hosted by Geraldo Rivera. I was able to get a seat in the studio to watch the taping of the show which aired on July 4.

In the early 1990s David was scheduled to appear on *Good Morning America* which was just downstairs from the office where I had worked. I planned to ask him to sign an 8 x 10 color photo that I had of him when he was appointed the National Youth Chairman of the Special Olympic Program in LA. I especially wanted to show him a personalized note card from his mom who had

previously lived in West Orange, New Jersey where David had grown up. In the 1970s I had obtained her address from a friend of mine and when David's grandfather passed away, I decided to send his mom a Mass card in her Dad's honor. Within a couple of weeks, she sent me a thank you note with some notations about David "knocking them dead in Australia" as well as an autographed photo of both of them.

I could barely sleep that night knowing that I would finally be able to meet him. The next morning, I nervously waited outside the studio. There was no one else around. Then I saw him walking down the long control room corridor towards me as I nervously stretched out my hand to introduce myself. He was very friendly and welcoming, and when he spoke, that beautiful voice immediately comforted me. During our conversation, his eyes were always focused on what I was saying.

I showed him the card his mom had sent to me, and as he read the note I explained why she had sent it. This was such a surreal moment for me. He then graciously signed the photo and said he did not remember where it had been taken. I explained it had been at the Special Olympics as he nodded in recollection.

As we started to say our goodbyes, I wished him well and once again extended my hand

and thanked him for everything. He then said to me, "My pleasure, thank YOU".

The next time that I met David was August,1993 when he and his brother Shaun were performing on Broadway in *Blood Brothers*. I brought one of the 11 "themed" scrapbooks I had made of him during my younger years. It was what I referred to as his "baby album". It was filled with articles and magazine photos starting with his birth certificate up to his 21st birthday. While David and Shaun were being interviewed on the set, I met Sue [David's wife] as she waited in the green room. She graciously invited me in as I began to show her the scrapbook. She commented how very much their young son resembled David's own baby photos. I told her to keep the scrapbook, she said that she could not take it, but I insisted. When David and Shaun entered, I introduced myself. I said to David, "I'm not sure if you remember me, but I met you almost in the exact spot about 10 years ago." He repeatedly nodded as he pointed to me and said, "yes, yes I do."

David and Shaun pointed out specific pictures in my scrapbook laughing as they reminisced. David could not thank me enough and immediately asked if I would like to see the play. I made a copy of the scrapbook for myself and passed the book on to their assistant when the tickets were delivered to my office. David had personally signed a playbill as well as three others where he had just simply

signed his name; again, another thoughtful gesture. Of course, the play was incredible and just the thought of sitting in David's guest seats while watching him perform on the Broadway stage was nothing short of astonishing.

Neither David nor I would have known how very much he would have affected my life. Never in my wildest dreams would I ever have thought that the home that my husband and I would eventually purchase would be only 18 minutes and 6.6 miles from that very address in West Orange where David grew up. How rewardingly ironic for this Staten Islander.

On the one year anniversary of his passing, my husband and I drove to his once childhood home on Elm Street and said a prayer. I greatly needed to do this for myself as I snapped several photos of that humble, little home.

So, in the reality of this thing that we all call LIFE and the daily decisions that we all make, it's only in hindsight that we can look back and see our own personal picture all come together. I can see mine so very clearly.

Above: Letters which Barbara received from David's mother, Evelyn

Below: Barbara's scrapbooks with picture from David's Nassau Coliseum June 1972 concert

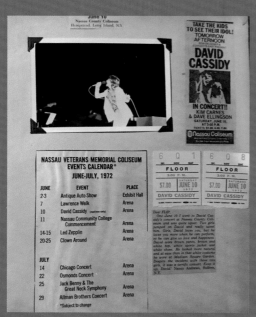

TERRY WING – SBStJ; SRN; RMN; Onc.N.Cert

Terry Wing was one of the officers in charge of St John Ambulance teams at David's White City concert in London on May 26, 1974. The tragic events which unfolded that day, and other mass crowd incidents he later worked at, made a lasting impact on the way Terry approached his work.

Terry spent more than 50 years in active operations with the SJA and was one of the founders of the Brighton Half Marathon, originally set up to help fund the building of the Sussex Beacon Hospice in East Sussex. He later helped organise the Brighton Pride Festival, drawing up operational orders and looking at risk assessment for the parade, to ensure maximum safety for the thousands who participate and watch. He currently works as a frontline SIA door supervisor (bouncer).

Volunteering to work at David's White City concert was important to me. It was a massive duty and one I wanted to do. With thousands of young fans and teenagers coming to a concert, it was always going to require a lot of experienced people behind the scenes to ensure everyone was looked after. I already had experience of large events such as football matches, Trooping the Colour and pop concerts so all of us working that very hot day, knew we might have a lot of excited girls anxious to see their idol, who might need medical attention.

White City was not a nice stadium. Built in 1908 for the Olympics, it was cold and damp, dark and dingy. We had specific areas to look after and my team were based under the seating in the terraces. The crowds poured in as soon as the gates were opened. As the day went on, we had lots and lots of casualties, some were very hysterical, or fainting in the heat. We were overwhelmed with work as hundreds of schoolgirls needed first aid or were taken to hospital with illnesses or injuries. We were emotionally drained by the end of the day.

I took a very short break because of the intensity of the work, walking through one of the tunnels leading onto the pitch. A plank walkway had been erected to get fans out of the terraces and onto the pitch. I saw some of my colleagues bringing out a girl who had collapsed. As a nurse I rushed over to help.

I had called in sick that day – I was a post graduate student nurse training at St Stephen's Hospital in London – because I wanted to do my public duty. I had forgotten to book my time off and it was easier to go "sick", but my name was splashed across newspapers the following day. I was seen treating a young girl who was swiftly taken to the Hammersmith Hospital, and someone must have given a reporter my name.

I later discovered the name of the girl I had been helping to resuscitate was Bernadette Whelan. She never regained consciousness and her death a few days later affected me deeply. Of all the people I have helped over the years, she is the only patient whose name I can remember. She made a lasting memory in my life.

If I see anything at all that could potentially be a risk to anyone else, I am on the case. Crowd safety is of paramount importance to me. I don't want to be in a position where I have to say to any organiser, "I told you so".

Since that day at White City I have worked at New Year celebrations in Trafalgar Square where two people were trampled to death, football matches, large shows and many events which attract thousands, but crowd management is always top of my list.

Stadium design and concert venues have been made safer, maybe not as a direct result of the White City tragedy, but the events that day of using a sports stadium for a pop concert made people sit up and think seriously about how to organise pop concerts at such venues, the welfare and safety of everyone.

Opposite top: David at White City. Photo: Barry Plummer

ANDREA PEARSON – UNITED KINGDOM

David's concert at White City in May 1974 was one of the greatest things I had ever been to. I would not have missed it for the world. My friend, Denise, and I were only 16 and travelled from Plymouth meeting other girls outside the stadium. All the girls were screaming and crying when David came on stage and I just wanted to see him. I was glued to the large screens set up around the stadium.

Fans pack into White City. Photo: @RichardImageArtPhotography

CAROL HAYWOOD – UNITED KINGDOM

I think it's fair to say that David was my first teen crush; first love really! I had a poster or two on my wall and would quite often spend my lunch money on a magazine if I saw David was in it. I had a Saturday job at Boots the Chemist kiosk at Waterloo Station. My boss would allow me to take my lunch-hour early so I could run home and watch *The Partridge Family*. My dear dad would record the shows for me on his Grundig reel-to-reel tape recorder (I still have the tapes).

I was over-the-moon when I was able to see David in concert twice at Wembley two days running in March 1973. The clocks went back on that Saturday overnight and I thought it was great I only had 23 hours to wait. Of course, looking back you can see how crazy the fans were, but at the time I was part of it, I never felt unsafe and just enjoyed living it, buying my programme which I still have, noticing it was one of David's bodyguards who sold me a poster, and of course screaming my head off during the concert and loving it! David "live", moving, speaking, real, breathing and singing for us...and he was so good.

In the 1970s I was able to enjoy "David moments", not least the fun of running around with other fans when we discovered which hotel he was in.

- I was in Park Lane when a London taxi stopped at the traffic lights. David smiled and stuck his leg up at the window showing his furry boots, and with that he was gone.
- I travelled to Heathrow to see him arrive, ran up and down back streets near the Thames trying to see him when he stayed on the boat.
- Spending nights huddled round an old battery radio trying to get a signal to hear his interviews with Tony Prince on Radio Luxembourg.
- During the Keep Britain Tidy campaign my mum, sister and friends took part in a walk across several bridges over the Thames, organised in David's name in aid of Muscular Dystrophy.
- At White City, David looked "small" but I could see him which was enough for me and just being there was amazing. The concert was incredible, and I was very impressed with David's ability on guitar and drums and I enjoyed him singing *Please Please Me*, *Delta Lady* and *For What It's Worth*.
- I was there when David was interviewed by Tony Blackburn at Broadcasting House (BBC) in June 1975. My sister and I were captured in a group picture by the press of fans who saw David leaving. I wrote to the BBC about that day, sending it in to Tony Blackburn's breakfast show and some weeks later, getting ready for school one morning, suddenly he was reading out my story. Oh, the excitement hearing my name on the radio.
- Standing in the street when David was interviewed by Peter Powell for Radio Luxembourg. David waved to us all.

I finished school forever that summer and it turned out to be an ultra-special day when I heard David was going to be at RCA (Curzon Street) in London that very afternoon so I went along. It was about the time *Get It Up For Love* was released (and then banned) in the UK. All afternoon fans were running around the building and screaming. I was standing at a side exit; a car pulled up and parked and then there was loud screaming coming from around the corner and fans near me ran, leaving me and others bewildered. David had obviously appeared.

Rare cocktail party invitation card

I felt sad, but the security guard winked at me and mouthed "stay there". Within 30 seconds, David came out of the side door heading for the parked car. I couldn't believe it! I couldn't speak, but I held out my hand towards David. He smiled and squeezed my hand tightly as he got into the car, which drove away instantly, leaving me quite breathless, faint and in tears. I was so happy!

Some fans found out he was off to Tramp for a promo party. David was already inside when I got there and I knew I wouldn't be able to wait, but after a while some people started leaving and a guy gave me his used invitation which is a nice keepsake of the day. I smiled all the way home.

My next opportunity to see David was at The Royal Albert Hall on October 22, 1985; and twice in Time in 1987. I think I was still very in awe of seeing David "live" and knowing he was right there on stage in person was magical. I saw him in 2005 on the Once in a Lifetime Tour.

I was deeply saddened and shocked to hear when David passed, not least as I had been married to an alcoholic and knew deep down some of the things David (and his family) would have gone though in his later years. A sad end for someone who, in my opinion, never truly got the recognition he deserved as a musician and who obviously still lived with demons left by the relationship with his famous father.

I'm sad I never got to meet him properly and actually wonder if we would have got on as he, I think, was probably quite stubborn. I thank the part of David that I was able to know for the love, the fun, his smile and, most of all, for the music. I truly hope David is now at peace and singing loudly in Heaven.

David greets waiting fans on a visit to Radio Luxembourg.
Photos: Liz Tiley

PAULINE GRIFFITHS – UNITED KINGDOM

I was besotted with David, had every solo single, LPs and all The Partridge Family music. My walls, even the ceiling, were covered in pictures. I even had a David Cassidy pillowcase. I bought every magazine he was in. I would sit and cry listening to his records, I used to sit crying listening to his records saying to mum, "I just want to be with him, Mum". She used to say, he's driving you crazy and you're driving me crazy. Mum didn't want me to go, at 17, to London on my own with my younger sister. The night before I couldn't sleep, so got up at 4am to get the train at about 6.30am. We got to London and everyone was brilliant with us; train drivers making the train wait. Just for us. People going out of their way to help us.

As soon as we got to the venue [Wembley Empire Pool] we met other girls all with the same in common, the love of David. One girl was telling us she had climbed the building trying to see David. That photo was also on the front of the *Sunday Mirror* with the photo of me

crying. It was an absolutely fantastic time, waiting for David to come on. All I did was scream and cry. I was on Cloud Nine.

The next day my dad come home from work, handed me the newspaper, laughed and said, "You would get your face anywhere". I was totally in love. I had never seen anyone so handsome but beautiful as well. I used to go in photo booths with his photo and have my picture taken, as if I was with him.

An old scrapbook cutting as fans storm the BBC

 I USED TO SIT CRYING LISTENING TO HIS RECORDS SAYING TO MUM, "I JUST WANT TO BE WITH HIM, MUM" 🙶

PAT MCFARLANE-ROWE – UNITED KINGDOM

Two days after my 13th birthday, I went to David's White City concert in May 1974, with my sister, Maggie Ellis, and cousin Shelley Hasted. We crawled through a window in the toilets and got into the stadium before it opened. We were able to get to the stand and watched the supporting act in rehearsal before being caught and chucked out. During the concert I got to the front only to be pulled out because of the crowd pushing forwards. Both legs at the top were badly bruised, but the excitement and thrill of that concert has always stayed with me and is reignited each time I go to any concert.

My sister and I were very lucky to meet David in his dressing room when he was starring in *Time* in 1987. We met him through my brother-in-law's connections and he was everything I thought he would be and more. He was genuinely interested in us, I was about 25 at the time, and just had my fourth child. David couldn't believe it and asked me all about them. We asked him about living in London and to be honest he kept turning the questions back to us. It truly was a magical experience that I will always treasure.

Even today when I think back to this night it brings a big smile to my face.

My love for David and his music have supported and helped me through many bad times in my life. Putting on a CD or a video/DVD in my darkest moments helped me smile and recall a happier time, and for this I will be forever grateful.

Pat McFarlane-Rowe (right) at White City Stadium two days after her 13th birthday with sister Maggie Ellis (middle) and cousin Shelley Hasted.

Below: Pat McFarlane-Rowe meets David in 1987

JIM SALAMANIS – AUSTRALIA

I own the red dungarees which David wore on his 1974 world tour. The spectacular outfit was for sale on eBay but without a photograph I had no idea if I was getting the real deal. The description fitted and turned out I was the only person to bid. I completely freaked when the lady who was selling sent me a photograph as it matched the poster I had of David wearing the dungarees on the tour. I think I paid a little over 300 Australian dollars.

The lady selling the dungarees wanted to build a tombstone for her sister who had passed away. In the 1970s she had been a huge fan of David and been to a few concerts. The costume allegedly was stolen by one of his bodyguards back in 1974. I think the girl's mother had paid around £50 for them which then would be considered a lot of money. Awful as it was for David to lose them, I was grateful that the money I paid went towards helping the family in the way it did.

Jim Salamanis with David's dungarees

Top and bottom: David was an exceptional drummer and singer. Photos: Barry Plummer

Above: David was faced with scenes like this all over the world. This was London Heathrow. Distraught, crying and waving, British fans see their idol David Cassidy leave Heathrow airport after his sell-out shows. Three thousand screaming teenage fans paid just 5 pence each to get to The Heathrow Roof Garden to wave David goodbye. Picture taken March 24 1973. Photo: Mirrorpix/Getty Images

In concert at White City. Photo: Barry Plummer

CLARICE LAMB – BRAZIL

I was about 10 or 12 years old when I first felt attracted by a boy. He was Keith, in *The Partridge Family* show. As I studied in an American school, and I used to hang out with the American students, I got a lot of material about David Cassidy. I guess I was the only Brazilian with a natural size poster in my bedroom.

The whole show was dubbed in Portuguese. I always waited anxiously for the song, when I could hear his voice. I tried to go to his shows, but maybe I wasn't mature enough or didn't have enough money, but the fact is that I never got to see him.

Every now and then I would search for him and see if there was a show I could go to. When he passed I realized that I had lost my chance so, I decided to honor him, and carry him close to me. My tattoo is his logo "DC" as a vase, or ground, for blooming flowers that grow into the air. I guess it describes my feelings towards the most beautiful man who ever walked this earth.

He was not only handsome, but a super talented and competent musician, actor, producer, writer. Perfection at every angle. That is what my tattoo represents.

GLORIA LONGINOTTI – CANADA

I got my tattoo on December 14, 2017, three weeks after David's passing which devastated me. I could not believe that my crush had died. It was like losing a member of my family. It took the tattoo artist four hours to do with breaks in between!! Not too much pain but any kind of pain would have been worth it for David. I was in tears when he did the tattoo, not from the pain but from his passing. When I saw David Cassidy for the first time and heard his sweet voice, I was hooked. I loved him then and love him now and always.

David had an impact on my life as a great, kind-hearted person, animal lover, and just a sweet all-round guy. It has made me take a look at my own life and to stop being bitter and to smile a whole lot more which I am doing. I have all of his books, dvd's, cd's and pictures of him that will be buried with me when I pass away which I hope won't be for a long time. I loved him so very much and still do.

BONNIE STRIPE – UNITED KINGDOM

I had a tattoo done of David's signature and some of his favourite flowers on my left inner ankle. It is special to me. This way I can have David with me always and whenever I look down, I smile and remember all the wonderful times I've had because of this amazing man.

KYM WINCHESTER – UNITED STATES

This tattoo is my tribute to David, and all he has meant to me, from the moment he entered my little girl heart, so many years ago. When I found out how sick David was, I prayed for a miracle. But I also prayed if he had to pass, please let him be unafraid and please let him feel all the love that was truly felt for him. Let his pain be set free, let him find the love and acceptance he never seemed to find here on earth. I love this man.

I knew I had to do something to have him be a part of me every day. So I planned out this simple tattoo. I have squandered so much of my own life – with pain, regrets, guilt, poor choices. When I heard David said, "so much wasted time", I wanted to honor him by turning myself around. No more wasted time.

The tattoo artist did his best to match the Partridge Family font, and I have David's Partridge on me, shedding one sad tear. When I go off path, I look at this tattoo. When I'm alone in my car, I talk to David and I say I hope he knows now how much he was loved, and how much he gave to so many.

People ask me about my tattoo every day, and I get to talk about David. Every day I feel he is with me, somehow, keeping me from racking up even more regrets. When I miss him, which I do every single day, I touch "his" bird. I hope he knows that, through his music, his beauty and his light he truly had an impact on this world and those of us blessed to have loved him. RIP my sweet angel. I love you so.

LIES HUIZEN VAN – NETHERLANDS

I have been a fan of David's since I was 16 years old, I am now in my 60s. David is my whole life since I first saw *The Partridge Family* and David singing. He helped me through my teenage years and tough times ever since. His music inspires me. I want him forever on my arm because if I die he is with me always and forever.

REGINA CHAPMAN – UNITED STATES

I can't believe songs written over 40 years ago still have that kind of impact on me and I am truly touched by them daily. So much so that I had a number of tattoos done: *Junked Heart Blues, Can't Go Home Again, Daydreamer* and *Tomorrow*. These songs are very personal to me. It may sound silly for a grown woman, but I feel even closer to David now with these words written on my skin.

USE THIS DOOR TO

A PLEA FROM DAVID CASSIDY

ASK DAVID ANYTHING!

Meet me here in Marabelle each week

ROCKING WITH DAVID

By David Cassidy

Photographs of DAVID CASSIDY FOR SALE
(including today's concert)

Celebrity Photos
P.O. Box 243
Brooklyn, N.Y. 11210

Photographs of many other celebrities also available!

Nassau Coliseum
June 10, 1972

DREAMS ARE SUMTHIN MORE THAN WISHES

CASSIDY— fans protest

Some irate DAVID CASSIDY fans popped into the FAB offices the other day. Their Mission? To inform us that they intended to picket the BBC in protest, 'cos the Beeb is dragging its feet over bringing back *The Partridge Family*. We agreed to help at once, 'cos we think TV is rotten without David and the gang too!

Anyone who lives near London can find out when and where the protest will take place by sending a stamped, self-addressed envelope to: DAVID CASSIDY PROTEST, c/o Miss C. Melite, Flat 2, Lancaster Lodge, Lancaster Road, London, W.11. You'll then be notified of the details. All letters should arrive by April 29th. The protest is planned to take place on a school holiday. If you don't live near London, why not write a letter of support to one of the organisers, Carmen Melite, Lorraine Frankie and Helena Zbroinska, at the address above? Every little helps, and it's certainly a worthwhile cause.

starpics

Danger! CASSIDY at work!

BITTEN, SCRATCHED, PUNCHED!

David Cassidy? He's just great!

Val Mumba goes to Wembley

Wembley, with exclusive pictures by John McKenzie

DAVID CASSIDY
DARLING DAVID

David Cassidy for ever
David Cassidy love you
David Cassidy for ever
David Cassidy for me
David Cassidy love you
David Cassidy for ever...

NEW Spotlight

WHAT NOW FOR DAVID?

MUNGO JERRY
ALICE IN WONDERLAND (OF THE WOMBLES)
The Rolling Stones

DAVID

WEENYMANIA!

Girls rush stage at David Cassidy's first British show

David's not off TV yet

WIGGLING CASSIDY SHAKES

pink pop bag

DAVID CASSIDY

SCRAPBOOK

ROBERT PATERSON presents

DAVID CASSIDY

BELLE VUE, MANCHESTER (061-223 2927)
Tuesday, March 13, at 5.30 p.m. and 8.30 p.m.
Wednesday, March 14, at 5.30 p.m. and 8.30 p.m.

EMPIRE POOL, WEMBLEY (01-902 1234)
Friday, March 16, at 8 p.m.
Saturday, March 17, at 12 noon, 4 p.m. and 8 p.m.
Sunday, March 18, at 4 p.m. and 8 p.m.

THERE ARE STILL A FEW TICKETS LEFT FOR THE ABOVE CONCERTS
DEFINITELY ONLY CHANCE IN 1973 TO SEE DAVID CASSIDY LIVE ON STAGE!

DISC

WIN A SLADE
ROLLERS POSTER

IN THE PIT WITH ROS

RAY STEVENS

DAVID CASSIDY

The Law and Billy Burgess

Widow M. K. Curtis joins Ben Cartwright in announcing the opening of a new school on the Ponderosa, an occasion marred only by the disrupting actions of a rebellious youth, Billy Burgess . . .

Ben	Lorne Greene
Hoss	Dan Blocker
Joe	Michael Landon
Candy	David Canary
M. K. Curtis	Mercedes McCambridge
Billy Burgess	David Cassidy
Doc Lyman	Les Tremayne
Tom Burgess	Bill Phipps
Billings	Charles Maxwell
Coulter	Sam Melville

Fabulous 208

WIN A PERSONAL TAPED MESSAGE FROM DAVID CASSIDY

David Cassidy
David Cassidy
Could It Be Lo

David Cass

OSMOND BROTHERS
YOUR JUNE CALENDAR
IT BROKE MY HEART WHEN...

WEEPY BOPPERS

By DEBORAH THOMAS

David Cassidy slips in secretly leaving his fans in tears

Adoration

EXCLUSIVE LOOK-IN

FANTASTIC DAVID CASSIDY COMPETITION

100 ALBUMS MUST BE WON

QUESTIONS

from our family—

...the best 2 minutes and 30 seconds of "breaking up" ever put together!

THE PARTRIDGE FAMILY

Starring SHIRLEY JONES • Featuring DAVID CASSIDY

"BREAKING UP IS HARD TO DO"

Produced by WES FARRELL for Vocal Rock Productions

inside: what it's really like on tour with David Cassidy

RECORD MIRROR

CHICORY TIP: 'We were daft to go heavy'

THE SUPREMES: 'But we're STILL Supreme!'

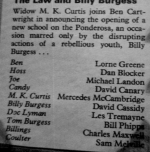

Photo: Barry Plummer

66 People were very afraid of letting me stretch out on my own, but I've got to keep changing. I have to outgrow my fans and then let them grow with me. I think it took a long time for them to believe that this was so. But I feel that my direction is positive. I have to grow and expand 99

Record Mirror, September 1972

2

★

MAGIC MOMENTS

My most treasured possessions from meeting David are the powder puffs and sponge I used when doing his make-up, and the tablecloth he autographed for me when he made appearances on BBC Television. I keep them locked in a tin. I was working as a make-up artist with the BBC, and had already missed my chance to meet him on *The Terry Wogan Show* where he performed *The Last Kiss* for the first time on British TV in February 1985.

A few days later he was going to be a guest on *The Kenny Everett Show*. A colleague and I were walking along a corridor and she whispered to me, "he is about to come through the door". I looked up, saw this man who I had been in love with since I was at primary school walking towards me. I just looked at him. All I could think to say was "Hello".

> ## 66 IF THE FANS GOT HOLD OF HIM, THEY WOULD TEAR HIM TO SHREDS AND HE MEANT THAT LITERALLY 99

He looked at me and said "Hello" back with a big smile on his face.

I turned into the make-up green room, and my knees instantly collapsed beneath me. Everyone I worked with knew how I felt about him and to meet your idol is often overwhelming. It was. How I managed to even speak to him I shall never know, it was almost a surreal moment. Since the age of 10 I had adored him, bought every magazine I could find with his picture in and plastered my bedroom walls with posters.

It was in the Green Tea Bar that I first really chatted to him. I was a lot more relaxed now, and he signed my tablecloth on which I collected signatures from actors and singers I was making up. There was a large circle in the centre which was reserved for David in the hope that one day I might get the chance to meet him. He signed it and as with the others I later embroidered over his signature. I told him I'd be making him up for *Saturday Superstore*. He seemed to be happy about that. I know I was.

Knowing I was going to meet him again for *Saturday Superstore*, I took along a load of my memorabilia – scrapbooks and photographs to show him and he was fascinated when he saw what I had done in the 1970s.

He told me he really had no idea his fans collected so much and decorated their bedrooms explaining that for him his life was like living in a bubble. David told me he did not know what the real world was like and every time he went out everyone just wanted a piece of him. If the fans got hold of him, they would tear him to shreds and he meant that literally. "A piece of my clothing, my hair, my body", he exclaimed to me adding all he wanted to do was sit and talk with his fans.

He did tell me he never really knew if people liked him for himself or the image they had been sold. He seemed a little scared of all that attention which must have been frightening and was surprised to hear the lengths fans went to for him.

He was completely interested in what it was like for his fans in the 1970s and he absorbed everything I told him. I had made a postcard with a ticket from his Maine Road, Manchester, concert in 1974 surrounded with pictures of him which he signed for me. The presenter, Sarah Greene, showed it on TV when she was interviewing him.

A few days later I found myself doing his make-up again, this time for Top of The Pops. Every time I did his hair or make-up we would just chat about

Above and right: Chrissie Webster and David

Previous page: Photo: Barry Plummer

anything and everything. David was always happy and laughing and fun to be with. I only saw him agitated once and sensed he needed to be alone.

In the late 80s I went to visit friends in Washington DC in the States. Radio station 104 was running a competition to win four tickets to the Monster Bash fancy dress party at the Old Post Office in Washington DC where he was hosting the event. The tickets went to the 104th caller to phone the station when they heard this specific sound they played on the radio. I told my friend I had to give it a go, and I was successful in my attempt to win them.

At the party he recognised me, which was lovely, asked what I was doing in the States. People said he always had a good memory for faces. I was thrilled he recognised me.

In April 2002 I met David again on *Star Lives*, a programme here in the UK similar to *This Is Your Life*. I did his make-up that day and his son, Beau's.

One thing I always remember about David was his lovely hair and silky, thick long eyelashes. At the time I did his eyes in the 80s, I wanted to make sure they looked perfect and natural. He had little bags underneath his eyes to the side which he was very conscious of and asked me to make sure I cover them up. He was fussy about his hair too, he did have his own hairdresser at the time in 1985. But the day he was on *Top of The Pops* turned to his manager and studio runner, and said, "I want Chrissie to do my make-up today", still makes me smile.

IAN RAVENDALE
– UNITED KINGDOM

In the mid 1980s I was a freelance television researcher, working on local and national arts, entertainment and music programmes for ITV and Channel 4. One of these was *Bliss*, a Channel 4 pop magazine we made at Border TV in Carlisle and I booked David as 'guest co-presenter' alongside regular host Muriel Gray for an edition of the show.

A couple of weeks prior to the recording, I get a phone call in the production office from a lady whose name I don't remember more than 30 years later but will call Carol. She'd heard on the grapevine that David was going to be appearing on *Bliss* and wanted to know if it was true. And if so, where could she get a ticket? I tell her, yes, it was true but there weren't advance tickets for the show and our regular audience just turned up at 10am and queued outside of Border Television and she was welcome to do likewise. If there was any problems, she could ask for me and I'd make sure she got in.

Ten days later I get another call from Carol and she asks whether David is still booked for the edition of *Bliss* due to be recorded a couple of days later. Is it OK if she comes up? I answer 'yes' to both questions.

The evening prior to the recording, I go over to the Hilltop Hotel in Carlisle where David was staying to talk through what would be happening. I wait in the lounge and after a couple of minutes he comes in, I get up, introduce myself and shake his hand. David is smaller than I imagined he'd be – 5ft 6ins maybe. He's got longish spiky dyed blonde hair in the style of the day and is slim with the taut physique of a dancer. We sit down and indulge in chit chat for a while.

What David is understandably most interested in is how we're going to present him. As with most of the TV pop shows of the time guests would mime their new release. Performers on *The Tube* played live but the production had a much bigger budget and a purpose-built studio at Tyne Tees in Newcastle which BTV didn't have. To get around this for *Bliss* we'd pre-record bands playing live for half-an-hour or so in front of an audience in Border's scene shed decked out like a rock club. We'd then drop a couple of songs from the live performance into the Friday afternoon programme.

As David was about to start on his first UK tour for 10 years and was about to release *Someone* as a follow-up to *The Last Kiss* to promote his tour, *Bliss* director Harry came up with the idea of having David playing his guitar and singing/miming in a cherry picker that we'd raise over the studio audience gathered in the souped-up barbecue/picnic set erected in BTV's car park. We'd keep the supporting arm out of shot so it looked like David was floating over the crowd. There was one detail I needed to play down.

Back in the lounge of the Hilltop Hotel I'm running through the set-up with David, and as I'm doing so, I'm thinking, "This sounds so bloody naff…." As I'm nearing the end, David leans back, draws on a cigar that's almost as big as he is and says; "Hey Ian, this isn't going to look…….. wanky, is it?" "No, of course not David……."

When David walks on to the set, he recognizes Carol, says hello, touches her on the shoulder and takes his seat next to Muriel. Bearing in mind he's probably caught on to the possibility that the cherry-picker routine could easily turn up on one of those 'Most Embarrassing

Moments' clip shows and has seen that the flying bucket is totally covered in pink balloons he could well have refused to play ball and insisted on doing his spot with both feet firmly planted on solid ground.

To his credit, David gets on the cherry picker, pink balloons and all and carries it off like a true pro and mimes *Someone* apparently flying over the car park while the audience of punks, new romantics and human puppets groove around 20 feet below.

A happy Carol comes up, says thanks and leaves for the railway station. Despite being a decent song *Someone* only had a UK chart run of three weeks, peaking at no 86.

I say goodbye to David and wish him well for the tour. I liked David. He was a nice guy and I was sorry to hear of his passing.

MARK ANTHONY – UNITED KINGDOM

Sometimes, an individual comes along who is totally unique. David Cassidy was a breath of fresh air for sure. Whether on TV in early guest roles on *Ironside*, *Bonanza* or as Keith Partridge in *The Partridge Family*. What you saw on screen was a kind, gentle human being who radiated a very special warmth. Yes, he was 'pin up' material with long hair and good looks, but there was more to him than just that. If you listen to his voice you can truly feel it. He was no ordinary singer. He could rock just like the best of them, while conveying something pure and almost angelic at the same time. Who can forget *Darlin'* or *I Write the Songs*, *Could It Be Forever* and *Daydreamer*.

> ❝ HE COULD ROCK JUST LIKE THE BEST OF THEM, WHILE CONVEYING SOMETHING PURE AND ALMOST ANGELIC AT THE SAME TIME ❞

He trod the boards of Broadway in *Blood Brothers* and in London with *Time: The Musical*, where he projected believable characters with true passion. What I remember most was David's great voice as it swept around the Dominion Theatre's sound system. That very special 'unique voice' that came out of my radio in the 70s along with his TOTP appearances.

David's command of the role was his right from the start, playing rock musician: Chris Wilder. The show was very much ahead of its time with great special effects including a huge projected floating head featuring a pre-filmed Laurence Olivier. His acting was very credible, I remember that very well. He was able to project a really special 'loving presence' which I'm sure was felt from everyone in the audience. I am so pleased I got to witness David 'live' in a really unique show, one that he easily made his own.

Thank you for the music and memories, they will live on for as long as we hold you in our hearts. And that is forever.

In October 1985 following his successful shows at The Royal Albert Hall in London, David performed at Blazers in Windsor. Sarah Robinson captured the excitement

CLAUDIA HELL – GERMANY

I cannot remember when I fell in love with David, but it just happened to me by seeing a picture of him. I was only nine years old and didn't really know anything about love at that time. If I ever met him in person, I think I would have screamed and run away, but I do want to say how much David saved my life while my mother was really sick. My love for him gave me so much happiness in a very sad time, and I always turn to him when I feel sad. He makes everything better. David was my first love and will be my last.

SHARON BELL-HORODYSKI – UNITED STATES

In the mid-1980s, David came to summer stock theater for a week in Ohio, as Joseph in *Joseph and the Amazing Technicolor Dreamcoat*. This theater company always met with people after the shows, so I talked to David every day for a week. Heaven! He was still just as completely cool and groovy. His voice in that show was phenomenal. I loved it when he would really belt out songs, in that strong clear voice. I secretly taped the musical numbers with a tape recorder by my feet.

The only photo I have of David and I was taken by a bystander, ironically, someone whom I met at that play after having met her at the first concert in 1971. David was signing my favorite album for me. I went to lean down, and at the same time, David went to stand up. We met in the middle, and he was laughing and saying, "Look at this! We don't know if we are coming or going!" He was tired and worn out after the show, but as always, good natured and kind.

I'd given him the sexy side of *Home Is Where The Heart Is* to sign, and he'd turned it over and signed the front. Wrong side, David! David was our first real exposure to sexy. He was not QUITE clean cut. There was an edge to him, which stayed through all these years. I'm sure our parents lost it when THAT issue of *Rolling Stone* first came out and had given up fighting it by the time *Rock Me Baby*, hit the charts. David balanced our naïveté with knowledge, guided us unwittingly from girl to woman.

I fell in love with David in September 1970 when *The Partridge Family* premiered on TV. I had certainly never seen a groovier guy or heard a more beautiful voice in my life. The thunderbolt hit, all bell bottoms and smelling of sandalwood, and sounding like the beach at sunset…and David stayed a part of me until this day.

In December, David came to Cleveland to be the Grand Marshall of the big Christmas Parade. My mom took my best friend, Vicky and I, complete pandemonium, but that was the first time I saw him in person, and he was even groovier than I thought he'd be. It was as if the winter sun was sparkling off his smiling face. Mom took us to the hotel he was staying, and we saw him up close as he left the building, no time to say a word. It was alright, I was speechless anyway.

The following June brought my first David concert, and we had very good seats thanks to the efforts of my mom, who was then knocked down outside Cleveland Public Hall by running girls, and skinned her knee, but soldiered on, happy that she could share this with her daughter and friend. My mom encouraged our madness and made sure I got a new dress for the concert. For my birthday mom had two of our best photos from that concert enlarged and framed for me. A souvenir of both David and my dear mom now in Heaven; and I cherish it to this day.

She took us to the hotel where David and his band were staying, although it turned out David was sick with his gall bladder, prior to his surgery. Nevertheless, Sam Hyman and the band of Brooks Hunnicutt, Kim Carnes and Dave Ellingson adopted my friend and I, treating us to Shirley Temple drinks while mom chaperoned, signing our autograph books, and singing songs in the hotel lounge. Sam took pity on us, telling us where and when they would be at the airport the next day.

My grandma spent that evening making a batch of her famous chocolate chip cookies for me to give to David. I had them in a tin, and

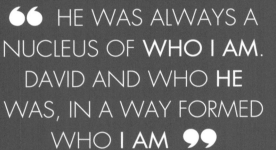

> **" HE WAS ALWAYS A NUCLEUS OF WHO I AM. DAVID AND WHO HE WAS, IN A WAY FORMED WHO I AM "**

we met Sam at the gate at the airport. I felt like I'd faint when David got off the airport cart and approached us. He was so sweet and kind, and we were probably total goofballs, but he overlooked it. We were actually speaking to him, and he spoke back, smiled, laughed, and appreciated the cookies. It went by in a blur, but is still one of my most cherished memories.

Mom, grandma and I were on a family vacation when we heard the Partridge Family was filming a show at King's Island Amusement Park. Dave Madden befriended my grandma, and they hung out together, smoking Chesterfield cigarettes and talking for hours about the good old days. Danny kept trying to chat me up, and I played pool with him at the hotel game room. But I only had eyes for David, who talked with a small group of us at the hotel after filming, signing autographs, and gratefully accepted teddy bears and gifts we had for him. I gave him a candle and incense bought specially for him at Spencer Gifts, one of the cool hippie stores.

Through the many years I saw David in concert whenever he came to Cleveland or Northern Ohio, I've seen him in Las Vegas, and in New York on Broadway. Maybe 20 times. He always made me happy, and looking back, now it seems like he was always a nucleus of WHO I AM. David and who HE was, in a way formed who I AM. Back in those early years, we were passionately interested in finding out more about David and if he liked it, we liked it too!

There were so many, many things that I exposed myself to because of David's influence in those early years. David said he liked a singer named Linda Ronstadt, who I then found out was incredible and she became my favorite female singer. Others, like BB King, I tried out and did not find them to my taste, and that fell away like snakeskin, leaving the parts that eventually became who I am. We drank 7 Up and ate cashews. I drew the line at lobster. David had a Mustang, then a Corvette, so I learned about cars. I learned about Los Angeles and The Valley, famous clubs and local singers; the theater, politics and New York City where he was from. He exposed his soft side, and let his fans know that he was a real person. There was, indeed, a little bit of him in every bit of me.

After seeing him in At The Copa with Sheena Easton in the early 2000s I watched him walk

through the casino after the show. I wanted to leave him alone and have peace without someone running after him. He had a water bottle in hand and looked tired, relaxed, and every bit as beyond groovy as he was years ago. I smelled incense and candles and heard yesterday's plaintive guitars in my head. I just adored him and loved him, no matter what.

I last saw David in concert in June 2016. I had tears in my eyes, singing, *I Think I Love You*, back to David with my arms outstretched. I felt such happiness, love and nostalgia, and I was so grateful that David was still in my life. When he announced shortly after that he had dementia, I knew it was a lie. I knew he did not, and that he was covering for something. I didn't suspect it was as severe as it was.

My 1970 love for David changed through the years, morphing from one thing to another, but always there and happy to see him, hear him, share in his life and talent. I was heartbroken in November 2017. Even as David left this earth, I was on line with other David fans, holding hands and grieving together as he taught us about acceptance. We are not perfect, so I don't know why we expected David to be perfect. He left us too soon, and I haven't quite gotten over it. Seeing the photo of David's ashes being scattered was one of the most startling and stunning things I have ever seen. Is that all there is? Oh My God, that's all that is left of David?

No, of course not... there are millions of women like myself, who were formed by who David was and who he still is. He lives on in his music, and in parts of us molded by his hands in our adolescence and through summer days of daydreams and of reality.

Someday, over the bridge we will all have great seats listening to him sing, laughing with him, giddy and getting autographs once again, basking in the sunshine, flowers, and love beads that was David. Now and forever I love you, my Darling David.

Above: Sharon's cherished framed photograph from her first concert

Left: David and Sharon Bell-Horodyski

LISA DAVIES, LISA DAVIES PROMOTIONS – UNITED KINGDOM

In the early 1980s George Michael and Andrew Ridgeley were at the height of their fame with Wham! As a young promotions manager with the CBS Epic record label, I knew them very well and it was not unusual for both of them to call into the office and spend time with us. One year during the height of their fame, Epic held a Wham! Christmas party for staff and some media at a club in central London. It was a fun night and I clearly remember at one point during the party I was standing in the middle of the dance floor with the glitter ball spinning round above me.

I wasn't dancing but in deep conversation with three others. I was distracted just for a second and I remember thinking, "Hey, I ought to take a mental step back here and remember this special moment", as in fact, a work colleague and I were standing there chatting with George....and his guest and good friend, David Cassidy. I had no idea David was going to be there and I had been a huge fan of his in the early 70s. He was the first and only pop star I really idolised, and I loved everything about him. Unfortunately, I had never met him before, but we stood there that night just having a completely normal chat, like old mates!

You can get a little blasé working in the record industry, as you are constantly surrounded by famous people on a regular basis but to be standing there in David's company absorbing his lovely smile and mild manner, was one of those surreal moments where you have to come back to earth and gather yourself. It was a great moment for me and one that will stay with me forever. I have no idea what we talked about, but I got that special feeling inside that takes your breath away.

I am sure he and George had a lot in common. That transition from a regular person to being propelled into stardom and not ever being able to easily walk outside your front door again without it being a military exercise takes some getting used to. Also, tackling the inevitable highs and lows of a long career in any sector of the entertainment world is like being on a massive roller-coaster. It's an abnormal and a crazy situation. Real fame, such as David had experienced from a very young age would have affected every aspect of his life forever more.

Unfortunately, I didn't ever get to promote any of David's music, though my path did cross with him several more times down the line at TV shows and other media events through the years. He was always very courteous and sweet to me.

I was very upset to hear of his passing and I cherish the fond memories of him that night at the Wham! party and the pleasure he and his music gave me as a young girl, introducing me to the world of pop.

> 66 REAL FAME, SUCH AS DAVID HAD EXPERIENCED FROM A VERY YOUNG AGE WOULD HAVE AFFECTED EVERY ASPECT OF HIS LIFE FOREVER MORE 99

LIZBETH MCANARY PIERCE – UNITED STATES

David was doing a play in Alberta, Canada in the summer of 1982. I was with a group of fan club presidents after the matinee. We were all taking pictures and David was leaning against the fence. I had given him a jacket the night before and asked if he had it here at the theater as I wanted to take a picture of him wearing it – even though it was 102 degrees.

My dad ran a Ford dealership and jackets were given to them as gifts when Ford were sponsoring the Indianapolis 500 in 1979. Dad handed out to his sales team and there were a couple left over. A Ford Mustang was used as the Pace Car and the Mustang logo depicts a galloping horse. I decided to give one to David, as he loved horses and at one point owned a Mustang.

He went and got the jacket which was so wonderful of him in the heat, and put it on. He was going to sit on the fence, but I told him to sit on my coat so he wouldn't get a splinter in his bum. He laughed and did as I suggested. I loved that laugh.

BEV GAZELEY – UNITED KINGDOM

David Cassidy. What did he mean to me? He was part of my life for 46 years which is longer than most of the people I know. He was my hero, my first love, no one has ever made me feel like he did. Unique, all consuming. I never met him but would love to have done so, just to tell him what he meant to me growing up. A friend of my parents gave me a poster of David in 1971 and I just melted, that's where it started. I loved his voice, he could have sung nursery rhymes and I'd have loved them.

His music helped me when I was feeling sad. In 1973 I moved to a new area with my parents when I didn't want to and played *How Can I Be Sure* on a continuous loop for five hours while putting all the posters up on my new bedroom wall until my Dad pleaded with me to play something different. But listening to David just blocked out the sadness and gave me a lift. I still have all the photos and posters as I couldn't bear to part with them. His *Cherish* album has always had an uplifting effect on me. Every Christmas morning it became a tradition to play *The Partridge Family Christmas Card* album. I still do. Hearing David singing *White Christmas* always sends shivers down my spine.

On Saturday mornings me and my friend (a Donny Osmond fan) would go into town and buy several magazines. We would then divide all the David and Donny pictures between us but if there happened to be one on the other

> ❝ A FRIEND OF MY PARENTS GAVE ME A POSTER OF DAVID IN 1971 AND I JUST MELTED, THAT'S WHERE IT STARTED ❞

side of another, we would have an argument about whose picture was better....I usually won and then watched *The Partridge Family* on TV.

In 1974 I heard David was going to be with Tony Prince on Radio Luxembourg. I sent a stamped addressed envelope and a photo to the radio station. To my delight I had a personal reply with my picture signed, "To Bev love David Cassidy". It's probably my most prized possession which is now framed and on display.

I never saw David at his peak, I almost had the opportunity for the Wembley gig but my parents weren't keen for me to go which is a big regret, but I did see David in 1985 on my 26th birthday at the Royal Albert Hall. To actually see him in the flesh was so exciting, but probably the most special time I saw him was a few years later at the Hammersmith Apollo. When he sang *Daydreamer*, I phoned my mum and held the phone up so she could listen, and I could hear her being emotional on the other end because she knew how much David had meant to me over the years.

For her, knowing how much I'd loved him for so long. For me, sharing that with my wonderful mum, who understood my dedication was immense. We both cried; a special moment that will always stay with me. This is a very emotional memory for me as I lost my mum and she knew. She understood. It was an instinctive thing to phone her and share that moment.

If I'd have seen David at the height of his fame, I'm not sure how I'd have coped. I think it would have been overwhelming. I do regret it, but I think I appreciated the nostalgia more in later years. Years ago, my one wish in life was to meet David and tell him how much he meant to me. Simple as. Yes, it's sad that it will never be possible now.

I did see David in *Time*. We were about five rows from the front. At the end when they were doing the encores, I suddenly had an overwhelming urge to rush to the front. David kissed a couple of girls and I was next to them, I puckered up and he left the stage! Devastated or what?! One of those nearly moments!! My life would have been complete.

To sum up what David Cassidy has meant to me; It feels like he has just been a part of my life forever. Indeed, could it be forever? I think so.

Above: David at the Royal Albert Hall.
Photo: Sarah Robinson

Below: Bev Gazeley proudly shows her prized possession

Photo: Henry Diltz

66 I was kind of disappointed that they put it on [The Partridge Family TV show being aired on ITV in the UK] because the whole thing stems from the fact that I was becoming popular there and my records were taking off. And so they expect me to be David Cassidy and I'm not David Cassidy on that show. I just felt badly because I made it there without the TV show **99**

Disc, February 1973

LIZA COPPOLA – UNITED STATES

The name David Cassidy once had the power to simultaneously bring 20,000 young females to their feet at his concerts, shrieking with affection and professed love for their dream man. Friday nights, precisely at 8.30pm, were kept solely for the latest episode of *The Partridge Family* television show where we could actually see our hero move, speak and sing.

So why David Cassidy? Well it was the 1970s and there were not today's distractions available for a timid, insecure and often sad, 13-year-old. David, I found, was the perfect "cure" for my woes and became the object of my affection. Though not a real boy (thank God, because I feared them) the fantasy that I leaned on for a couple of years, got me through some tough times.

Now allow me to speculate, but I do believe that "we who loved David" had something particular in common and that is this: the need to escape our teenage troubles and enter a safe oasis that was ours alone. For me it was a place to block out the rage of an alcoholic and controlling parent. To retreat, all I had to do was shut my bedroom door, turn up my Partridge Family records on my player, sing (and soon learn to play guitar) and lose myself in the music and my thoughts surrounded by his beautiful and smiling face.

The first and most poignant time I met David was in 1989 at a CD Radio Release party for *The Partridge Family Greatest Hits* record. I had won a ticket to the party via the sponsoring radio station. As I waited in line at the venue for my chance to speak to David and sign some of my memorabilia, I kept thinking to myself: Is that really him....standing right in front of me....moving and speaking....the untouchable.... unimaginable....real David Cassidy? Yes, it was. And when I finally reached him on the stage, I was as flustered as I would have been at 13 and managed to squeak out that because of him, "I learned to play guitar". That's all I remember saying.

I met David again

Below: David's mother, Evelyn Ward, studies Liza Coppola's scrapbook about David

Above and opposite: Liza meeting David in 1993 and 1989

in 1993 backstage at the Broadway show he and his brother Shaun starred in, *Blood Brothers*. He seemed healthy, calm and peaceful and he happily posed with me (and my very large pregnant belly) for a photo.

In early 1994, I was having lunch with some new friends in a diner in Forest Hills NY when the subject of David Cassidy came up. My new friend mentions that her mother is a dear friend of Evelyn Ward, David's mom. Hearing this I nearly choke on my food and go into my years of obsession in less than a minute. She then casually asks me if I would like to meet her. I all but casually say, "Are You Kidding Me ?????!!."

Some time later, meeting Evelyn was a most special time for me not only because she was David's mom, but as it happened, it was just a few months after I had my first child. I of course brought my baby and some of my memorabilia to meet Evelyn in her apartment in New York City.

We (my friend and hers) delighted in my 13-year-old comments written under some of the photos in a scrapbook. She was completely delighted by it and we laughed over my admiration and affection for him. She did enjoy seeing pictures of herself. There were some pictures of Evelyn from a teen magazine that were taken backstage at my first David concert at Madison Square Garden (March 11, 1972). The date is clearly on the cover of the scrapbook. What was most poignant and memorable about our time together was taking my baby to nurse in private to Evelyn's bedroom where she joined me and shared her own memories of David as a baby.

Loving David Cassidy has been an unusual blessing in my life. Because of him I possess the gift of musical ability and I also have a kindred and lifelong friendship with a David Cassidy "pen pal" that began in 1972. I will always remember my teenybopper years with joyful fervor and David

Cassidy will always make up a part of who I am. When David died, a part of me died too. I am blessed to have been a part of his legacy.

ANNE MARIE WOODRUFF – UNITED STATES

I was born in December, 1966 and as far back as I can remember I have loved David Cassidy. Many images are conjured in my mind when I think of him, images that intertwine with precious childhood memories and feelings of innocence, discovery, hope, excitement, joy, and even heartbreak. I remember those shaggy locks, those super groovy clothes, those eyes, and that unique, breathy beautiful voice that would draw me in like no other. Images: running, playing, bubblegum, 45 rpm, family security.......truly "Summer Days". Even as I would grow and change, I would always return repeatedly to listen, remember, and appreciate.

Throughout all of these years, somehow collecting PF and DC artifacts and collectibles has made me feel as though I could hold on to all of those moments, if only for a little longer. As an adult, how excited I was to see him live on several occasions. Meeting him, of course, outside of the Music Box Theater in NYC after *Blood Brothers* was the best of all – truly a dream-come-true. I remember my idiotic words, as he signed my playbill and smiled for a picture with me: "Will you take me for a ride on your bus?" Geez. In my defense, I am surprised I could speak at all.

November 21, 2017 felt like the death of so much more than a person; it felt like the death of an era, of a feeling, of a childhood. I am so thankful that he lives on forever in music and memories.

Anne Marie Woodruff meets David

GINNY LOPEZ – UNITED STATES

In late 1990 I happened to hear on the radio that David was going to be at a popular disco club in Houston called Bayou Mammas on November 21. I had to get there to see him, meet him, and talk to him. The excitement at the prospect was simply overwhelming.

Inside, the disco lights were almost blinding; people were dancing on the floor area; the music was incredibly loud, and around the dance floor it was very dark. David was in there somewhere. I followed the crowd, mainly excited girls like me and there he sat signing everything placed gently in front of him. He looked so beautiful – his long, colourful hair captured in the lights. It was like seeing a mirage. I had to blink twice to convince myself this was true. He signs some albums but it is dark – maybe we will both be blinded by the lights and not easily see each other. Maybe he will be blinded by true love!

I approach the table and somehow manage to say: "Hi. Can you sign this?" I showed him the big gloved hands of a long clown shirt I am wearing. Maybe David thought of his song, *I Am A Clown* when he saw it, but he cheerily said: "Sure!"

Shaking, I hand him my permanent Sharpie marker and he signs his name on the big white gloved hand of MY shirt – it was long enough to reach the table when he is signing. I am so very happy. I can only smile, and he smiled back. In a moment of impulse, I lean forward over the table and give him a gentle kiss on his right cheek. It was a beautiful moment. His skin was baby soft.

I turn around and take a few steps towards the dance floor but it's too dark to see where I am walking. I stop, someone taps me on the shoulder and asks me if I have David's pen. I hold tight to my marker explaining in between giggles. "It's not his, it's mine". Someone shouts: "Found it!"

For a brief moment I had kissed David's cheek and that has stayed with me all these years. I found paradise. I will never forget how wonderful that evening was, how warm and caring David was.

WERONIKA – POLAND

I was born in 1962, in Poland, when still a communist country. We didn't have *The Partridge Family*, western records, teen magazines and we couldn't travel abroad. I didn't know English at all, but it was enough just to see David's face in German magazine *Bravo* and hear *How Can I Be Sure* on the radio, to fall in love. Subconsciously, I always looked for the kind of boys, later men, like David. I mean slim built, not tall, long limbs, adventurous and….sexy.

I started to learn English, we had only two lessons a week when I was in secondary school, and I couldn't buy English books, but I wanted to know what he was singing about. We teens in the 70s helped each other and slowly I started to get to know more about him and got to know some of his songs. But it wasn't easy. At the time (the end of the 70s) it looked like David disappeared. I heard *The Last Kiss* in 1985, but I was also very busy with my life, marriage, university, children, work, difficult situation in Poland. It was hard just to get food.

So, it started for me again in 1998, when I saw (I have satellite TV) a BBC documentary *David Cassidy: Teenage Dream*. That was the first time I really saw how everything looked like in the 70s, how much a global superstar he was, and I fell in love again. But it was undercover. I was a serious teacher, mother etc, but with new technology, I could at last really get to know David Cassidy and his music.

I read a lot of interviews with him and one sentence stuck: "Do what you really love doing. Don't care what others say, don't be afraid". I can't say I changed my life only because of

David Cassidy, but his example, his courage helped me to make decisions. I completely changed my life, found new ways how to earn money, stopped work at school, moved out from the centre of Warsaw to the country.

After November 21, 2017 I was in shock, couldn't find myself a place, so I decided to go for a two-week tour around the UK. It was my dream since the 70s and I also wanted to see with my own eyes some places connected with David. I saw The Dorchester Hotel, as well as The Phoenix and Dominion Theatres, Royal Albert Hall and other places he played in. But it was also a sad experience. I felt his presence.

ROXANNE NEWKIRK-LINN – UNITED STATES

On December 16, 1998 I had one of the best days of my life: I got to have lunch with David Cassidy. I had won a contest on a radio station here in Cincinnati. I remember getting to the restaurant and being seated with about 20 women including myself and my sister Debbie. When he walked in, he was wearing all black and was so handsome. I remember him talking with us and when we sat down to eat, he sat right down next to me. My sister said the look on my face was priceless. I got to eat lunch and rub my elbow against his as we were eating.

We talked as we ate but we were not supposed to talk about *The Partridge Family*. He signed memorabilia, albums, pictures and such for us. Then we sat at a table one at a time with him and had our picture taken with him and he autographed a picture for us. He was the nicest and most handsome man I have ever met. To this day I remember it like it was yesterday. I will never forget that day.

ANGELA KEEN – HAWAII

I was an 80s kid, but I grew up in the shadow of my only sister who was a 70s kid. I was in kindergarten around 1974 as *The Partridge Family* ended its show. In the 80s, David made a comeback with his song, *The Last Kiss*. That time in my life was memorable because I began having interest in boys.

His popularity faded but when I got a job as a radio DJ in 1986 at a station that played oldies from the 70s, I once again played a few of The Partridge Family and David Cassidy songs.

Flash forward to 1995 or 1996. I was a TV news reporter and news anchor in Honolulu. I would often receive invites to VIP events. I was invited to a luxury shoe store opening in Waikiki. They often have stars help draw attention to these events. Their star was David Cassidy!

I remembered my days watching him as a child and reruns later as I got a bit older, not to mention my radio DJ days. It was a heart-pounding and heart-warming experience to see him in person. I had my hair especially done in an updo just because! He was so gracious to visit with me. He gave me his autograph and we took a photo. Sadly, my eyes were closed in the photo. I will always treasure that moment in my life.

That Magic Moment for Angela Keen

DAVID RIEUWERTS – UNITED KINGDOM

I would like to tell you about the time Keith Partridge wrote a letter to David Cassidy, with a little help from me that is. It was back in 1995 after David had appeared on the John Dunn tea time show on BBC Radio Two to talk chiefly about his role in the West End musical *Blood Brothers*, but in which he also took the opportunity to describe Partridge as, I quote, "an airhead" who was, "More interested in his hair than anything else!"

Now Keith had taken a lot of flak over the years, mainly spouted by males of varying ages and backgrounds; teenagers anxious to maintain every semblance of street credibility, pop pundits who wrote in the 'trendy' music press and the multitudes of young men interested only in listening to 'serious' bands.

They figured Keith was too whiter than white for his own good, that his songs were nothing more than trite manufactured candy floss pop and they laughed at him for being in the same band as his mom. I mean, what kind of a guy would want that? All this criticism Keith had taken on the chin, but David joining in the chorus of disapproval too? The one guy who knew what it was like to be Keith more than any other? Surely not. Such a thing was just plain wrong!

Keith was a good sort really. Who could ever forget the episode when, as the eldest male in the family, he had taken his responsibilities seriously by introducing his reluctant younger siblings to the joys of string quartets and art galleries in an effort to further their education?

Then there were the episodes when he always appeared more concerned about the welfare of his sister, Laurie, especially when she was dating a different guy on an almost weekly basis, than any brother we had ever met in real life.

> 66 THEY LAUGHED AT HIM FOR BEING IN THE SAME BAND AS HIS MOM. I MEAN, WHAT KIND OF A GUY WOULD WANT THAT? 99

At one stage he even tried writing a classical concerto to impress a girl who thought the Partridge music was pleasant but too simplistic. In all the guy really tried but received nothing but criticism and was now getting it in the ear from the man who played him on screen.

So, I helped Keith write a letter to David, put it in an envelope for him and addressed it to David Cassidy, c/o The Phoenix Theatre. London.

I placed the letter through the pillar box at the end of our street on December 13 1995. As I turned away to walk back home it suddenly dawned on me that David Cassidy might actually get to read it and my mind suddenly transported me back through time until, for a few moments, I became my younger self again.

It is 1972 and I am 12 years old. I am in my grandparents' cosy house on a dark winter evening and I am flicking through a magazine I have just bought that afternoon. It is called *The David Cassidy Magazine*, November 1972, issue six. I have purchased it because my younger brother, sister and I have previously clubbed together to buy the number one single, *How Can I Be Sure*, a lush ballad which Cassidy sings in a unique breathy yet strong style and is flawless. The pages of my newly acquired magazine show David on stage, by the pool, on the set of *The Partridge Family* and scuba diving.

It is exciting and takes me into another world. On top of all that David looks like the coolest guy I have ever seen with his fashionable long hair, slim fit shirts and jackets. I want to look like that! I want that haircut and I want to wear those kind of clothes. At 12 years old it looks like I have my first pop hero, a real-life role model, and though I don't realise it at this time he is one I will follow to the end of his life.

I am aware David's fan base is screaming girls rather than boys, but it doesn't bother me much. Just to make me feel more at ease issue six carries a letter from a lad called Eddie who states he is a fan. What is more, Eddie's letter is in reply to a guy called Neil who had a letter published in issue four to say he bought Cassidy's latest album *Cherish* and that the media should not just assume David only has girl fans. From that moment being a boy Cassidy follower presents me with very few problems.

The world catches Cassidy-mania very quickly. Everywhere I go his smiling face looks back at me; from newsagents' shelves, posters in shop windows, record stores and dozens of photographs stuck on my sister's bedroom wall. The girls at school cover their books with photos of him and my sister takes all her drinks from a mug bearing his likeness. I can even spot Cassidy's handwriting, featuring as it does on countless signed photographs in magazines and on some of his later album sleeves.

When the premier pop music programme in Britain, *Top of The Pops*, reaches its milestone 500th edition it flies Cassidy in from America to celebrate as the special superstar guest. Cassidy emerges from the plane in an immaculate white suit, talks to DJ Tony Blackburn on the tarmac and then sings the tracks of his latest double A sided single which hits the number one slot the week after.

If all this were not enough, we watch David every week in *The Partridge Family*, the story of a mother bringing up five kids single-handed, albeit in

Dear David,

Recently (Wednesday December 6th) I heard you on the BBC Radio 2 John Dunn Show calling me, of all people, an "airhead". Hey, I bet you never guessed I'd hear it but I'm here in England and I did! Man, I could hardly believe what I was hearing, and I think you should have a heart and apologise.

I mean we were once so close it was as though we were the same person, now you go around saying I was "whiter than white" and you never dug my music. David how could you say this? Who else could sing classic songs like 'I Think I Love You' and 'Point Me In The Direction Of Albuquerque' and deliver them the way I did? Some boring Grunge artist? Some rapper with his baseball cap on back to front? No way man. Our music was great and still is.

Listen David, I have a lot to contend with at the moment and I can do without you calling me an asshole in public too. I mean Laurie is dating that Lester Braddock again and you know what a reputation he has. Can you remember back in 72 when she had to knee him in the nuts for coming on too strong at Muldoon's Point? I'm real worried that she will have to use the same tactics again.

Also, mom is up to her old tricks, she keeps giving lifts to this teenage college kid who has a crush on her then pretends to run out of gas on dark lonely roads. When your mother acts like that it's real embarrassing for a guy, especially when word gets out around college.

Hey, let's not get too depressed. At least the chicks around here still love me, and my singing and they all have a lock of my hair, so it isn't all bad news!

You see David, stars like us don't come along very often. Sure, the kids all loved me, and I played a part in your success, but they loved me because you were the guy who brought me to life.

Okay so I'm not in with the in-crowd but I never was, I just did my own thing and let the people be my judge. No, I didn't do drugs. No, I didn't shave my head and have a goatee beard whilst singing about some political issue or other. No, I didn't chant an incomprehensible dirge over a drum machine. And you know what? There is a whole generation out there who are eternally grateful.

You still enjoy great success David, but I was there some of the time and we had fun. Look back at what we achieved together with pride and remember that old saying of ours, 'C'mon Get Happy'. That's a great philosophy to hang on to.

Your old friend, Keith Partridge

a glossy cinematic world where the sun always shines, great tunes are sung and a multicoloured school bus is parked outside the house ready to take the Partridges on their next adventure. Back then the chances of writing to Cassidy and him even seeing the letter, let alone answering it, would have had odds somewhere on a par with being able to fly to the moon and back.

One afternoon in mid-January, I found an envelope addressed to me laying on the floor by the letterbox. I knew who it was from instantly without having to open it. The handwriting was the same as I had seen years ago on all those posters and albums and just to confirm my assumptions, written on the back of the envelope, were two words in black ink which left me in no doubt. They simply read, 'From Keith!'

Inside there was no letter but a colour flyer for *Blood Brothers* which was personally signed. Even as an adult man it was a surreal moment, to think that the guy I had idolised as a kid and was loved by so many millions of people had actually read the letter and must have spent a few moments of his life writing out my name and address.

I hope David understood that the letter was asking him to be proud of his portrayal of Keith Partridge and not to think unkindly of the character or the music just because it wasn't accepted by the so called 'serious' pop critics and fans.

Keith gave David the chance to introduce his great singing voice to the world and to demonstrate a fine talent for playing light comedy as can be witnessed in many episodes. I have often wondered if the letter ever had a positive impact on how David viewed his efforts with *The Partridge Family*. Alas, I will never know but he certainly seemed to embrace it far more in his later life. I genuinely consider him to be one of the finest pop singers ever. As an actor he was obviously very talented too and, yes, *The Partridge Family* played a part in proving that.

My regular forays into secondhand record stores have unearthed some Cassidy/Partridge Family gems over the decades and enabled me to purchase material I could not have afforded as a youngster. On one occasion back in the eighties I walked into a town centre charity shop to find staring invitingly at me a full set of *The David Cassidy Magazine*, all 43 issues in pristine condition for £4, including my long lost issue number six which takes me back to that day in my grandparents' house when for the first time, I'd truly discovered my own pop star and boyhood icon.

I was more than happy to receive such a personal acknowledgement and of course that blue envelope with 'From Keith!' written across the back is my most cherished souvenir. I hope Keith was happy with the outcome.

JASON MULLEN – UNITED KINGDOM

I worked at the Phoenix Theatre in London as one of two assistant managers from 1994 to 1997 so covered the whole of David's run in *Blood Brothers* from 1995 to 1996. We got a few guest stars in the show during the period I was there including David Soul, Bernie and Linda Nolan and Lyn Paul from the New Seekers, but it was David Cassidy who got the most attention from fans.

I had heard of him of course but being born in 1967 and only a little boy at the time of his fame remembered him as someone whom the teenage girls (who lived in the same council flats as I did) were a little crazy about, many had posters on their walls of course.

I met him not long after he joined the show and liked him, but also found he was quite a shy reserved person and my impression was he could be a little overwhelmed sometimes by the fans who waited for him outside. I seem to remember though he still had time for them and did stop for autographs, photos etc. The fans, not surprisingly, were mainly ladies (some with their own teenage daughters) and a few men too, all by now in their 40s but at one time followers of him during his Partridge Family days.

A lot of my duties were dealing with the public at performance times. We also liaised directly with the stage management and *Blood Brothers* producer Bill Kenwright (who had been responsible for persuading David to do the show) on many matters. Sometimes I acted as a go-between David and people who wanted to meet him and took autograph books to be signed to his dressing room or dropped messages around to him. He was always very relaxed and signed any things we had.

One personal memory that stands out concerns a colleague of mine who had found a 1972 David Cassidy annual in a second-hand shop on Charing Cross Road. She very sensibly decided to get it signed and asked me to go round with her. We knocked on his door and he momentarily seemed a little surprised to see us and the book. However, we went in and sat down.

He began flicking through the annual, pointing at the photos saying things like "That was the private jet I had" or "I remember that photo being taken" and some comments about his 1970s clothes too.

You got the sense he had enjoyed those days but was not bitter that his fame wasn't on the scale it had been. He signed the book for my colleague, maybe she still has it?

The fans who came to see the show were by and large well behaved and resisted screaming when he came on, but the last night was probably the craziest. It seemed everyone who liked him had booked.

The show got its usual standing ovation only this time was followed by flowers thrown at the stage, and memorably a pair of knickers. These landed in the front stalls and were retrieved by a member of staff who found they still had the M&S label on them so were thankfully clean and new. I was handed these and as I was due back stage to help with David's exit, took them round to show him. He smiled but politely declined the offer of keeping them.

By this point now the fans who had left the Theatre were on Stacey Street outside the Stage Door. There had to be at least a hundred there. David needed to make a quick getaway and a car had been arranged. Iain the Company Stage Manager asked me to help.

We got David and explained the best way was to make a run for it to the waiting car (being a Beatles Fan I had watched *A Hard Day's Night*) we would both flank him once out of the stage door. Final goodbyes to the other actors and we opened the doors to some excited fans. It was Cassidymania with flashes from cameras and screams.

I recall dashing for the open car door, one excited lady grabbed my shoulder saying: "I just want to touch him". I replied "Get Off" (belated apologies to the lady concerned but things were a bit tense) and then took hold of David's left arm, he ducked down and both Ian and I pushed him into the back seat of the car and shut the door.

We watched as it drove off both thinking we had never seen that level of excitement on the last night of a show and never would again.

CINDY LYNN – UNITED STATES

I met David twice. The first time was in 1981. I was in high school and decided to go see him in *Little Johnny Jones* with a friend. I was too young to attend any of his live performances, so I was really looking forward to the show which was great. I felt I needed more when it was over so asked an usher if there was a place to go and meet. He said, "sure, go downstairs, go down the hall and at the end will be some red ropes. Just wait there and he will come out". We only waited a few minutes and then he came out. I was awe struck! Looking as handsome as ever with a plaid shirt on and still some of his stage makeup. I waited my turn impatiently to get a picture with him. Finally, it was MY turn!

He said hi and signed an autograph for me, then I asked for a picture. He said "sure!" And I guess he wanted to get the picture just right because he kept telling everyone to move back and it took a while to get it. I was thinking, "boy he was making a big deal about this picture." But I loved every minute of it. David taught me to take chances and just maybe you will get what you want. I did that night.

The second meeting was when David was in Chicago in *Blood Brothers* in 1994. I went to two shows. The first with my husband and daughter; the second with my friend, Betsy. Before the show, we had sent roses backstage for him. We were not sure if he would come out but decided to wait in the lobby after the show. Our luck paid off and he came out in his black leather jacket holding the flowers we gave him.

We said hi and got some autographs. As he was signing, he asked if my name was Candy. I said no it was Cindy but you're close. (Wow!!) He said I looked familiar. I said we met in 1981 at *Little Johnny Jones*. We had a longer conversation this time and I almost got to go to lunch with him.

A few days later the phone rang, my husband answered it, then said, "it's him." I said "who??" "David Cassidy," he replied. My knees started to shake. I said hi. He said, "Hi this is David Cassidy. How are you?" Well, I could have passed out! He was actually calling me at home. I could not believe it! But I had to remain calm and not sound like an idiot. I said, "I'm fine, how are you?" He asked if I still wanted to meet, but he was running short on time.

He asked how far away I lived from the theatre. I was about 40 minutes away. It was the last night, he had to leave right after the show and didn't think we had enough time to meet. I think he said some other things, but it was all a blur. He then told me he hoped things go well for me and to have a good life! I thanked him for calling.

Must have been a few minutes but I could not believe that David Cassidy just called me at home. And the only witness was my husband. I was in Heaven the rest of the day. Lunch would have been great with him, but a phone call was a good backup. I will never forget it.

LIZBETH MCANARY PIERCE – UNITED STATES

When David was playing Joseph at The Royal Theater in New York City I had to go. I stayed the whole week in March, 1983, meeting so many fans from around the world. CT, one of David's bodyguards at the time came and found me, standing outside and gave me a note from David to meet at Joanna's. We were standing next to each other and he said something was different from the last time he saw me. I told him that I had lost 150 pounds. He immediately turned and hugged me. Such a wonderful hug, so warm and caring. He whispered in my ear that he was so proud of me. I didn't want to let go.

LYN GOODWIN –
UNITED KINGDOM

I saw David do a concrete handprint in Disney MGM and spoke with him at an 'audience with' David Cassidy afterwards. He was such an amazing talent. I've been a lifelong fan of David from the age of 14. I saw his 2000th show in EFX in Las Vegas and after seeing him in *Blood Brothers* in London got the chance to meet him. David won't be forgotten – my grandchildren ask me to play David Cassidy in my car, particularly *Could It Be Forever* (live version) and *Daydreamer*.

RONNA AUSTIN –
UNITED STATES

This picture of me with David Cassidy was taken in 1991 in Oklahoma City at a local music event that he emceed. At the time, I was a writer for *Backstage Pass Magazine*. I was there to do a few interviews. Having been a teenager in the '70s, I was stoked to be at the same event as David and hoped I would get to meet him.

David was extremely busy, and a lot of people wanted to meet and get a picture with him that day, so I wasn't sure I would be able to get anywhere near him.

However, later in the day, I noticed he was standing alone and approached him, asking if he would mind taking a quick picture with me. This, of course, was before the age of digital cameras and cell phones so, fortunately, our staff photographer was available to take this picture. I didn't get a chance to chat with David at all. We just quickly took the picture and the moment was over. But he did put his arm around me which was pretty thrilling.

Above left: Promotional leaflet from handprint ceremony

Above right: Lyn Goodwin's programme and ticket from the 2000th EFX show

Left: Ronna Austin with David. Photo: Bonnie Guthrie

I have always joked that David and I color-coordinated our outfits beforehand. I say it with a straight face and so, some people actually believe me. I eventually tell them I'm joking — but we did look a little like a couple, didn't we?

ONE WEEKEND AT WEMBLEY

The only difference between DAVID CASSIDY and Elvis, said the man, is time

GARY STOCKDALE – EMMY-NOMINATED COMPOSER/SINGER – UNITED STATES

In 1990, I was playing in a band called The Jenerators with an old friend of mine, Billy Mumy, who was one of the two main towheaded child stars of my generation (the other one being Ron Howard of *The Andy Griffith Show*). Billy starred in the famous Twilight Zone episode and went on to play Will Robinson in *Lost In Space*. But by his teens, Billy was also a musician and a songwriter, and toured with such bands as The Beach Boys and America. In 1991, David was experiencing a bit of a career resurgence with a new song, *Lyin' To Myself*, so he was planning to go out on tour, and needed someone to put a band together, and music-direct. Mumy suggested me, and so I got the gig in the summer of '91.

Having gone to college in the early '70s, I have to admit I didn't really follow David's career (The last thing a young arts student was doing with his nights in the early '70s was watching prime-time TV). I knew he was a teen idol, and I would see his face on *Tiger Beat* magazine and the like. And, of course, I heard the hit records, but, at the time, that was music for teenage kids, and I wasn't into it.

So, when I got booked on the tour, I assumed I knew what his fan base was; figuring that the tour would be mostly people in their 40s who remembered David from *The Partridge Family*. What I didn't realize though, is that, during his prime years, David was as big as any rock star had ever been. He was beloved. That became clear to me from the huge crowds who would come to every show we did. The ages ranged anywhere from people in their 50s, to young people in their early 20s. And some of those older fans brought their kids.

We rehearsed at S.I.R. in Hollywood, and then started out on the road in August. Opening for us as a comedian was David's former co-star from *The Partridge Family*, Danny Bonaduce. We hit New York City first, and before our first show at The Bottom Line, we appeared on two TV shows, *Live with Regis and Kathie Lee*, and *The Geraldo Rivera Show*. We played to very full and appreciative crowds.

In Chicago, we played Park West. After that gig, all of us went to a private thing at the Hard Rock, and wound up jamming on a couple of tunes with former Rolling Stone, Mick Taylor, who seemed a bit mystified that he was on stage with David, the former teen

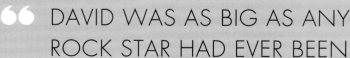

DAVID WAS AS BIG AS ANY ROCK STAR HAD EVER BEEN

heart-throb. The band, Bobby Huff on drums, Roni Beck on bass, and my friends, Mat and Kelli Gurman, who I had brought into the band, all got along great, and we enjoyed our days in each new town.

After the tour I went back to my work scoring films and TV in Los Angeles, and singing in recording sessions for records and movies. Mat and Kelli went on to work further with David. I saw David a few times after that, the last one being at our Jenerators' bandmate David Jolliffe's wedding. This was after the press reports had come out about David's problems with alcohol, but when I saw him he seemed in good spirits and full of plans.

David was a star in his time, and greatly beloved by his fans, who stuck by him through thick and thin. We had people who would literally follow our tour from town to town, they were so dedicated to David and his music. They loved him. And, for a time, he was one of the biggest pop stars in the world. I enjoyed playing for him, and with him, and I'm grateful he took me with him on that crazy ride.

MAT GURMAN – UNITED STATES

David made a point of spending time with his mom when we were in New Jersey at the start of the tour in 1991. He told me that it bothered him that most people did not know that Shirley was not his birth mom. He loved Shirley and had a great relationship with her, but he also was very close to his birth mom and it distressed him that she did not get the respect she deserved so he went out of his way to let people know. He loved her very much.

The day of our first show at Club Bene, even though David had to go with Victor to do radio promo, he also found time to see his mom and spend time with her. He was a really compassionate man with a huge heart.

He told me that while he was endorsed by Ovation guitars, he was giving guitars to everyone, all of his friends, many of who were not around later in his career when things were not so bright. He seemed a little hurt about that.

He loved it whenever an old friend would come to a show, especially some of the writers of the big hits he sang. He was so proud to introduce them, especially Tony Romeo when we were in NYC playing at the Bottom Line. David had a huge heart and was a fine, compassionate and generous soul.

Years after we had worked with him, my wife Kelli joined him in Keys for a show at The Canyon Club in 2007. He was so thrilled to see her after about 15 years. He just lit up. I was not there but he asked about me and Gary Stockdale, how we were doing and what we were up to. His joy was infectious and so sincere. He gave Kelli a big hug.

That was the last time we heard from him or saw him.

Top right: David rests his head on Mat Gurman's shoulder. "We were flying back east from LAX [Los Angeles Airport]. This was a moment. This photo is very dear to me," recalls Mat.

Right and opposite page: David at Club Bene. Photos: Mary Pomarico

Far right: L-R back: Roni Beck, Kelli Gurman, Mat Gurman, Victor Bridgers, Gary Stockdale. Front: Bobby Huff, David Cassidy. Photo: Victor Bridgers, courtesy of Mat Gurman

✦ We were touring in Victoria, BC, playing at a club called Harpos. On that 1991 tour, which had Danny doing stand-up comedy as the opening act, David was wearing some black leather pants that laced from the front and a silver studded black leather jacket.

David had a few problems with the pants holding up since they were actually from the old days when he was touring and filling stadiums. Harpos had a raised stage, probably about six feet from the floor so the audience standing in front of the stage were looking up. We were 3/4 of the way through the set list when I noticed a guy staring up at David with his jaw literally dropped and mouth open, amazed expression on his face. The guy did not move.

Between songs I asked Kelli (my wife and one of the keyboard players on that tour) "do you see that guy staring....". Just then, David called to me (I stand right next to him during the show) "get me a towel". This didn't make sense to me because there were towels all over the place, even by his feet. I thought I must have misunderstood and asked one of the roadies to get him another guitar strap.

When I handed the strap to David he snapped at me, "No man, I need a towel!" I said: "There are towels right by your feet". In a muted and embarrassed stage whisper, he said: "I split my pants". I gave him a towel which he quickly stuffed between his guitar and his pants, looking a bit like a kilt.

We finished the set and talked about it but did not share it publicly. Several days later Kelli and I were watching a late-night talk show where Morgan Fairchild was one of the guests with David. She began to roast him about the incident as if she was

at the show. Later, David asked me if it was me that spilled the beans. I told him it was not me. He found the whole thing amusing. David had a great sense of humor.

✦ I had baby sat for him and Sue once in San Francisco. Beau was a toddler. I was there to play for a show with David. I was playing a board game and changing the rules by being invisible. Beau found it a very funny idea. When his dad came back in, Beau played a trick on him saying, "You can't see me because I'm invisible!" David was puzzled and said to me, "Are you messing with my kid's mind?" It was pretty funny. I doubt Beau would remember it, or me for that matter, but it was a precious moment I have never forgotten.

We had just had our equipment delivered from somewhere in Canada. Everything in the cases was ice cold. We were getting set up to get a sound check. My guitar was freezing as was a small light green polishing cloth I kept in my amp. I went to use it and found it really slimy and wondered what had leaked all over it. I had been noticing this over the last few shows but this time, it was ice cold and really got my attention.

I went to wash my hands cause this stuff made them sticky. When I came back and we started to play a little, I watched David walk over to my amp, pick up the polishing cloth and blow his nose in it several times. I was horrified! I said to David: "Have you been blowing your nose in my polishing cloth"? He chuckled and said, "Oh, sorry man, I thought that was for me". "That explains the slime. You may keep it", I told him.

Top: David at Hershey. Photo: Mary Pomarico

REGINA CHAPMAN – UNITED STATES

I had just started my junior year of High School in 1970, about three months shy of turning 16, but on September 25 something in my world changed forever. There he was on my TV. The most beautiful boy I had ever laid eyes on. He was so beautiful, those eyes, that smile. There was something different about this boy. Something safe, soft and tender. His voice was so breathy and soft. Like you could almost feel his breath on you through the TV as he sang..... just to me of course.

I would just lay on my bed staring into David's eyes as I listened to his music. He was safe and I didn't have to be so brave and tough, the way I did at school. I can only imagine what my friends would think if they knew about my love affair with David and his music (in my mind) he was mine all mine and no one knew it.

The TV show, his music and posters kept me company and let me love him safely and without judgement. I could talk to him, relate to him in so many different ways. I would read the stories in the magazines, but I read my own stories in between those lines. He was my safe place for a long time, a connection was made but he never knew it. I will treasure that about my teenage years with him, always.

It's 1989 and I'm listening to my favorite radio station KLOS, the Mark and Brian Show in LA, California. David was on the show, funny and charismatic and back the following year playing his new song *Lyin' To Myself*. While on an early morning TV show in November, 1990 with Mark and Brian they mentioned David would be at Tower Records in LA that day. I grabbed my two boys and while in line my oldest James (13 at the time) asked David to sign a poster and he graciously did that for him. I know my knees got weak. I was so nervous and honestly can't remember a thing I said to him. He engaged with Dean (then 5) smiling and asking him something. I know we shook hands and I remember him asking my name. I guess I must have said it so faintly that he thought I said Gina because that's how he signed my CD. "To Gina, Much love, David Cassidy". This is my most prized possession! I never realized in a million years just how much it would mean to me.

When I heard he was sick, I started listening to his music again and remembering how I felt as that 15-year-old girl. I was praying for a miracle. Then, he was gone. I felt like my heart had been ripped out. This was something I had never felt before about an entertainer on any level. I couldn't understand it. I still don't. Sometimes my heart actually hurts from the loss. I find myself in tears when I hear certain songs. My teen years have been ripped apart.

As I listen to David's music, I have once again connected with him as I did when a young girl. I realize now, just how much his music means to me and has always meant to me. It's more than just songs. It's the lyrics, the feelings in them. I listen and can hear my life in those songs.

> **❝ I WOULD JUST LAY ON MY BED STARING INTO DAVID'S EYES AS I LISTENED TO HIS MUSIC. HE WAS SAFE AND I DIDN'T HAVE TO BE SO BRAVE AND TOUGH, THE WAY I DID AT SCHOOL ❞**

YASMIN WENDLING – UNITED STATES

After seeing David in Las Vegas in EFX, one of the staff came over, asked if I was Yasmin and escorted us to his dressing room. I stood by the door trying to breathe normally. Not possible, knowing that at any minute he would open the door. He was standing by the bar. My friend told him I was his number one fan and he loved it. He was very gracious. We sat and talked for an hour or so. He was very grateful for my devotion and I was in a dream. I showed him the photograph of my sons. One is named Ricky after one of my favorite songs, *Ricky's Tune*, which he wrote. My other son is named David. He signed, "To Ricky & David, Much Happiness". I have that picture framed and hanging in my hallway.

Yasmin Wendling meets David in Las Vegas. Notice David has a framed montage on the wall behind him from his Madison Square Garden concert

HOWARD PATTOW – UNITED STATES

At the end of the day David Cassidy is the reason I am an entertainer today. When I was a kid, the first two rock albums I had in my fledgling record collection were Paul McCartney & Wings' *Band On The Run* and the Partridge Family's *Sound Magazine*. The music on the *Sound Magazine* album captivated my young ears. Many years later, that childhood love of that music would

Sound Magazine
A Tribute to the Partridge Family
For booking and info, contact
Howard Pattow

inspire me to produce a Partridge Family tribute band, named after that particular album: *Sound Magazine*.

Thinking back, I would say

I enjoyed watching the television program for the music. The song was the prize at the bottom of the cracker jack box. You had to sit through the show to get to the song. Watching David Cassidy sing – it just seemed like he was having so much fun – the joy of performing is extremely catchy – and it certainly planted seeds in my own psyche about how one properly works a stage and an audience while performing live: the smiles to the family members as the song is being sung.

David Cassidy had the perfect voice for that material. And nobody pronounced the word "you" with more pop intensity. He could really sell a song. I don't know how much of his vocal approach was due to his own singer's instinct or due to the guidance of Wes Farrell and co. It's interesting that my two first albums were Cassidy and McCartney and I produced a Partridge Family tribute band. I am currently performing as John Lennon with numerous Beatles tributes.

66 People were saying, 'well, he's like Elvis' about me, then they'd say – 'no, he's like Sinatra', maybe because I'm singing ballads. I really don't like to be compared to anyone too much. I just think I'm myself. I'm not trying to be anybody else **99**

Disc, February 1973

3

★

TOUCHING LIVES

CHASING DA VINCI – UNITED STATES

Chasing da Vinci is made up of multi-instrumentalist siblings who in 2009, won a national talent contest on CBS Television in the United States. Appearing as J4, the family from Tennessee, performed a variety of songs every week during the Singing Family Face Off, on which David was a judge. When they performed, *I Think I Love You* during the competition, David observed: "I am a little overwhelmed. It was the first number one record I ever had, it was the first song I recorded, and I have to tell you, you were so much better than me. I loved your vocal, the choreography that was going on."

When we were told we were going to New York City for the first time on that chilly morning with the cameras in our faces, I don't think any of it had yet registered with us. In fact, I'm pretty sure it never did for any of us. I (Jessi) was 15, Jeddi, 13, Josiah was eight and Sophi just six. Everything was new, exciting and overwhelming.

We were going to be flown to NYC to perform on CBS Early Show, we already knew David would be one of our judges. We had been watching other contestants on the show in the weeks prior. Because Sophi was so young at the time, I remember having to watch *Partridge Family* reruns in preparation for meeting him because she had no idea who he was! There were a lot of dinner meals spent watching that show before the first meeting.

I remember when we first met him personally after our first performance. The studio lights at CBS were so bright and he was standing in a small group of people with his back to us. I remember thinking it was amusing he was wearing ripped jeans, because at 15 most adults his age didn't like or approve of ripped jeans when I wore them.

He turned around and smiled at us and encouraged us, saying once again how well we performed, knelt down on Sophi's level, hugged her and said she was just adorable. There wasn't ever time for one specific moment of conversation, but week to week we always looked forward to his encouraging words towards us and his big smile.

We consider ourselves very fortunate and blessed to have met him before his passing. He made a lasting memory and impression on all of us we will never forget.

CHRIS PHILLIPS – LONG-TIME FAN – UNITED KINGDOM

David was a man who cared a great deal about others. I know this because my family have been on the receiving end of his kindness. At a time when we were in the depths of despair, David came into our lives with a true gift of love. Our daughter, Johanna, was murdered in 2005. The impact of her death was devastating for us. We could not comprehend what had happened. It felt like I had been hit by a train. You shouldn't be having to bury a child at the age of 21. Life is precious.

We were invited onto the morning breakfast programme, GMTV, to talk about domestic violence. David would be a regular guest on the show and a few days after we had been on, they announced he was going to be in the studio. I was frustrated to think we had missed the chance to meet him. I have been a fan since I was at school in the 1970s, and meeting him at this time in our lives would have given us something to smile about.

Previous page: David at Epcot 2007. Photo: Lizbeth McAnary Pierce

I contacted the production team we had met. Knowing what we were going through they said they would see what they could do.

Out of the blue I received a signed CD and a personal note from David. I was gobsmacked that David had been told about our family tragedy, and gone out of his way to write to us. That meant everything. Our heads were all over the place and here was my hero, David, writing to me. The CD is my prized possession. I've never played it and never will. It is far too precious.

On hearing David had died, I simply sat alone that morning and wanted to think of some way to thank him for helping us. If it hadn't been for the events that happened to me, I would not have started my tribute page on Facebook. It was my way of saying thank you to him.

When at school I bought all the girl teen magazines. I kept it quiet that my room was decorated like a girls! But David got me into so much trouble. I grew my hair like David's, I dressed like him, all these girls wanted to go out with me and their boyfriends were not happy. It caused me so many problems, I couldn't go out with my best mate, Stephen. I didn't have problems getting girlfriends, but one guy just came up to me one night and punched me in the face. I began to wonder what life must be like for David.

I saw David for the first time live at Wembley

Empire Pool in March, 1973. The atmosphere was electric. He never released *I'm A Man* which he performed that day. It was such a good rock song and he nailed it. *The Higher They Climb* was probably his best studio work. Back in the 70s was the best time to see him. It was so exciting to read the dates he was coming, sending off a postal order and waiting for the tickets to arrive.

Left: Chris Phillips

Below right: The sealed and signed CD

Below left: Letter from Wembley confirming 1973 concert tickets which everyone who was successful in their application, received, as referred to by Chris in his story

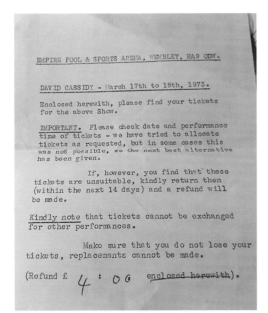

MICHAEL LEFNER – UNITED STATES

We moved from Tucson, Arizona to the very remote town of Bethel, Alaska in 1968. Bethel is 400 miles west of Anchorage and the only way there is by plane. Back in those days we didn't have a radio station (except the Armed Forces Radio Network) a newspaper, television, and only three flights per week from Anchorage to receive our mail etc. The world could have blown up and we wouldn't have known about it for a while.

Our high school did have a small weekly publication including a record dedication page and I remember dedicating a song called *I Think I Love You* to a girl I had a crush on. But I didn't know who sang the song. I really didn't start hearing about *The Partridge Family* and David Cassidy until I went to college in Oregon from 1972 to 1977. I think I watched *The Partridge Family* on TV for the first time in 1976.

The first albums I bought were *Notebook* and *Sound Magazine*. I can still remember listening to *Notebook* for the first time and concentrating on learning each and every song. After that I was hooked and bought every PF and David Cassidy album I could find – and have been a huge fan ever since.

While in college I bought my first David Cassidy solo album, *The Higher They Climb*, at the Oregon State University bookstore and I've always remembered what the cashier said: "This doesn't sound anything like the Partridge Family". I didn't know what to think about that, if he meant it was a good thing or not.

I remember watching the TV movie *A Chance to Live* one night while the rest of my family went to the local county fair. I wanted to see David Cassidy instead, so I stayed home. I have become a huge collector of PF and David Cassidy memorabilia as well and just wished I had an extra room to display everything.

I finally got to see him in person when he appeared at the Seven Feathers Casino in Canyonville, Oregon in 2008. It was a dream come true and my wife and daughter came with me as well. I had my kids watching the PF on TV in the 90s so they were familiar with them as well.

> 66 I CAN STILL REMEMBER LISTENING TO NOTEBOOK FOR THE FIRST TIME AND CONCENTRATING ON LEARNING EACH AND EVERY SONG 99

Michael Lefner with some of his collection

ELIZABETH AND GEORGINA KORN – AUSTRALIA

Twins Elizabeth and Georgina won the hearts of the world when in 2006 they were invited onto a TV show in Australia, *Where Are They Now?* The programme looked at what had happened to some of the world's biggest stars over the years. The girls – who are among David's biggest fans – were guests on the show, interviewed in the studio in a replica of a 1970s teenage bedroom where the walls were covered with posters of David. In 1974 Georgina had won a David Cassidy Lookalike competition. They had no idea they were about to meet him.

Elizabeth: During our interview we were asked if we knew what David was doing now, and we said touring in the United States. We had no idea he was going to walk onto the set so when he did, we were speechless. He hugged us and we sat there in shock. We chatted like old friends, laughed, he sang *I Think I Love You* as a ballad to us on his acoustic guitar, and looked so proud when we spoke about his father. After the cameras stopped rolling, we got to give him really big hugs, kiss him on the cheek, tell him we still sing his songs, how he made our lives immensely happy and we were never going to forget him. He was clearly moved as much as we were and wiped away our tears.

Loving David when we were teenagers was clean and innocent. It was blue skies and sunshine. We are very lucky to have lived through that time and experience. For us no one equalled to that time or him. The connection has been there since the beginning and will last forever and a day.

Our experiences may not have been available to everybody, but meeting David lifted our souls for a long time, and still does. When you hear his songs, it takes you instantly back to that innocent time. We sing his songs today as though time has stopped, nothing has changed. Maybe things were difficult at times, but that part of you was the best time anyone could have.

Georgina: David made our lives so very happy. I have to stop myself sometimes and ask: "What is my life without David Cassidy?" He was for us the spark in every day. I will love him and his music forever. I don't think he ever really knew the inside of the hearts of those who loved him, not in a hysterical sense but we really did think he was the coolest, nicest guy who sang these gorgeous songs filled with happiness.

Celebrities and huge stars like David who are in the spotlight and so adored never see it from our angle. They often don't know what it is like to love in that degree, to have all that adulation, to have that gift of making people so happy. I would look at his posters and say, 'Do you realise what you have done to us, what you have meant to us?'.

Elizabeth: I don't think he ever knew the full extent of how deeply he was loved – really loved.

The pose Georgina Korn copied which won her the David Cassidy Lookalike competition

He came into our lives at a very impressionable time. We were just young girls going to High School and did not expect someone like that to come into our lives. When we were at school, Georgie had a folder, the cover of which was the advert for the Melbourne Cricket Ground, March 10, 1974. Inside the folder it said, "he's mine, all mine", it was a message to everyone: Hands off!

Georgina: That's right. I do remember a girl at school turned to me and asked rather indignantly, if I ever thought I was going to marry him, or even meet him. I insisted I would, one day. She told me I was mad and said I would never meet him. I never forgot that remark. I met him three times. I would never, ever had believed that meeting David would ever have been a remote possibility. I wish I could go back and tell her, well look at me, I did meet him.

The best and happiest time of my life came when

> 66 WE WERE ADVISED TO CONTAIN OURSELVES, NOT TO SCREAM WHEN HE COMES ON – BUT PLEASE, I SAY, DON'T SUPPRESS OUR HAPPINESS 99

I entered a David Cassidy Lookalike competition on an afternoon kids show on Channel 7 called *Do It* hosted by Ian Buchan in 1974. My aunt had taken a snap Polaroid photograph of me imitating David, but we never thought anything would come of it. I came home from school in my art shirt which was covered with David's name to find a stamped addressed envelope in my handwriting. I nervously opened it to read they wanted me at Channel 7. We had no telephone then, so they had to write. I cried endless tears of happiness. I was so grateful because I loved David so much.

Elizabeth: We went over to the studio and when Georgie stepped out of the car all these girls started running towards her thinking she was David. It was a little frightening. There were three other girls in the competition, they took pictures of everyone and said they would be in touch.

Georgina: When they told me I had won I was beside myself. The winner was supposed to meet David as he was here for his concerts, but that never happened as the laundry woman at the Southern Cross Hotel had stolen his underwear, or so the story went. I was given a poster and a copy of his *Cherish* album which he later signed.

Elizabeth: Mum and Dad took us to the MCG where 75,000 fans were packed in. Seeing David was an absolute joy; it was like a vision, unbelievable happiness, just instantly. I remember him being so skinny and so much smaller than what I had imagined in a red t-shirt and blue overalls. There was nothing of him, but he raced around the stage and we were hysterical.

He came back to Australia later that year and again in 2002 when we were lucky enough to meet him at the airport and in the audience for *The Rove Show* taking David some Australian themed gifts. We were advised to contain ourselves, not to scream when he

Elizabeth and Georgina Korn on *Where Are They Now?*

comes on – but please, I say, don't suppress our happiness, we need to be able to express ourselves and he's got to know how we feel.

Georgina: David had a beautiful spirit about him. Deep down inside he was a lovely, kind person who had that beautiful joy and happiness about him.

Elizabeth: I don't know what happens to us when we go to those concerts, but in 2002 I wanted to let him know how much we loved him. I went down to the stage and started pounding my fists screaming, "We want David". I wanted him to feel the same adulation that he had in the early 1970s. People followed what I was doing. To see and hear him sing again, our hearts were jumping out of our chests and we were alive again. He just made us so happy.

Top left: Elizabeth and Georgina Korn

Georgina (top) and Elizbeth (below) in front of the Partridge Family garage door Georgina painted

Left: David holds a press conference at the Southern Cross Hotel in Melbourne as fans clamour to get inside.
Photo © Scott Hicks

JOANNE RIZZO – UNITED STATES

My earliest memories of David Cassidy were when I was 13 years old. I remember watching *The Partridge Family* for the first time and instantly being drawn to him. It was like a magnet. He had it all......... the voice, the look, the sparkle of charisma, the personality, the walk, the hair, the eyes.......I can go on and on. He was a dream for any young girl. I was IN LOVE! I never got tired of listening to his songs, the way he emphasized certain lyrics, the tone of the voice, the emotions.

I was lucky enough to see him live at both Madison Square in March 1972 and the Nassau Coliseum in June. How do you describe the experience? It's indescribable. It gets to every part of your being. As a young girl he brought me happiness at times when I lacked self-confidence and was very shy around people. I retreated into a land of joy and happiness and I loved every minute of it.

The 80s and 90s were full of raising my three young children so the next time I was able to attend a show was Atlantic City in 2001. I attended his Tarrytown show having a very unique after-show experience. My partner and I walked our way down to where our car was parked and we noticed a very distinct car parked right outside the restaurant where we just had dinner earlier that evening.

It had a sign in the front window. When the driver noticed we were looking, he quickly removed the sign. We decided to go back in for dessert hoping it was his band inside the restaurant. Sure enough the entire band and David were all seated at the same table where we had eaten. He was kind enough to autograph our ticket receipts from the show.

BB Kings will always be a stand out for me. We were always SO close to the stage and David enjoyed being in New York so much. He always told stories of his memories here and it made his show so touching and intimate. His enthusiasm never died. He gave his fans ALL he had at every show. I consider myself SO lucky to be part of this time in our lives.

The highlight was being at his very last show at BB Kings in March 2017. I bought the tickets so early never realizing that it would be his VERY last show. I enjoy keeping David's memory alive through the music bringing back the times gone by. He was an extremely rare and talented young man who was never given the recognition he so desired.

> I RETREATED INTO A LAND OF JOY AND HAPPINESS AND I LOVED EVERY MINUTE OF IT

Joanne Rizzo at the Meet & Greet at Westbury Music Hall in March 2013

LINDSEY JUPP – UNITED KINGDOM

I didn't know him as Keith on *The Partridge Family*, I didn't see the shows......to me he was David Cassidy the voice and the dream. I was too young to go to the first UK concert but I continued to collect every album and posters from the pop magazines. My bedroom walls were only for David and they distracted me nicely from school homework and puberty.

He disappeared from the magazines and I left school to go to work, but I still regularly returned to listen to my albums.

1985 and *The Last Kiss*, which he performed on *Top of the Pops*, rekindled so many memories. My husband bought me the single and again the albums were played once in a while. Then cds came along and my children somehow seemed to know the songs as familiar as nursery rhymes.

When I was expecting my first child I saw *Blood Brothers* in London and was spellbound. I hadn't seen his acting ability before. In the last scene he ran down the gangway and passed by my seat. I could have touched him!!

In 2002 I saw DC for the first time in concert at Hammersmith – I was so shocked how all the words to the songs were right there in my memory and he was awesome. I saw him again in Bournemouth for that same tour, took my mum who knew all the words too having listened to my records played over and over in the 70s, and again in 2012. His music is part of me, it's there as a comfort in sad times as well as good.

I can now see that his work schedule with concerts was phenomenal, the demands made on himself and by others was unbelievable. His show in Vegas and his success he had there for years, he was always striving for more and reinventing himself. To me he had it all, he was able to take a song and make it his own. So clever, and so sadly missed.

KIM SOUTHERN – UNITED STATES

In 2003, I had tickets to see David in concert at a golf resort in Ellicot City, MD. I was going with my friend and fellow "Cassidiva", Tama. We had second row center seats – only about 10 feet away from the stage. It was a relatively small and intimate setting and we both agreed that it was almost like a private concert. This was the closest I had ever been to David.

He looked great and spent quite a bit of time talking and interacting with the audience. He thanked everyone profusely for coming to the rescheduled show. Someone sent up her 7-year-old daughter to get an autograph, and David grinned and said, "Sure mom, the old sucker punch! Sending up the kid to ask me, knowing I can't refuse her!" It was adorable.

When he got ready to sing *I Think I Love You* near the end of the show, many of us approached the stage. David walked back and forth along the edge of the stage to touch our hands. NOW, I thought, this was the closest I had ever been to David, and it was surprising to me how small he was in person. I turned and said to my friend, Tama, "He's an elf!" HE HEARD ME! He laughed, thank goodness, and said – "Yeah, I looked a lot taller on TV, didn't I?" My face must have been beet red.

Having had a couple of gin and tonics before the show, my inhibitions must have been reduced, because as he was walking back towards me, still touching hands, a sudden urge came over me and I reached up and ran my hand, ever so gently, along his abdomen above his belt. OMG. He gave me the funniest

look of surprise! I put my hands over my face in embarrassment and said, "I'm so sorry!!" He said, "Don't worry, sweetheart," squeezed my hand again, and kept walking along the stage.

When I got home that night, my husband was waiting up for me. He said: "How was the concert?" I replied: "I TOUCHED HIM." My husband stuck his fingers in his ears and said that he didn't want to hear anymore. I will never forget that evening. My inner little girl was squealing in delight.

JILL MARIE ADAMS – UNITED STATES

David has been a part of my life for 50 years and my son Jason's biggest mentor and influence since he was 2 years old. I met David long before Jason was born when we moved to California, yet my memories are mostly since Jason would listen to all my Partridge Family and David Cassidy cassette tapes.

Many young fans, including Jason, were bullied for loving him, but he was bullied anyway so he never denied it. He says it takes a real man to like David Cassidy, so I made Jason a shirt which he wore proudly. Jason has met David many times. He became his biggest inspiration and an often-distant mentor.

When Jason was just two and a half, he wowed everyone at a pre-school banquet singing *I Think I Love You*. Soon after that he developed epilepsy but performing on stage gave him the confidence he needed to deal with the challenges of living with it. He was only seven when he found a flyer for the children's theater group, Showcamp and the stage gave us a place to cheer him. He later won a scholarship to work on a degree in Science and Theater Arts at California's Glendale Community College. I am sure without David's influence his life could have

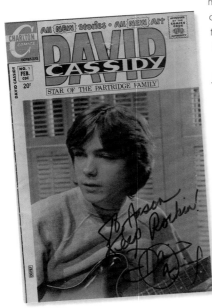

Jason Adams with David and the comic book he signed for him

been very different. Thank you, David for making a difference in the life of a child.

David noticed Jason at The Orleans in Vegas, put his hand on his chest and said, "Hey Buddy" as he leaned over and gave Jason three good manly handshakes. Jason was so happy. He hadn't been feeling well and this lifted his spirits. David had the kind of energy that heals. On one occasion in Las Vegas when girls rushed to the stage, Jason stood to the side. David asked the girls to make room for his little buddy and shook his hand. That made that trip for Jason.

Jason met David and his family at the recording of the TV series, *Ruby and the Rockits*. When Jason sang *How Can I be Sure* at a taping of the show, David, the rest of the cast and crew gave him a standing ovation. David said something his dad told him, "Talent will prevail". Jason took what he said to heart. David kindly autographed Jason's David Cassidy comic book which he kept in mint condition, as well as a photo declaring Jason is his favorite fan. David will always hold a special place in our hearts.

God bless you in Heaven, David, where we know you are not judged, and being accepted as the amazing talent that you are. We miss you.

KAREN BYROM – UNITED KINGDOM

Karen Byrom and David meet and greet Glasgow 2002

I first "fell in love" with David when I was just 13 – someone at school was passing round a *Jackie* magazine, and I was immediately enthralled by those soulful eyes looking out at me from the page. Funnily, I don't remember watching *The Partridge Family*, though I must have done – but with a sister and two brothers, there was always a fight for TV time in my home.

I shared a bedroom with my older sister, and there were strict demarcation lines! My walls were covered in Cassidy pix – yes, even the giant posters that came in three parts, and whose colours never quite matched – while hers held posters of hideous sci-fi creatures she put up just to scare me! My father said my David pictures were more frightening! But he and mum did buy me *Cherish* on vinyl that Christmas. *Ricky's Tune* was my favourite song, possibly because I knew David had written it himself.

I was never lucky enough to see him in concert at the height of Cassidymania. When his first comeback UK tour was announced in 2001, I wasn't even fussed about going. But my friends and I decided it would be a good girls' night out, so off we went to Glasgow. I'd forgotten what a wonderful singer David was, and how that treacle-rich voice could make you feel you were the only girl in the room. My crush was reborn.

But I was an adult now, with no time to moon. I bought his album *A Touch of Blue*, put it on my ipod and got back to real life, thinking he'd probably never be back in the UK.

Then ...! I worked on *My Weekly* magazine, where my friend, Maggie Swinburne, was celebrity editor, and she commissioned an interview with David from writer Peter Robinson. As a result, she talked to David's publicity people and blagged me a "meet and greet" at his next concert in Glasgow in 2002.

By that time I was 43, but I was more excited than my 13-year-old self might have been! I prepared for it as if it was my first date, even borrowing a black dress from one of my chums,

just as we used to do when we were teenagers.

The actual meeting went by in a blur. Up close, David looked just as I'd imagined. I told him I loved his music, he gave me a handshake and a chaste kiss and signed my programme, his publicity woman took a picture on my camera, and then it was over.

I was ushered back to the concert hall, where I joined my pals, who were just as excited as I was. I just had to tell them all the details when the lights went out and David came on. What a brilliant concert. I was on an adrenalin high all night. I remember texting my friend from whom I borrowed the dress, I MET HIM! HE KISSED ME! I've seen David Cassidy in concert several times since, and while naturally none met the excitement of that night, I remained a fan.

When news of his death came I felt so sad – I'm glad I have those great memories of the first man to touch my heart.

> ❝ I REMEMBER TEXTING MY FRIEND FROM WHOM I BORROWED THE DRESS, I MET HIM! HE KISSED ME! ❞

David relaxes at home in Encino with his much-loved English setter, Bullseye. Photographer, Ed Caraeff, recalls: "The time I spent with him, he was down-to-earth and unpretentious. I knew he had famous Hollywood showbusiness parents. He was easy to shoot and very comfortable in front of the camera." Photo: Ed Caraeff/ Iconic Images

KAREN BYROM

My penpal, Debbie, and her friend, Jan, in South Shields were also massive David fans. They were lucky enough to attend his Manchester concert in 1973, and they also got a mention on *Blue Peter*, when they sent him a hand-embellished blanket for his beloved dog, Bullseye. Neither she nor I expected that it would ever get to him, let alone be handed over to him on television. David was invited into the studio for the judging of the Blue Peter Keep Britain Tidy poster competition. The producers promised to pass on autograph books, presents, letters and cards sent to the studio. Presenter, Peter Purves, wheeled over a pile of gifts to David. On unfolding the blanket, David said, "Oh it's great. It's lovely, really lovely". I so wished that I could be with Debbie and Jan to share their excitement. She later told me they'd screamed the house down.

LOZZA – UNITED KINGDOM

I started off a fan in 1973. I lived in the UK and my grandad drove a black London cab and was happy to indulge my obsession with DC. He made it so that I went to nearly every show at Wembley Arena in 1973 and at the tender age of 14 he took me to Glasgow, White City and Manchester. I went to the "Day out with David Cassidy at the Isle of Wight" in 2008. I was very nervous but David was charming and put me at my ease.

He asked when I had first heard about him so I told him that in 1973 I went to nearly all of the Wembley Arena shows to which he said "really". Then I told him the story of my grandad taking me to all of the UK shows in 1974. He reached forward, held my wrist and said: "he must of loved you very much". I said that he did. David then said: "he sounds like a wonderful man" – I replied that he was wonderful but sadly long gone.

I added that being able to come and see him (David) helped keep grandad's memory alive. He smiled and said: "you are beautiful". I had many meets with him in the years after that and he was always charming.

PHILIP CLARK – AUSTRALIA

David Cassidy for me was first a role model and then a tremendous lifelong source of inspiration. His music and work are seared into my consciousness and indelibly woven into the fabric of my life. As trite as that might sound, that IS the genuine impact he had on me and the gift he unknowingly gave to me and millions of others. He gave me positivity, hope and joy when I had very little. His impact will remain with me for the rest of my life.

When David passed away it was a deeply emotional time for me and the millions like me the world over who had admired this great, hugely talented human being who was haunted by his flaws, his life's imperfections and his tortured relationships, particularly with his own father, and the loss of his dear mother. I felt desperately sad that a man who had been so loved by so many had died not fully realising the tremendous impact he had had on a generation of people the world over.

In 1970s terms, I came to David Cassidy fandom pretty late in the piece. I lived in England at the time when David hit public consciousness, but initially he passed me by. I was disinterested.

At the age of 11 in the autumn of 1972 I started high school, a huge and tough all-boys school. I struggled to find my place and acceptance among the 1,000 students. By 1973 I had a new best mate. We created our own safe space amidst the chaos and hung out together every chance we could. The first time I went to Bob's place and saw his room I was dumbstruck. His walls were covered in pop posters dominated by David Cassidy. For a teenage boy back then it was (ridiculously) taboo for a boy to admire David. I reacted the way I was conditioned to which was to exclaim "YUK".

Late in 1973, when I was almost 13, David released *Daydreamer* and arguably his best solo album from the Bell years *Dreams Are Nuthin' More Than Wishes*. Both went straight to #1 in the UK and for some inexplicable reason I was suddenly hooked. In an instant David Cassidy became my favourite pop star. I read everything I could to learn more about him, bought posters and hung them on my wall. I listened to his music, wondering retrospectively how I could have ignored this fantastically talented artist.

With hindsight and wisdom, I recognise now that on the threshold of my teen years I was searching for a role model, someone whom I could admire and seek to emulate. I was impressionable, struggling to make sense of a world that could sometimes be cruel. I'd been bullied and got into more fights than my sensitive, introverted, shy, fearful self could deal with. David Cassidy struck the right chord with me. His image then (manufactured as I now know it was) represented everything I wanted to be. He was musical, a rock star, popular with girls and seemed to have everything a young guy could ever hope to aspire to. And his voice and those songs of yearning that he so often sang back then reached into my sensitive soul, spoke to me and for me.

British boys did NOT, could NOT like David Cassidy. He was soooo popular with girls that I think it left boys nowhere to go but to hate David with as much passion as the girls they wanted to date loved him. It was a backlash, a counter statement. They resented David's strong influence.

The inference that any guy who admired David must by definition be sexually attracted to him is preposterous. I definitely did not follow David for the same reasons as girls did. Back then I wanted to BE him, not be WITH him. Interestingly, that male backlash phenomenon was uniquely British because when my family moved to Australia at the end of 1974, nobody cared that he was my favourite singer and in fact a number of my new male Aussie mates had some of his records and regularly borrowed mine.

My connection with David Cassidy was a safe, private place where I could escape. I got lost in his music. I was tremendously excited

when something new about him came on TV. David Cassidy meant (and still means to me) what The Beatles and Elvis has meant to millions of people the world over, irrespective of their gender.

In 1993, with the pluck and determination of a lifelong fan, I rang the Music Box Theatre where David was performing in *Blood Brothers*. Mustering as much confidence and assuredness as I could, I asked to be put through to David. Amazingly they put me through to the stage manager. He placed me on hold, spoke to David, came back and said that David asked me to call back the next day at exactly the same time and he would speak to me then. I did and when David came to the phone my heart was pounding through my chest.

He was amazing and thanked me for my support. We talked about the show, how we could get him to Australia for a concert tour, our children. I was blown away. I recorded the conversation on cassette tape and it remains a very precious possession. I was on cloud nine.

In 2000, my friend Jim and I flew to Las Vegas to see David in At *The Copa*. It was the first time I had ever seen David perform live and I was completely beside myself with excitement. After the amazing performance his PA took us back stage. When I saw David come into the room, it was completely surreal. He gave me a huge hug. The three of us talked with David for 45 minutes or so. He was very generous and gracious.

As we were leaving, David was sitting in an armchair. I knelt down beside him, took his right hand in mine and told him how much I had loved him, how much his music and performing had impacted on my life and how I never dreamt that I would ever have gotten the chance to thank him in person. At that moment, my inner teenage self was ecstatically leaping for joy while my adult self, tried to remain poised. David

> ❝ I KNELT DOWN BESIDE HIM, TOOK HIS RIGHT HAND IN MINE AND TOLD HIM HOW MUCH I HAD LOVED HIM, HOW MUCH HIS MUSIC AND PERFORMING HAD IMPACTED ON MY LIFE ❞

graciously thanked me and said that every day was a wonderful affirmation of his impact when he had the chance to connect with fans like me.

On that same trip, Jim and I had the unique opportunity to have lunch with David's lovely mother Evelyn. She was extraordinary, very beautiful and full of anecdotes and reminiscences from her remarkable life. She was clearly very proud of David. Two things in particular I learned from her that day: 1) They almost migrated to Australia in the late 60s; 2) They saw a psychic when David was a young teen who told Evelyn that David was one day going to be famous in every corner of the world.

David did another concert tour of Australia in 2002 and I was invited to attend his Sydney press conference and took my wife with me. It was surreal to be there in my home city with David Cassidy in the same room. I was completely and pleasantly surprised when David exclaimed, "Philip, you're here. How are you man?" He hugged me and my wife and we chatted for a couple of minutes. I walked out of the venue on cloud nine.

I saw him in Wollongong, Melbourne, Newcastle and Sydney. Every concert was an amazing experience. It was heart-warming to be in venues surrounded by thousands of people who all cared about David and were having the times of their lives. The Melbourne and Sydney concerts were particularly wild with fans pushing forward and sometimes screaming so loudly you had to block your ears. My son, himself a guitarist, came to two of the concerts with me and was totally impressed with David's musicianship and guitar playing.

A few years later David secretly came to Australia to appear on the local *Where Are They Now?* TV show. When David left, the audience gave him a standing ovation. I was fortunate enough to be sitting next to the exit and as I reached out to shake David's hand, he looked at me and said: "Philip! How great that you're here". The fact that David recognised me again and that we had that moment was so special for me.

KAREN BLOOR – UNITED KINGDOM

This treasured picture was taken on November 16, 2008 at the Hammersmith Apollo during a Meet & Greet. I told David that I had waited 35 years to meet him and he said: "awww bless". Little did he realise the story behind our meeting. When I saw the meet and greet offer on eBay, I bid on a pair of tickets. As the auction didn't finish until 5.30am I decided to set my alarm to watch the results. In my excitement to secure, I upped my bid to £1,000 (or so I thought) but had actually typed in £10,000.

However, it was a fortunate mistake as the final price was just over £1,000 and believe me it was the best money spent giving me a night to cherish for the rest of my life.

Karen Bloor with David. Photo: Sue Bond

MICHELE CRUZ – AUSTRALIA

I loved, loved, loved David Cassidy, who was a huge part of my childhood life, he made it a better place. He was my first and only posters on my bedroom walls. I loved the way he looked, the way he spoke, his gorgeous laugh and his perfect singing voice that made me feel like he was singing to me.

I was there at the Melbourne Cricket Ground on March 10, 1974 right up near the front getting squashed and loving it. I remember wearing my very first bra to the concert and I had overalls on very similar to his. I will never forget the thrill of being so close to him.

In the 70s I entered a competition on an after-school TV show, hosted by a woman called Trudi, on which I won an autographed t-shirt and poster from David. My drawing was David sitting on a kangaroo. When the prizes arrived, the t-shirt was so big for me. Can you believe I was so worried David would think I was fat….I will never forget it.

In November 2002 I saw David live again at the Vodafone Arena, in Melbourne. I was lucky to be very close to the front of the stage again, and it

Left: T-shirt signed by David
Below: Michele Cruz with David

was just so special to see him. He made my heart flutter with millions of butterflies as he did in 1974.

One of the highlights of my life was actually meeting David Cassidy in 2002. I was invited to a press conference held at the Como Hotel in Melbourne. I was sitting three metres from my idol – I LOVED IT!!! When we chatted and had photos taken, I still thought he was perfect as I did back in 1974 when I was a child. David Cassidy had a huge, positive, beautiful, impact on my life.

RIP sweet, beautiful David. Singing with the angels now. I'll love and miss you always.

MARY MCSHEFFREY – UNITED KINGDOM

I was 10 and like so many others fell in love with David on *The Partridge Family*, excitement growing before each episode was aired; saving my 50p pocket money to buy records and magazines; my bedroom walls plastered with his beautiful face; amazingly being allowed to go and see him at Wembley in the early seventies. Playing his music in my bedroom would often make me cry. I remember listening to a little transistor radio at school break to see if he had moved up or down in the charts.

My friend Jeanette and I took a day off school to go to the Grosvenor House Hotel in London. I was about 14. We managed to get into the hotel with two other girls. Once inside we opened the first door we came to and all shuffled in – to find it was a broom cupboard essentially. We all just hunched down, hearts beating in our ears not knowing what to do next. The door opened and a weary looking security guard saw us off the premises. Later on, outside David came out onto the balcony, waved to us and made it all worthwhile.

I went to White City in May 1974. David was just a dot in the distance. I can remember the excitement and anticipation and a tingling feeling waiting for him to come on stage. I bought a rosette and scarf which I treasured for years.

I went to see David in *Time* and *Blood Brothers* in the West End and to see him perform at The Royal Albert Hall. But it wasn't until 2004 that I would actually touch him.

Seeing him in concert, listening to those old songs again took me back to a carefree happy time of my childhood. I will always be grateful for that.

In 2008 I had a meet and greet on the Isle of Wight and met him backstage at Glasgow two days later. Stupidly I half expected him to recognise me from two days before, how unrealistic was I? There were about eight of us meeting him in Glasgow. We were able to have our photo taken with our own camera. I stood next to David and he put his arm around me. His driver/security guard was given the task of taking the photos. He couldn't work my camera initially and as he tried to do so David was rubbing my arm. I remember thinking you can take as long as you like – I've got David Cassidy's arm around me.

David's voice can still move me to tears. David Cassidy didn't know me, and I didn't know him, but I am forever grateful that he was a part of my life growing up.

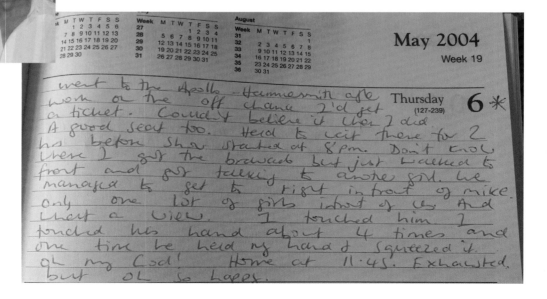

Above: Mary McSheffrey with David

Right: Mary McSheffrey's diary entry

DIANE OSWIN – UNITED KINGDOM

Mum was the lady who stole David's heart – at the age of 81.

She was the catalyst for my adoration for him. I was the youngest, but it was mum who bought all the magazines, records and tickets for the family to see him at the Empire Pool, Wembley in 1973. She was a superfan, probably a bigger fan than me and my sister.

Mum brought up four kids and David was probably a bit of an escape for her. David in the 1970s was such a big thing at the time, it was so wonderful. Our lives at that time evolved around David, we could not wait for the next magazine to come out, the next programme he would be on, the next record to be released. It was sooo exciting. You can still feel that feeling you got in your stomach – we are very blessed with the happy times and the music he made.

But mum certainly made a big impression with him when we met him in 2008. After my sister, Christine, saw the advert in the national press inviting fans to join him on the Isle of Wight mum took us over and at 81 it was a big thing for her to do. She did steal the show with him. It was lovely of him to give her that time. She charmed him as much as the other way round.

It all seemed unreal in a way that having been fans since we were teenagers, we were going to meet him in our 50s. David wasn't there when we arrived, I think he came over on a speedboat. When he appeared on the stage it was just amazing to see him. He spoke about what this day and his fans meant to him. It seemed important to him we had the chance to meet him. Fans would go onto the stage one by one to spend a few minutes with him, have their picture taken and we were so excited. But then he said he would not have time to get around everyone. At that point I gave a big wolf whistle and shouted: "Come over here". He jumped off the stage and came over to our table.

I was a professional cake maker and made him a cake using the *Dreams Are Nuthin' More Than Wishes* album cover design. David could not take the cake with him but donated £100 to the Make A Wish Foundation. He was very taken with the picture, said Bullseye was his favourite dog, had been so special and how much he meant to him. He seemed very natural and relaxed talking to us and I felt very comfortable talking with him.

He turned to mum – she told him her name was Margaret – and asked her how old she was. She told him: "I'm 18, but I am your biggest fan!" She was just playing around with her age, and he found that amusing, asked her who her favourite singer was. She told him Elvis. He agreed. She was mothering him and offering advice on his sore throat. He really took to her and at one point told her, "I love you".

It was amusing that all us ladies had been preening ourselves in the bathroom waiting to meet him that day, and our dear mum stole his heart. She never forgot it.

David had a real depth to him and his fans really did mean a lot to him. The way he was with mum and all of us, it was all so nice for him to meet people who were very dear to him, without it being scary. He was this enigma and people could not get close to him. He was terrified he was going to get a cold, but he would put his arms around us. He was lovely.

For mum to have met him in the latter stages of her life was so amazing for her. She always said there was something special about him, something different – he was exceptional. Mum said he had a sort of mission in his life, but it was perhaps too much for him. The way he looked – he was so stunning – the music, the TV series, it was like a perfect storm both positive and negative. He ticked all the boxes about what young girls fantasied about. Before him we had nobody.

The frenzy around him when he came to the UK just built

Above: David meets Christine, Diane and Margaret Oswin on the Isle of Wight

Below: Special message just for Margaret

and built, so when he did the concerts in 1973 it was out of control. We had never seen anything like him before. A few years later we got jobs at the Strand Palace Hotel in London but it was just chance he was in London. We saw him come out of another hotel with Kay and he acknowledged us putting his hand up, and then again after the premiere of a film Kay was in.

He still has a presence on this Earth. God Bless you David and thank you for giving us all you did, and still do. I hope you are at peace now.

CHRISTINE OSWIN – UNITED KINGDOM

David's LP *Dreams Are Nuthin' More Than Wishes* is actually the theme of our life. David's energy had a big impact on our family. It helped us focus on our hopes and dreams. We never ever let go of dreaming to meet him. The positive energies he sent out will be in the world forever. I do believe we live our lives by never giving up and holding onto the dream, it will eventually come true. Mum always told us that. Meeting David was one of those dreams.

I was an apprentice hairdresser and went on to have my own salon. Diane went into catering, had her own business and made fabulous cakes. Our brothers had mechanical businesses and then became musicians.

I remember looking at the picture of the little girl with the dog which was the pull-out print with the *Dreams* LP. I made a wish and had three beautiful daughters who had their hair up like the girl in the print. I also made a wish I wanted to live in Devon, and that happened.

The day the tickets arrived to meet David on the Isle of Wight, *I'll Meet You Halfway* was on the radio. I wrote this letter:

Hello David,

Welcome to dear old Devon, the next place to Heaven.

I am delighted at last after all these years to meet you. Sometimes we have to wait a long time for wishes to come true, don't we?

A few weeks ago, I was sitting in the Ship Inn pub on the back beach in Tinmouth when I had a Déjà vu moment. What happened was, as I looked through the window there was a young boy with a dog sitting on the wall looking out over the river. It was such a lovely picture and it took me back to my memory of the front cover of your LP *Dreams Are Nuthin' More Than Wishes*.

About half an hour later I picked up a newspaper in the pub with an advertisement to meet you on the Isle of Wight, so of course I had to come.

When I was 17, I entered a competition in *FAB* magazine – we all had to collect money for charity and the one who collected the most got to meet you. All the rest were supposed to be invited to a party. But then we got a letter saying unfortunately the party wasn't going to happen.

At the Isle of Wight, when David came over to us, he put his arm round mum and just seemed to be in the moment. I thought that was the real person, especially when he was talking to mum, he was just a boy. She told him to take Manuka honey and Vitamin C for his throat.

Top right and far right: David engages with fans at the Isle of Wight. Photos: Lizbeth McAnary Pierce

Below: Special book made by Christine Oswin for David

He was lovely, warm and kind; just an ordinary bloke who wanted to be loved and understood. He just wanted people to be real with him.

I wrote to him in 1973 and sent it to the fan club. I put my heart and soul into the drawings and everything else. Over a year later it came back with a covering letter, which I didn't keep, and I don't know if it was true or not, that said David enjoyed reading this and wanted you to have it back.

Years later I made a book which I gave him in the IOW. He looked through it, said it was "really lovely" and while he couldn't take it with him, he did want to sign it "so it reminds you of me" he told me. And he did: "To Christine, Much Love, David Cassidy" on the front.

After meeting David, I wrote a little poem:
I think it was Saturday
When I went to see David Cassidy
My mum, brothers, little sis and me
Wembley, London, the concert to see
We screamed and screamed with all our might
We saw David was far out a sight
Oh David, please look my way
In my heart you'll forever stay
I'm the one you're singing to
Not her in front in the queue
To meet you was my deepest dream
But now all I can do is scream
I wish my wish would all come true
It has but now I'm 52.

Above left: David signed the book made for him

Left and above: Diane Oswin shows David the cake she made for him and with the cake

LYNN PARSONS – BROADCASTER

I was working for Smooth Radio in London on November 11, 2008, when I interviewed David for a series we were running. I invited my friend to come along as she had loved him as a teenager too. He was warm and engaging.

When I was very young my Dad, who happened to share David's birthday, had given me the album *Dreams Are Nuthin' More Than Wishes*, which had a front cover of an original painting of a small girl with her dog sitting side by side looking over a lake. I took the album with me to the interview as it was the first album I had ever owned. David was surprised to see it and said, "Oh for goodness sake, let me sign it, shall I sign the picture of me and Bullseye?" I was confused. Then he slid the painting of the girl and her dog out and underneath was a beautiful photo of him and his English Setter, which I had truly never seen before. He signed the picture, and only recently on looking back at the message did I notice he had called me a 'doll', It made me smile as I've never been called a doll before or after that moment.

When I see a picture of David with his shiny long hair in the 1970s it is how I remember him. The posters on our bedroom walls and on the front covers of teenage magazines *Jackie* and *Fab 208* were served up by record companies including the question and answer features from favourite colour and food to what sort of girls he liked.

When I met David, he explained he hadn't been that person at all. On that day in the studio, when our eyes met, they were the same eyes that had stared down at me from the poster on my bedroom wall. I didn't love him any less, but I found myself disappointed that he wasn't the person I had been sold a dream on years before. The interview lasted about an hour and he was happy to have photos taken.

Afterwards I felt ashamed that I had felt disappointed, asking myself the question 'How dare you feel that way'. David had a beautiful spirit that had been misrepresented back in the 70s and I had no claim on this man. But I felt deeply saddened on his behalf that he had never achieved his true potential. He had wanted to be taken seriously as an actor.

In my experience, when you meet someone who is successful for singing or dancing or writing or painting, they are either driven or slightly introverted and often have an enormous ego. I did not think that David had an ego at all.

Since that meeting in 2008 I have read interviews where David made it clear about just how damaging those teenage years were for him and of course the knock-on effect on his life. I felt sad again that I had fallen for the record company hype that had been served up in the 70s that had contributed to an unhappy life for David.

I was fortunate enough to see David in the musical *Time* in London's West End. And the audience couldn't take their eyes off of him. He was a brilliant actor but didn't get the opportunity to fulfil that dream in this lifetime.

It was an honour to meet David in 2008, after all he had played an integral part in my childhood, if only from the bedroom wall. When he passed away, I was very, very sad.

Opposite page: David at the Desert of the Sun Arena, Primm, Nevada June 2007. Photo: Darrell Lloyd/BACKGRID

Above: Lynn Parsons (right) with her friend Danah Hatt

Below: Lynn's signed album

REN'EE GIVENS – UNITED STATES

I first fell in love with David when I was about 12 years old. Like every young girl I bought every magazine with David in it, plastered all over my bedroom walls was his beautiful face. In 1971 I had his concert ticket in my hands at Evansville, Indiana and counting the days to finally see him in person. The concert was cancelled because he needed emergency gall bladder surgery. I was worried about him. We were told it would be rescheduled but that never happened.

In 2004 my family were driving down town. I saw a sign at our casino that David was coming there on my birthday. I screamed out: "I have to go". My ex brother-in-law worked as a security guard there and got me a ticket. His wife went with me. It was my birthday, August 7. I took a picture out of my scrapbook with me.

It was general admission, so we got there early. I was talking to these other ladies about how they had to cancel his concert in 1971, and that I've been waiting almost 34 years to see him. When we finally got to sit down those ladies saved me and my ex sister-in-law a seat close to the stage. He came on and I thought I was going to faint. It was so good to finally see him in person.

As the concert went on something inside of me told me to hold the picture up I brought with me. He saw me holding it up, told the band to stop and asked me to come up to the stage. I was shaking and crying as if I was that 12-year-old girl seeing her first love. He put the picture by his face comparing it, asking the fans: can you believe this is me? He asked me how old I was then, I said 12. He just laughed and smiled that heart-melting smile. I asked him to sign it as it was my birthday. He said: "Happy Birthday". It is one of my most treasured possessions.

I would have loved to seen him in 1971 but waiting for 34 years, he was definitely worth the wait. I will never forget seeing him and coming to the stage. I will love David Bruce Cassidy until I take my last breath. He is and always will be in my heart. He is forever missed and loved by me.

CHRISSY LAYTON – BRISBANE, AUSTRALIA

Right: In concert by Chrissy Layton

Far right: Chrissy Layton and friends with their thank you message

I remember how upset I was not being allowed to go to David's 1974 concert because my mother thought I was too young. I did make up for that when I saw David many occasions in the *Time* musical when I was on a world working holiday, and again when David toured Australia in 2002.

A group of 30 of us waited at Brisbane Airport when he came here in 2002. David hid his face behind a bag hiding from the media, but I found myself following a girl I had just met. We ended up in the airport car park with David and two others. I said something like, "All your fans are here". And I can honestly say he was the perfect gentleman.

He thanked each of us with a kiss and I respected David's wishes not to take a photograph. I gave him an envelope with an article of mine which had been published. Having forgotten, as he left the car park, to give him a CD my boyfriend made, I called his name and ran after him. I told him I was not here to harass him, I just forgot this. He took the CD and said, "thank you, sweetie".

For his concert I made a poster saying, "Thank you 4 the kiss yesterday". To my delight he grabs my hand and then my poster holding it up during the show and said something like "I enjoyed it too".

> ## TO MY DELIGHT HE GRABS MY HAND AND THEN MY POSTER HOLDING IT UP DURING THE SHOW

To: stretton@netspace.net.au
From: Ruth McCartney <ruth@mccartney.com>
Subject: Message Boards

Dear Sue,
My webmaster Ruth McCartney is online all the time and keeps me up to date on some of the global DC chat and message sites and I understand through the grapevine you are going through a rough time with your son. My best wishes go to you and your family - keep your chin up...

Love,
David

SUZANNE (SUE) MCCONNELL – AUSTRALIA

Dearest David,

Where do I begin to say all I want to say to a man who was such a huge part of my life?

David, you were my first love from age 13 when The Partridge Family came to New Zealand television screens in 1971.

You were my shining light and my refuge from the darkness that was my home life of abuse from both of my parents.

The hours I spent with my best friend playing records after school and on weekends was my sanctuary.

My very first concert was at age 16 seeing you live at the Auckland Town Hall in February 1974, what a night that was and one I will never forget.

Life moved on for me, moving to Australia, marrying in 1984 and starting my own family; two boys I named Matthew and David for obvious reasons. My David, unfortunately, was born with severe disabilities and spent a great deal of his life in hospital, one year being particularly challenging.

Through an online email group, you found out and took a moment out of your precious time to write to me, an email I will treasure for the rest of my life.

I got to thank you in person for that email two years later when you returned to tour Australia in 2002, meeting you at Melbourne Airport, another moment in time I will treasure.

When the news came that you were in hospital, I prayed so hard that you would recover, only to find days later that you had passed away. My heart was broken, but David, I know in my heart you are finally at peace and all your troubles are no more.

Love forever,
Suzanne (Sue) McConnell

erybody Wa... ece of David ...

POP FEVER

Part 5 of RM's series on the pop revival: DAVID CASSIDY

IT was a normal day outside the Dorchester — except for a couple of hundred vivacious teenage girls perched on the walls, kerbs and parked cars like a horde of pigeons roosting in wait. In wait for what? The Monkees left the country years ago. Didn't Pop Fever die?

SUPERSTAR David Cassidy is quitting the pop business. His British concerts later this month will be his last.

It is the final chapter of one of pop's most remarkable success stories, and the news will stun thousands of devoted British fans.

David is just 24.

He told me at the weekend: "The party's over. I can't go on pretending to be something I'm not.

"I want to leave at the top so that my memories of these last crazy four years will be happy ones. And this seems like the ideal time and place to do it."

Confused

Crazy

Don't

Hundreds of girls besieged

make some concert appearances.

And already the Dorchester Hotel in London's millionaire Park Lane, is brushing up on its security.

The Dorchester staff are used to the veteran stars, but young Cassidy is a different proposition.

Last time hundreds of girls, aged between ten and 14, besieged the entrance and blocked the revolving doors.

The switchboard was jammed with calls from...

along the hotel corridors trying to spot their idol.

As for David, he tried to remain unconcerned as he relaxed in his suite wearing faded jeans and T-shirt and padded the thick pile carpet in his bare feet.

Bad crush

But he couldn't escape attention when he wanted to go out.

So bad was the crush he had to be shepherded through a back door covered completely by a blanket, police witness...

worked, but at the last moment someone recognised his boots and yelled out "That's Dave."

Next second he was surrounded by clamouring, grabbing, clawing girls, begging for an autograph or hoping to "win" a button, shred of shirt or hair from his head as a "souvenir."

"The hair pulling is the worst bit," David said. "I've got a sensitive scalp and I go mad if anyone pulls my hair."

David is physically on the small side, standing 5 ft 7 ins, in his socks and weighing in at 8 st 13 lbs.

He was born on April 12, 1950, in Englewood, New Jersey, to Broadway stars

Jack Cassidy and Evelyn Ward.

When he was five, his parents divorced and he moved to Hollywood with his mother.

The break up left its scars with young David.

"I had a lot of rejection from my father when I was young," he says. "I never saw him after he divorced me and my mother. I didn't hear from him for a year.

"But I don't feel any hostility towards him. I'm a good friend of his now. But I feel that a little boy should not be shunned like that."

David's father has certainly helped him since he

David's back on song

by David Wigg

...D CASSIDY, the ...an pop idol who ...his last concert ...nce in London in ...t year, is making ...back.

...ur years of being ...r of his own ...darling of the ...ers, 25-year-old ...nt into hiding. He ...long hair and ...at's the best ...ever done. You ...how good it ...!"

...had enough. ...allowed to ...ex-Beach...

David Cassidy

new album on Sunset Boulevard which will be in contrast to anything Cassidy has done before.

It is being produced...

the group America, ex-Beach Boy Carl Wilson and Ritchie Furley.

Cassidy will visit Britain between June and July for TV and radio appearances.

I understand he is now anxious to be accepted as an entertainer and musician—not just a teenage idol.

But it sounds as if it is going to be difficult for him to shake off that image completely.

THE SUN, Monday, May 6, 1974

QUITS ...LAST

...nal
...will
...ain

...ant to be able to ...and say: 'Her ... great trip that ...on't want to feel

...e way to achieve ...get out now—... plans for, the ...id said: "I am ... ing to get man- ... couple of rela- ...hat are very ... to me

Happier

...on't have to ... in rags ... split up when ... my mother ...vorced twice ...ry ugly. But ... marriage

I just want ...mal life if ...ling than ... been able

...day, I

POP SHOP

walked through New York's Central Park, and went to Zoo. I saw all those animals, and they looked the way I used to feel

But I have no clear picture of what I will be doing in five years. Or even tomorrow. I may go back to acting, but only if I get offered the right kind of material.

"People keep sending me film scripts about a boy and his dog, and stuff like that. And I have been sent a couple of really pornographic ones — sort of like David Cassidy's Last Tango in Acapulco. I don't think they are me, either.

And his farewell:
I want to say good-bye to the kids. Or may-be sing it. And I want them to be in no doubt that I mean it. I have no doubt that this really is the end of it all.

"And I don't want them to be sad. Because I've not I have never been happier in my life."

Town

'A scene of panic and fear' — John Beattie

...have been much worse.

For a start the image of the White City, abused at an one end of the ground. The terrifying for other end was completely simply with the fans pushing forward from the middle of the ground to get a better view of David.

But it was then we were packed into central grass area of the stadium who came off worse. A steel barrier blocked their way between Press enclosure and the high stage.

The supposedly lucky ones who had managed to clamber to the front of the barrier on the 'unfortu-nate' — they had to bear the full weight of thousands of kids behind them pushing forward.

Standing in the enclosure and watching the terrified faces of the front-runners I could see a jovial pink colour to red and then a fatalising blue, my mind drifted back to a somewhat similar situation which happened, not at a pop concert, but at a football match in Glasgow a couple of years ago.

Around 60 people died on that fateful day — crushed to death at an exit stairway during a Rangers/Celtic

match on New Year's day — the terrified looks of the kid's faces on Sunday was similar to the looks on the faces of the helpless who died in Glasgow.

Fortunately a full-scale disaster didn't happen at the Cassidy concert but there's no doubt in my mind that it could have. Promoter Mel Bush and his organisers should have thought more carefully about the dangers and the consequences.

The grass area was sectioned off badly — surely more sections and more barriers could have been the answer and maybe the stage should have been situated in the middle of the ground than confining everybody else to the terraces.

All right, the kids were partly to blame but after all, they paid over £2 for tickets which should have entitled them to protection at any costs. The security boys didn't have a chance to control the crowd — in fact a couple of them treated it all as a big joke!

I asked one security bloke who thought he'd have a bit of a lark and subsequently, he started throwing bucketsof water over the fans directly behind the barriers.

...another sat on top of the unfortunate victims and thumped away on her chest with his fists before the girl was carried off to a stretcher.

Engineered photographers fought with security men and each other trying to get a picture of the stricken fan while cried St. John ambulance men screamed: "bloody animals," at them.

"I'm not too sure how that young girl put on but I heard later that she had "died" for heart stopped beating but a doctor had massaged it back to life on the way to Hammersmith Hospital.

The show ended as it was started. Young girls crying and screaming while a steady stream of security men carried them away to again rest safety!

It this is what live music and massive pop concerts are all about then, sorry — I don't want any part of it.

Cassidy row

A row broke out this week when several RRM readers ... complained about the security arrangements at the David Cassidy concert at White City.

...From RRM April 13th 1974...

Some people were literally screaming out for water and the panic developed.

The horror of the situation was only driven home when Cassidy appeared on stage.

After several numbers he abandoned the bedlam and told famous "Beef" jock, Tony Blackburn tried pathetically to get the crowd to move back.

He didn't help matters when he announced that unless everybody controlled themselves, the concert would be stopped. The boorior moment and the Press threatened because enveloped in a sea of bodies all trying to comfort their companions until help arrived.

Suddenly, amid all the confusion, two uniforms was completed in my eyes. One young girl was pulled from the crowd and a security man, obviously shaken shouted: "She's dead, she's dead — this one's a gonner, look at her she has gone green and is cold all over.

At that point six ambulance men rushed to the scene and as one tried much too mouth resuscitation.

...POP STAR David Cas-sidy turns breakfast into party time for two little girls.

It wasn't surprising that the girls—both handicapped — could hardly concentrate on the bacon and eggs when their idol joined them at the table in the B.B.C. canteen yesterday morn-ing.

David met them before appearing on Ed Stew-art's Junior Choice radio programme.

But after all the kids' stuff he turned to more grown-up matters — the broken romance that has made him decide to give up live concerts.

David revealed that he dated a beautiful girl back home in America for nine months.

But the affair ended

because 24-year-old David had to be away so much on concert tours.

"She just couldn't live with my sort of life," he added.

David said that the girl—he refused to give her name because she is now married—was the only person he had ever wanted to have a per-manent relationship with.

"I haven't had much time to get involved with anyone else," he said.

"But I don't plan on living all my life alone with a guitar. You can only get so close to a guitar."

Picture by DEREK CATTANI

...rue superstar

John Beattie

...his arm round the two delectable ladies who joined the onstage so backing vocalists.

The first couple of songs were unrecognisable amid the noise, but he tried hard with the boys which was coming out of the P.A. system or to the most help a few...

By this time darkness had fallen and the vocals had no the floodlights were switched on but the spotlights were still firmly projected on Cassidy — it was hard to believe that such a little bloke standing onstage creating such a human uproar in the space of one little hour.

In quick succession he went into Daydreamer, I'm not sure if he was trying to adopt a more gritty sound here but it didn't come over the way it does on record and the gradual decline of his vocal powers seemed and turned to now effective backing vocals.

Cos I Be Sure...

One of his main influences "was the Beatles" he told the crowd, "I've been moulded to to this number for four years," he chucked as the band went into the blues number that wouldn't be ready to react to that manner.

An aging gentleman on the boo end didn't seem too pleased at the rip-off of the song — it was too plain to shout his way through to the little man. But it was not to be. Further numbers included Cold Feet and Easy Rider before I finally strolled quietly rolled through on a breeze of rampaging girls crashed around any conditions looking rapidly which might have been falling their marvellous eyes.

Despite the event, I hope that this isn't the end of Cassidy. His earlier stage act suggests that he'll miss the 'live' thing once kids. Not that we're likely to see him as a loony act — those kids are rarely dead.

I reckon he's the guy who's catering years to come. He can

Cassidy's best

DAVID CASSIDY : To-morrow (RCA 2645).

It's Paul and Linda McCartney's song and an-other Cassidy / Bruce Johnston production. This is by far the best of the "new" Cassidy we heard yet. His vocal is very assured throughout and he does wonders with the high notes. The whole effect is very Beatle-ish and at one point towards the end I could have sworn he was about to launch into Carry That Weight. Very catchy, very clever (what with the well...oohs and

66 I had a meeting with David Bowie. He called me up and said, I want to produce you. I said well, OK, let's have a talk about it. Then I thought, well, why does he want to produce me? I asked him and he didn't really have an answer – he just said, well, where do you see yourself in five years? It never came together. But it was like, too definite. I didn't like that. It's probably for the best that it didn't happen. I believe in doing what feels right at the time. I just want to keep recording and producing myself until somebody comes along who I think can do it better than me 99

Sounds, July 1975

THE DAVID EFFECT

KRISTAN HAYWARD – UNITED STATES

David Cassidy was such an awesome singer and had such natural talent. He had a beautiful voice and there is no one quite like David Cassidy – he was one in a million. David had a huge influence on my life because I was an only child. When I was younger than 10, the show was too sophisticated for me but as I got older I started to watch it. I really fell in love with David Cassidy in 1977, when I first really realized who he was, and I wanted to know everything about him. I loved his music.

I met David in New York City in 1983, at the back door of the theatre where he starred in *Joseph and the Amazing Technicolor Dreamcoat*. It was a dream come true for me to meet him. David was upbeat, friendly, asked me if I had ever been to New York before – I told him yes and that I was on my way to college. He asked me where I was going, and I told him Penn State. "That is a good school", he added before signing my playbill.

I spoke to David on the air when he was on the radio in Pittsburgh in 1990. He was always so gracious to his fans. I later saw him in concert in Clearwater, Florida at the Ruth Eckerd Hall where Danny Bonaduce opened for him – it was fantastic. I saw him at the Treasure Island Yacht and Tennis Club in Florida to give an intimate concert on April 13, 2012, the day after his birthday. I bought two tickets over the phone and a few Happy Birthday cards for David. I loved picking out cards for him hoping to give him one at the concert.

On the day of the concert, as I was getting ready to go, a man in a white convertible drove by our house. I wasn't sure, but I thought it may have been David. There was a beautiful sunset – the sun was setting in a magnificent array of colors. We were seated at tables of around 10 people – David sang 10 to 11 songs and did a wonderful job. I could not believe he was only about 200 feet away from me.

I prepared his birthday card for him prior to going to the concert and I wrote in it:

"Dear David – Happy Birthday to you and many more. I love listening to your music and I love the sound of your voice. Thank you for coming to Treasure Island – Florida loves you! Love, Kristan Hayward." The meet and greet later never happened but I handed the card over to be passed onto him.

David has had a very therapeutic effect on me. When I hear his music or see him in any picture, it makes me feel good. He makes me relax and feel really happy. He is such a beautiful person. I will always love him. I had a Mass said for him at our local diocese.

ALISON HAINES – UNITED KINGDOM

I was 6 years old when I first saw David; it was early 1972 and that moment will remain with me forever. I can still recall exactly how it felt at the time. I was watching *The Partridge Family* for the first time and when David appeared on the screen, he took my breath away. But then, the moment he started to sing, I was transported to another world.

My childhood and home life were filled with violence and abuse and then all of a sudden, this little girl realised she had found someone made of sheer loveliness. I dreamed that David would magically appear and put his arm around me, or hold my hand, and everything would become okay.

With his talented acting and beautiful voice, David became a safe place for me at a time when I truly needed it most. That he was not consciously aware of the contribution he was making to my life matters not; David had something about him that was extremely special, something otherworldly in fact. He gave me the strength

I needed to survive those difficult years. In a childish and innocent way, I fell in love with him at first sight. But of course, we all grow. When *Rock Me Baby* first came out, I actually didn't like it much because I was far too young to fully appreciate it! As my life moved on, I started to lose touch with David until much later in my life.

In 2003 I was at a checkout at a garage and David's CD *Then and Now* was for sale at the desk. I bought the CD, played it and everything came back, including all the old emotions. This time I decided, I would stick with David once and for all.

In April 2011, I received the email announcing David's UK tour. The moment those tickets went on sale, I reserved my front row seat and a place at the Meet and Greet. I wished I could go back briefly and tell that little girl: "You know, one day a long time away in the future, when you are 46 years old, the moment you long for will happen, you will finally meet David".

So, on November 9, 2011, I had my photograph taken with David just before his show in Birmingham. I was surprised at how emotional I felt; we exchanged a few words and that moment where David and I were close together with our arms around each other meant so much more to that little 6-year-old girl than I can ever find the words to express.

I am so sorry David that you had to sacrifice so much for us, that you spent your life trapped in the control and insane pressure of the music entertainment industry.

David brought such incredible joy and light into this world and into millions of lives. His legacy is not only his songwriting, musicianship, acting and other talents; it is the hope and love that he instilled into our hearts. I, for one, can never thank him enough.

> 66 I HAD MY PHOTOGRAPH TAKEN WITH DAVID....... I WAS SURPRISED AT HOW EMOTIONAL I FELT.......THAT MOMENT WHERE DAVID AND I WERE CLOSE TOGETHER WITH OUR ARMS AROUND EACH OTHER MEANT SO MUCH MORE TO THAT LITTLE 6-YEAR-OLD GIRL THAN I CAN EVER FIND THE WORDS TO EXPRESS 99

Previous pages: Photos of David in concert 2010, courtesy of Lizbeth McAnary Pierce

MICHAEL SMITH – UNITED STATES

Becoming a David Cassidy fan started at the age of 10. My cousin first told me about him and the show and so I started to watch. I thought the music was fantastic. I would get my portable cassette player and hold it in front of the television speaker and try to record the music onto cassette.

Some years later I decided to make a bucket list containing only three items. One was to meet David Cassidy, two was to shake his hand, and three was to have my picture taken with him. In early 2015, my daughter had me take her and a couple of friends to Indianapolis, Indiana to see a band they wanted to see. After coming back home, I was inspired to try and see Dave in concert.

I found that the last date he was playing in 2015 was in Bloomington, Illinois, about three hours away, but I figured that was about as close as I was ever going to get. I wrote to the venue asking questions about the event. One of the ladies that worked there would write back with the answers. One of my questions was if there were going to be a meet and greet. Finally, in one of her emails back to me, she said there would be a meet and greet for about 12 fans, and she wanted me to be a part of it. I couldn't believe that I was going to have the opportunity to finally meet him.

As the night went on the venue began to fill and the lady who had been writing to me found us and took me and my wife to a room where some other people were

Michael Smith completes his bucket list

sitting. After a short while she came back and said that we were going to go backstage to meet him. We stood in a line and just a few minutes later he walked around the corner waving to us. It was a surreal, unbelievable moment.

I remember looking at my wife and saying, "there he is". I've been waiting 45 years for this and now the time has come. I was the first one in line and he had mentioned that he was trying to get over a cold.

I reached my hand out to shake his hand but he fist bumped me. Then he put his arm over my shoulder and we had our picture taken. As I backed up, I told him how I've been a fan for 45 years and it was such a special moment for me. He replied, "that's great bro, what's your name?" I think I told him, but I honestly don't remember.

In hindsight, I wished I had told my wife to start recording when he first came out and then I could've had the whole thing on my phone. I'll never forget it.

> **❝ I REACHED MY HAND OUT TO SHAKE HIS HAND BUT HE FIST BUMPED ME. THEN HE PUT HIS ARM OVER MY SHOULDER AND WE HAD OUR PICTURE TAKEN ❞**

ANGELA GARLAND – UNITED STATES

I was only 11 when I saw David on the first episode of *The Partridge Family* – what a handsome boy he was. I found out later on he was much older than I thought. I didn't care. I was totally smitten with him. I loved his singing. I started buying all *The Partridge Family* albums, saving all my allowance money for that purpose. I have continued to be mesmerized by David all these years.

I never got to see him live until 2015 when my daughters drove me to Manalapan, New Jersey for a free, outside concert. My dreams had finally came true. We got some meet and greet tickets to meet him in Newark, New Jersey, before a concert on June 25, 2016. It was just a few blocks from his grandparents' house in West Orange, where he had lived with his mother for some time.

When it was our turn to walk in and meet David face to face, I thought my heart would pop right out of my chest, it was beating so fast. He spoke with us just briefly, and we had our picture taken together. I will cherish it forever.

Angela Garland and David

ARACELI – SPAIN

I just turned 13 some days before *The Partridge Family* was first aired in Spain. I fell in love with David's gorgeous face and that sweet voice instantly. I was totally crazy about him, he meant the world to me. David came to Spain in March of 1973 but he just performed on a TV show. I rediscovered him in 2005 and two years later saw him in concert for the first time in Manchester on the Once In A Lifetime tour. When he walked on the stage I couldn't believe he was there in front of me.

I saw David live six times and each one was a special experience. At Glasgow 2008, I was filming and he just stopped, looked at me and that was the first time we made eye contact. Other times he blew us a kiss as his car was driven away from the Hammersmith Apollo; he picked up my Spanish baseball hat which was thrown onto the stage; he handled my birthday present to him.

But the most amazing experience came on April 11, 2011, the day before David's 61st birthday at the Planet Restaurant in the Novotel Hotel where I saw him sitting two tables from me at his birthday party. I was so nervous being so close to him that I nearly tripped over all the chairs.

While I was still wondering what I was going to say to him, he suddenly turned to me with his arms open wide and said: "Hiiii!" I was so surprised, all I could say was: "I came from Spain, David" and we both gave each other a BIG hug holding us tightly while he whispered in my ear: "Awwwwwww, sweetie!". It was like MAGICAL; David was there, holding me!! And he even let me kiss his neck.

He was so nice, friendly and lovely to me. And so funny too. I had always thought I may have fainted if I ever met him, but I wasn't nervous. He made me feel sooo good, it was like talking to a friend you see every day.

The day David died, I lost my friend, the love of my life, that dear person who I had loved all my life. I shall never, ever, forget it. When you admire a person as much as I have David, and continue for so long, you buy his records, attend his concerts and finally one day you get to meet him. You feel when they die you have lost a friend, a companion. People may not understand it, but April 12, 1950 has made me smile many times. November 21, 2017 will hurt my heart forever.

ROSA BRINN – UNITED KINGDOM

I first met David at a book signing on March 7, 2007 at Waterstones in Oxford Street. I rang my mum directly afterwards and burst into tears. I couldn't talk, she thought something terrible had happened to me!

Roll forward to Wembley on November 11, 2012 for a Meet and Greet with my idol. It was a moment to cherish. I dumped my bag on the floor and stepped towards David who, to my utter amazement, walked towards me and held out his arms – David Cassidy was giving ME a greeting hug. Hardly able to breathe, I leaned forward to give him a kiss on the cheek but to my absolute horror he backed away! I let out a rather loud disappointed "Oh!".

Rosa Brinn off to see David in concert

David turned and must have seen the devastated look on my face. "Oh honey, it's not me," he said apologetically. "It's these guys here. We have to be quick to fit everyone in, we haven't time." While he was saying this, he put his arm around my shoulders and pulled me towards him, so my arm automatically went round his waist. I remember thinking how hot David felt and how soft his shirt was. A quick smile and click – the moment was over.

I turned to say thank you but I'm not sure whether he heard or not because he pulled me into a full and proper bear hug. His manager was walking towards me about to pull me away and I reluctantly let David go and went back to collect my bag. I was not supposed to be standing where I was as everyone was ushered out after their photograph had been taken, but no one seemed to notice, and I watched others having their moment with him. I was making sure I made the most of every minute with David.

It was an excellent show, exactly as I had expected and worth every penny. It took two days for the experience to really sink in and then I couldn't stop talking about it.

I had really been cuddled by David Cassidy. Also, I had a sore throat which gradually developed into a cold. David had a cold that night and had given me something after all! It was the first cold I've ever had which I actually cherished.

CHERYL PANGBORN – UNITED STATES

My first memory of David Cassidy was taking the *Up To Date* album to my kindergarten class for show and tell. My mom wrote my name on it in big block letters with a black marker. I still have that record. From that time on I never let go of my love for David. My most fond memory is when I got to see him in concert in Palm Beach, Florida. This was literally a dream come true.

My best friend found a darling shirt that had the same pattern as the Partridge Family bus, and I had a purse with the same pattern. We were so thrilled to be there. We even snuck around

the back of the theater after the concert to see if we could get a glimpse of our idol. Sadly, we didn't, but we did meet Danny Bonaduce who was on tour with him and that made us smile.

I lived in Fort Lauderdale and I knew so many people who ran into David around town in the early 2000s. I dragged my friends to all the places he had been seen but I never did run into him.

His passing made me so very sad because he truly was my first love. I still listen to all the old songs and they never grow old to me. I know he had some difficult years toward the end. Seeing his downfall was a heartbreak burnin' my mind. I still see that groovy, far out looking boy he was, and I won't ever forget him.

66 HIS PASSING MADE ME SO VERY SAD BECAUSE HE TRULY WAS MY FIRST LOVE. I STILL LISTEN TO ALL THE OLD SONGS AND THEY NEVER GROW OLD TO ME 99

JEANETTE DEGIULIO – UNITED STATES

When I was 10 years old, my dad died. I was devastated.

In May 1972, my mom took me to see my dream come true, David Cassidy at the Salt Palace in Salt Lake City, Utah. After the concert I looked forward to teen magazines, decorating my room with posters and new release of albums. I never missed *The Partridge Family*. David gave a very sad little girl something to look forward to at a very dark time in my life. He gave me my smile back.

All throughout my life I checked to see how my childhood hero was doing, buying his new music. I married and had three children. My daughters would visit their grandma and listen to my old albums. They know almost every song by David.

Years later in my 50s I had seen where David was working to save the retired thoroughbred racehorses. I went to a livestock auction with a friend in 2015. At my age I had not planned to own horses again, but I saw this thoroughbred, went to look at him, he put his head over my shoulder. He was weak and thin.

I remembered David's mission to save these horses. I bought the 17-hand thoroughbred racehorse. Months of love and proper feed restored him to great health. I never thanked David for the many ways he made my life better. He truly will always be my hero.

When I received his papers, I was shocked to see Secretariat in his blood line, David's favorite racehorse.

LUCIE FITCHETT AND VICTORIA WILLING – UNITED KINGDOM

Lucie Fitchett and Victoria Willing met at school in north London when they were 11 years old. A defining part of their friendship was a teenage crush on David which 38 years later they used as the basis for a play, *Could It Be Forever?* which received five-star reviews.

The pair had gone their separate ways after leaving Camden School for Girls building successful stage and TV careers. Lucie left behind her unfinished A levels to pursue a passion for contemporary dance and training as an actress. She went on to work in all areas of the business as an actress, producer, director and writer. Victoria studied French and European Literature at Warwick University before training as an actress at the Drama Studio in London. She has appeared in theatre productions and various television series.

> **DAVID STRUCK A NERVE WITH US AT A VULNERABLE AGE, THAT TRANSITION FROM A GIRL INTO A WOMAN, A BOY INTO A MAN**

When they reconnected after 30 years, invited to a dinner party by mutual friends, they reminisced about their teenage love for David and decided to write a play around that adoration as a starting point. In a case of art mirroring life, the comedy-drama is based around a reunion of old school friends Stephen, Mel, Katherine, Andy, Sean and Becky who step back in time recalling a week when David came to London. It moves forward to the present day, allowing the characters to examine their lives and whatever happened to their aspirations. Did they achieve what they wanted and how different, as time goes by, have they become? Their first co-production *Could It Be Forever?* was given its premiere at the Edinburgh Fringe Festival in 2010. Out of the blue and unsolicited, David told them he was "honoured" and "extremely flattered" to be the inspiration behind the production.

A page from a weekly magazine the girls wrote "for fun" when they were 12/13 years old

The Mood Board they worked from when working on their play

Victoria: We both had an innocent infatuation with David when we were at school. He was so beautiful, you could not take your eyes off him. He was unthreatening because he looked rather feminine, but he was also a bit raunchy, a bit dangerous.

In our play, the friends meet for the first time in years because Sean wants to bring them together. David appears in the story by chance when they find an old David Cassidy magazine. Some are still smitten, some indifferent, but the memory of him during a week in 1973 soon proves to be the force that binds them.

The characters and the audience are thrown into the past which forces them to look at some truths in their lives. It looks back to how everything has changed, how friends have changed, how they have grown, whether their values are the same, their dreams fulfilled.

They drift back to the days when he would visit the UK for promotional visits and concerts in the early 70s. They remember how crowds of screaming girls would gather outside the Dorchester Hotel in 1972 singing all day and night. No hotels would take him because of this, and on his next visit he had to stay on the *Ocean Sabre* on the River Thames. He wasn't safe there either with fans lining the Embankment and jumping into the water to reach him.

They recall how he made them feel, the memories igniting hidden desires and fantasies, the human cost of friendships in a period of our lives where everything was much simpler.

At the reunion they fall into a collective memory of one week when David was in town. We had older actors playing themselves as teenagers and we played ourselves. In the play they learn about themselves and who they have become because of what happened to them back in 1972/73 and where they are now.

Lucie: I think people responded to something spiritual with David, the seeker in him.….there was something – charm or charisma does not cover it. We wanted to project that in the play. It centres around when he was staying on the *Ocean Sabre* on the Thames. Fans lined the banks of the river, waved and screamed and called his name to encourage him to come out on deck. Some tried to swim across to reach him. Our play explores all those emotions of what he meant to so many. For me, even though I had moved on by then, when he married in 1977 it weirdly felt like the death of a dream. I had a feeling that part of my life had gone.

His final words when he died, "so much wasted time" are so right for his story. You can hang something on those words, more in your 50s or 60s than as a teenager. David struck a nerve with us at a vulnerable age, that transition

---

CAST OF CHARACTERS

Stephen - Age early 50s and 15

Andy - Age early 50s and 15

Sean - Age early 50s and 15

Becky - Age 50 and 14

Mel - Age 50 and 14

Katherine - Age 50 and 14

ACTORS AGED AROUND 50 PLAY THEMSELVES AT BOTH AGES.

David Cassidy in the flesh (with a blanket over his head) played by actor playing Sean

Voices of:

David Cassidy - Age 23 and 60

Seventies Newsreader

Loudhailer voice

Various crowd - fans / security / police.

n.b. text in bold indicates audio only.

/ indicates overlapping lines with following character.

The play is set in London in 2010 and in 1973.

SCENE ONE
2.

1973 - Wembley Arena, London - a Sunday evening in Spring.

At a distance, the sound of teenage girls at a huge arena pop concert. The STAR, David Cassidy, has left the building, but the crowd still shouts for more. Stamping begins, and swells.

In semi darkness, teenagers Mel, Becky, Katherine, and Stephen run on. They are barely visible perhaps just silhouettes?

MEL
(Shouting) Stage door's round the back!

BECKY
Come on Stephen!

KATHERINE
Ow!

Katherine trips up over her long skirt as she tries to run.

The sound of the getaway van revving its engine... a hysterical young female crowd... burly security guards, desperate to keep control, bark orders -

ALL MEN
"OUT THE WAY! LEAVE HIM! GET OFF! COMING THROUGH!"

Girls are screaming, crying, shouting; Imperceptible words of adoration, with the occasional -

BECKY MEL AND KATHERINE
(off) **"DAVID, I LOVE YOU!"**

Suddenly David Cassidy rushes on, his head covered by a blanket. We can see his cowboy boots and tight jeans. He legs it across the stage, and off.

Blackout.

BECKY
(Off) Stephen! Look out!

STEPHEN
(Off) Ow! Christ!

KATHERINE
(Off) Stephen, are you alright? You're bleeding.

from a girl into a woman, a boy into a man. His words are very relevant now we look back, to how we saw the play evolving and allowing us to look back at our teen years and ask if we got what we really wanted as we got older, what we were searching for as teenagers.

Victoria: We did try to develop the modern part more and to create a story that reflects the past and shows how the passing of time has affected them all. But no matter how much we did, how hard we tried, the really gorgeous parts were when the kids were role playing with each other. When they pretend to be David Cassidy, when they are in the playground listening to the chart countdown at lunchtime on a Tuesday, when Steven takes Katherine for a date at the Wimpy Bar.

Lucie: We used to make up fantasies at school, talk to each other about scenarios. One idea for the play was that we have a ceremonial wig that becomes the "David wig", and whoever puts that on becomes David, so it was a great theatrical device because it meant we could have these girls role playing, taking on the different roles themselves.

Victoria: It was from Lucie's very pure idea about the fantasy – Lucie came up with a few scenarios which were fantastic because each one I put alongside each of the three female characters.

Mel, who was the slightly raunchy one and had a drink problem later in life, had the raunchy Rolling Stone magazine story where they go out, drink champagne and he pulls her up on stage.

Then Catherine was the hippy one, enjoying time with him riding on horseback with his horse Apollo, wearing the puka shell necklace which David made famous after collecting shells on the beach in Hawaii. In the fantasy he makes one for her, puts it round her neck and they ride into the distance – together.

Becky's fantasy was auditioning for, and

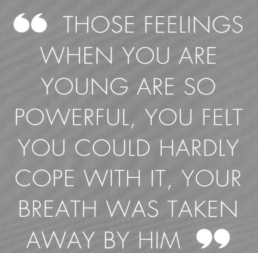

66 THOSE FEELINGS WHEN YOU ARE YOUNG ARE SO POWERFUL, YOU FELT YOU COULD HARDLY COPE WITH IT, YOUR BREATH WAS TAKEN AWAY BY HIM 99

winning a part, in *The Partridge Family*.

Lucie: In the first read through we did at the Soho Theatre in October 2009, there was still a David type of character who was set apart from the action, which gave the audience an insight into how he saw what was happening around him.

Victoria: It is about David, but it is not about David. There are other elements, it is not about his life, it is about his fans' lives and how he represented everything they wanted all those years ago. He is still the one person who unites them, he is almost a spiritual figure. It is not about him as a person. The soundtrack includes music from those years because although it is about that time, David is central to it.

When we heard David knew about the play and the kind words he had to say about it, we were excited beyond words. We had no idea he even knew about it, but someone had told his team about what we were doing. It was amazing to read what he had to say.

The serious message is about looking back on your teenage years, reliving a moment in time which then was very innocent, and in our lives, David was everything. On a serious note, can the past make us see what is important now?

Lucie: Once the play got to Edinburgh and the audience reaction we received, it was a complete justification. Our first review was five stars and the piece had such a magic to it. It wasn't just David Cassidy fans in the Gilded Balloon at the Festival, but a mixed audience, it had a real energy and spirit which was really something special.

We did revisit the play and rewrite it in 2014. We had a reading at Trafalgar Studios in London – the same characters but this time it was set on a boat on the Thames, forcing the characters to be together in one place as before but this time more relevant to the memories. Again, the characters reflected on their teenage years, but time had moved on. Mel's drink problem had escalated and everything in their lives which we touched when they were teenagers was magnified. It was very well received too. Writing the play about him and us, his fans, literally changed our lives.

Victoria: Those feelings when you are young are so powerful, you felt you could hardly cope with it, your breath was taken away by him. I remember thinking when I go to the concert at Wembley Empire Pool in 1973, I am NOT going to stand on my chair and scream. Within three minutes I was doing just that and couldn't stop myself. I was caught up in this wave of hysteria. The two friends I was with did the same.

Lucie: David had so much all-round talent. I always thought given the opportunity he would have wiped the floor with them in *Godspell*, as an example of the theatre work he could have perhaps done. He would have been stunning.

David wasn't a child actor but was reacted to in the same way. He had done that and as his career moved on, he was not allowed to grow up and be this grown up person as he was trapped in this child actor role. It would have been fine if he had done a couple of series of *The Partridge Family* and then moved on. The difference with David is that he was an idol and had a successful career as a singer, who sang rock music so removed from the TV series that really launched his career. He was not just an actor, he was not just a singer and musician, he was not just an idol. In many ways that was his downfall.

People didn't know how to view him later on. It isn't widely known how many important songwriters and performers wanted to write for him or work with him. Had he been able to pursue that, maybe his story would have ended more positively.

Victoria: There was so much interest and possibilities with our original play, and the rewrite, it was disappointing we never got to take it on tour and allow more people to see it. What matters is the reviews which were wonderful, and knowing how much, even though he never saw it, David appreciated it.

Victoria Willing and Lucie Fitchett in a photo booth as teenagers and recreating the picture today

David's message

I am extremely flattered to be the subject of a new theatrical production with a wonderful pedigree that is debuting at the Edinburgh Festival, which I consider one of the most prestigious and artistically credible theatre showcases in the world.

I have been aware of the Festival for decades now and have been so impressed by original plays and productions that have been presented there.

Being the subject of the artistic imagination often humbles me and makes me feel very grateful. Knowing that I've had a significant impact on other human beings, I have always tried to bring light into other peoples' lives. Projects such as this merely confirm this belief.

I am honoured and thank the creators and hope it fulfils their expectations, as you all have fulfilled mine.

With much love and thanks,
DC

EIKEI HIEI – JAPAN

I first saw David Cassidy on TV when I was watching *The Partridge Family* in 1973 and I had a crush on him. I was 10 years old and I've been his fan since then. He came to Japan in 1974 to have several concerts but I was too little to know that, I missed a big opportunity to see him in concert in Japan. I never got to see him back then.

I had wanted to see him in concert since I was 10 years old and at the age of 48, finally my dream came true in 2011. I saw him in concert at Hammersmith Apollo in London, and met him for the first time at his pre-birthday party the day before the concert at the Novotel Hotel in London.

I couldn't believe that a gorgeous man I had been dreaming of for almost four decades was standing in front of me and talking. "Is this real?" I asked myself. I was totally ecstatic, but I tried to focus on what he was talking about. "I'm here to show my appreciation to my fans and I'll meet each and every one of you. I really wanted to do this for you and for me," he told us.

I felt he was humble and really cared about his fans. He was absolutely gorgeous on the inside and outside.

After his speech, he started played the guitar and sang, *Ain't No Sunshine*. Finally, I saw his live performance. I was just overwhelmed by a feeling of happiness and joy. He then walked around the room to have a short "meet and greet" with each fan. He was such a sincere superstar.

I still remember my "Special Moment" vividly. After he sang a few phrases of *Addicted to Love*, he suddenly came close to me from the stage. First, he gave me a kiss on my right cheek and then gave me a big hug (for 12 seconds!) I almost felt faint with excitement! It was all so sudden that I couldn't say anything but "I came from Japan". He said words of appreciation for all my support and loyalty for the long years. The night was the one of the most unforgettable and best memories in my life.

I really appreciate all that he brought to me… music, love, dreams, power, courage, joy. He influenced my life in many ways either directly or indirectly. I can't mention them all, but actually he taught me "dreams come true".

It was not easy for me to have been his fan in the days without the internet, it was very difficult to get news from him in Japan, however I kept on loving him and his music. It's because of his amazing talent and his brilliant work. His music will live on and he will be in my heart forever. I'm honored to be his fan.

ELAINE MENDELECK – BRAZIL

The year that changed my life was 1971 when *The Partridge Family* was first shown in Brazil. It was a series that charmed a whole generation of young people here. For the first time I knew what the expression "Prince Charming" meant. David Cassidy was perfect. I had never seen such a handsome man in my life and I can say now, with all the experience of more than 55 years, that I have never met anyone who could match him at that time.

When the series ended, it was very difficult to find news about David here in Brazil, but I did not give up: I made my father import solo albums that were not sold in my country and I got news of David from friends who lived in the United States.

It was thanks to Facebook that I met several fans of David and made wonderful friends in Brazil and the United States. It was thanks to one of these Brazilian friends who came up with the idea of traveling to New York to watch David's show in 2012. I just did not believe it when finally, on a sunny afternoon, I walked into the BB King Club to buy my ticket for the show. I leave the club carrying that ticket as if it were the most precious thing in the world. And it really was.

On the night of the show I could not believe that finally, after almost 40 years, I would finally see my great love in person. Walking into the club, sitting at a table in front of the stage and realizing that the big moment was coming, left me with my heart beating so fast that I thought I was going to faint right there. I held on but I was not prepared for what came next: I suddenly came face to face with my great love. Even after so many years, David was still perfect. I could see those eyes so beautiful, there are no words that can describe them. The smile was unique. The talent, the charm and above all the love and kindness with which he treated all his fans. I found the human being a thousand times more charming than the fantasy I had of him. Those moments were magical.

I've seen many things in my life, but I can say without a doubt, that seeing David was one of the most wonderful moments that I've been through. And today, I can still feel the warmth that came from that divine artist and fantastic human being. There will never be anyone like David Cassidy.

David captured on stage by Elaine Mendeleck

DAVID'S SIGNATURE HOT DOG

A piece of David will forever have its heart in Toldeo, Ohio.

Customers who step into Tony Packo's see one thing when they walk through the door: hundreds of hot dog buns.

The restaurant became famous when it was mentioned in several M*A*S*H episodes. Character Maxwell Klinger, who was played by Toledo native, Jamie Farr, mentioned the famous landmark in 1976, "If you're ever in Toledo, Ohio, on the Hungarian side of town, Tony Packo's got the greatest Hungarian hot dogs."

Actor, Burt Reynolds, started the tradition of what is known as "bun signing" in 1972 when he visited the restaurant and autographed one of the famous hot dog buns.

Since then actors, musicians, politicians and athletes have left their mark and the walls are adorned with these signature buns – foam, air-brushed look-alikes in vacuum-sealed cases – including one from David.

He signed the bun in Branson, Missouri in October, 2016. "I was the only one on the list for a meet and greet," recalled Lizbeth McAnary Pierce. "David greeted me and laughed about signing it, and said that the shirt I had brought along, was way too large. I was working at Packo's at the time. That was the only size my boss had given me to give to him. I told David to wear it as a night shirt and he laughed adding, "I don't wear anything to bed!" We both laughed. He signed the bun which I brought back to Toledo, so he adds another piece of history to Packo's walls."

David with Lizbeth McAnary Pierce and the signed hot dog

TO AUSTRALIA WITH LOVE

It had been difficult to explain that they had to go to London and collect David Cassidy.

The man seemed puzzled, but his curiosity got the better of him. "Really? Why?" he sighed, raising his eyes to the ceiling.

"He has to stay here while he waits for a flight," she explained calmly. "It won't be for long. He won't get in the way or be any trouble. You will never know he is here. You'll be at work all day. It is all very secret. No one must know he is here. There is nowhere else he can stay."

Leaning back in his chair, arms folded, he waited for an explanation.

"I did promise I would help but I never thought for one moment I would actually end up doing this," she said trying to sound apologetic, adding they would have to take his car as the extra space was going to be needed.

"He does not travel light then?" her husband asked.

"Best to be sure we have enough space," she added, explaining she had already made arrangements to collect him the following week from an, as yet, unknown address in London, from a man she only spoke with via emails.

A week later they drove up to London to collect David, a figure literally larger than life in the eyes of many. His appearance on the street, had curious onlookers turning their heads for a second look. They managed to get him into the car without drawing too much attention, but he refused to be covered in a blanket, "I spent my life under one in the 70s," he had once lamented. It was a tight fit, and David had to rest his head on her shoulder for the two-hour drive. But this was the start of a much longer journey.

The days "in hiding" turned into weeks and weeks into months. All too soon the call came that it was time to move on. The long-term plan had always been to head to Australia. The cost had been prohibitive, and his accommodation had to be secure, so he waited until everything was in place on the other side of the world.

Once the funds to cover his journey arrived in the UK, flight arrangements were made, and all the necessary tracking put in place. The lady attached a rustic luggage label which read "To Australia With Love".

The 15-day journey from London which included stops in Germany, New York, Louisville, Honolulu and eventually Australia was likened to a final world tour.

One evening in September, 2015, Jim returned home from work to find a new house guest standing in his room. "Welcome home, David," he beamed.

The life-size David standee had originally been used for the promotion of Allison Pearson's book, I Think I Love You. *Jim Salamanis won the item on ebay where it was listed as "collection only". Editor, Louise Poynton, offered to collect on Jim's behalf.*

Jim Salamanis with his well-travelled David standee

DANNY CALVAGNA – UNITED STATES

I was infatuated with singing and music since the first time I set eyes and ears on Elvis when I was two years old. The Beatles changed everything musically for everyone and then The Monkees on television brought the fun of being in a band to life for all of us that were beckoned by the music to play and sing. We all wanted to be in a band.

It was September 1970 when I was 15 years old and had been playing and singing in bands for a couple of years that *The Partridge Family* came into our living rooms. There was David Cassidy not much older than I and of course the rest of his musical family.

It was not long that every girl I knew had a David Cassidy poster and were buying every record and every magazine with David. I have to say that it was not cool to play Partridge Family songs in a band at that time. I did not dare, but secretly I wanted to be David Cassidy. I would not even whisper that let alone state this aloud. He was a guilty pleasure. A voice that I wished that I had.

Fast forward 40 years. I have been a musician and singer all of my life. I decided that it was time to have fun and go out on a limb musically. I started a band, 45rpmNY. This was going to be my guilty pleasure band.

The first thing we decided was that The Partridge Family songs were going to be the cornerstone of the set list. This was surely going to be a challenge. Who wants to hear a band cover Partridge Family songs? Who will come to these shows? What will all my super cool musician friends think?

Well let me tell you. People came in droves to see the band that did Partridge Family songs. My musician friends came out of the woodwork to tell me David Cassidy and The Partridge Family were their secret guilty pleasure, that they all wanted to be David Cassidy. I realized the magnitude of what David was to the real musicians of the time. He was our true north, our direction.

Every night I see the joy and happiness that this music brings to people from all walks. We now do a complete tribute to David Cassidy show and I am in touch with so many people that love

David and cherish his music and his memory.

For me this is how I thank him and his many, many fans all over the world for so many wonderful memories. Our "C'mon Get Happy Show" has generated so much love and excitement from so many people I know David would be proud to know that he will bring joy and happy times for many years through these shows.

MARK WAYMAN – UNITED STATES

I met David Cassidy through Rex Smith and David's brother, Patrick Cassidy. We share a mutual interest in racehorses, and David attended one of my parties at the House of Blues West Hollywood. I live in Las Vegas, and get a note from David that he had an upcoming show at the Silverton Casino. He invited me to the Green Room prior to the show. When I arrived, we talked for a few minutes, then told him a 15-year-old girl I sponsor in Make-A-Wish was a huge fan and had binge watched *The Partridge Family* on Hulu.

He thought that was hilarious, so I said, "I'll get her on the phone right now and prove it." David responded: "Show starts in 10 minutes. Can't do it." Not an issue, told him I had front row seats and would see him in the showroom. As I'm walking down the hallways to the showroom David comes running out of the Green Room and shouts: "Wait, come back in here. Get her on the phone." He looks at his manager and says, "The show is going to start five minutes late."

So, I ring her up, and without saying David Cassidy, state, "My friend David wants to say hello." David takes the cell phone and talks to her for 10 minutes. When he hands it back I can tell she is crying and I asked what was wrong. She responded, "He called me sweetheart".

Mark Wayman with David

Secret UK hideout for David Cassidy

CASSIDY is Coming!
Darling David arrives in Amsterdam tomorrow (Friday) to begin his first all-scale European tour giving his fans this side of the Atlantic their first taste of Cassidy in the flesh on stage.

Security precautions usually reserved for visiting heads of state have been lined up so that David can undertake the tour without being physically harassed by over-enthusiastic fans.

"We've got to keep our movements pretty secret, David said this week, because if my fans knew where I'm staying or what time I'm arriving in different cities, not only would I be in danger, but

a concert at Antwerp Arena on Wednesday afternoon.

On Thursday the band-wagon flies from Brussels to Madrid where David will appear on the Estudio Abierto TV show and the next day goes back to Germany to give two concerts at the Offenbach Stadthalle in Frankfurt.

He goes to Luxembourg for radio shows next Saturday and gives two concerts in Rotterdam the next day.

The big news for his British fans is that David's entourage gets into Manchester on Monday week (March 12), but without the elusive Mr

time have been whisked off to a secret address in the British countryside where he will be residing during his stay in this country.

Unlike his last visit to Britain, David will not be staying in a yacht moored in the middle of the Thames in London. David was concerned that once again fans may try to swim to the yacht, so the decision was made for him to stay "somewhere in the country."

David will be in this country from March 12 until the end of the month and during his stay he will be appearing at Belle Vue, Manchester (two shows on

following day), and Empire Pool W (where he will show on March 16 two shows on March

Already lined David are t appearances i country, on Top Pops, on March Blue Peter the fol

All of David's c HAVE SOLD OUT all shows, the first the concerts will be up by American du and Dave.

To coincide with th Record Mirror produced a souve page biography wit colour shots of

Super Pup rocks across Europe

CASSIDY T-SHIRT
YOURS FOR ONLY
$3.95
POSTAGE PAID

BRAVO
Streit!
Werding/Marcus
Neuer Starschnitt!
SLADE
Dr. Korff:
Schwangere Mädchen
Led Zeppelin kommen!

FREE COMPETITION devised exclusively for FAB 208 readers in co-operation with Supersoft
WIN A Super TRIP TO HOLLYWOOD

1,000 OTHER PRIZES TO BE WON

HOW TO ENTER

mer teen idol David Cassidy has been recording country/pop at Nashville's nd Emporium Studio with Grammy-winning producer Larry Butler, who also te many of the songs on Cassidy's upcoming LP.

TV Times
MELBOURNE
MARCH 2-8, 1974

STAR PUT-ONS!
ut-out school labels
HE GREAT GABLE
ill Collins series
SCAPE FROM
HE BRADY BUNCH
Robert Reed at home

ENGLISH EUROPEAN EDITION
FAN No.27
EXCLUSIVE! LATEST & GREATEST
DAVID CASSIDY PIN-UPS!

DONNY ALAN MERRILL DAVID E
MARTY PAUL & DANNY
RUSS NODDY SPECIAL SHAUN'S SEXY PHOTO FILE

Μαντρεύεται ὁ Ντέηβιντ Κάσσιντυ

Why I can never walk alon

By JOHN BLAKE
PARIS, Monday.

POP IDOL David Cassidy is living in fear of kidnap attempts. Detectives are probing two incidents in which gangs have attempted to drag him into cars.

Now 24-year-old Cassidy is under constant guard by a team of private security men who follow him everywhere—even when he takes a shower.

The kidnap attempts have

DAVID CASSID
TELLS OF HIS
FEARS AFTER
KIDNAP GANGS TRY TO GRAB H

talked about them before, I don't want to give ideas to

to record any more tra now got the money

do it my way -or else

DESTINY
The secret of David's success
What your daydreams mean
An invite from Emperor Roskin
Are you a flirt?

RM European Tour Souvenir Special
THE CASSIDY FILE

David **CASSIDY**
Could it be Forever?
My Story

the partridge family
the complete first season

WE'LL MEET AGAIN... WE HOPE!

FRIENDS OF DAVID CASSIDY [AUSTRALIA]

Music Star
DAVID

Cuttings Book

B.B. King
DAVID CASSIDY
LUCILLE'S GRILL
LUNCH · DINNER · LATE NIGHT

MARCH 4, 1974
David Cassidy's Australian tour was about to start, with the first concert at Randwick Racecourse in Sydney. Airport officials were concerned his arrival would cause the same scenes of panic as had recently occurred at Heathrow, where hundreds of screaming fans were injured.

I LOVE DAVID CASSIDY

Who are SUPERFANS

TIGER BEAT'S OFFICIAL **PARTRIDGE** Family Magazine

DAVID CASSIDY
HERE HE IS! THE LITTLE KING OF THE WEENIES AND TEENIES

AT LAST! everything you must know about DAVID
DAVID'S CONCERTS: got your tickets?
SUSAN'S HIDDEN HOME!
SHIRLEY'S FILM LIFE!
DANNY & BRIAN: super fan's chart

ackie
PART 1 OF YOUR SUPER DAVID CASSIDY POSTER

NASSAU COLISEUM

D A V I D

Photo: Barry Plummer

66 Anyone who loves the film *Casablanca* as much as I do has to be a romantic. When I was recording my new album at the Caribou studios we had these videos that played old films. I played *Casablanca* all the time and drove everybody else crazy. I was sitting in my room crying all the time 99

Record Mirror, March 1977

5

★

LOVE AND LIGHT

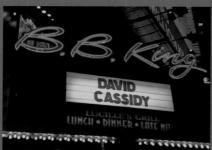

FINAL CURTAIN – CINDY DAVIS – UNITED STATES

I saw David at his last concert, at BB Kings on March 4, 2017 which was the most amazing experience of my life. David had already announced this would be his last show, he was retiring due to his health and later telling us he had dementia. I was crushed beyond belief. I cried my eyes out that morning but at the same time I also had a strong inner drive to see him one last time. He needed the love and support from his fans more than ever at that point.

I wanted to give David a gift at his final concert, something extra special and out of the ordinary. It needed to stand out and catch David's eye. I decided to write him a letter explaining how much he means to me, and always will. I felt he deserved to know. It was to be extremely honest and heartfelt. It needed to make him smile and feel unconditionally loved. I stayed up very late for a few nights pouring my heart out into that letter. I could never repay David for how much he improved my life, but I knew this letter would be a good start.

He ran onto the stage in his true DC style, all

smiles full of energy, passion and enthusiasm. The audience immediately stood on their feet for David out of pure love and respect. We clapped and cheered, and it was easily sensed that he greatly appreciated it. He was just that kind of person. He never took his fans for granted. We mean as much to David as much as he means to us. Nothing else existed to me whenever David was on stage. Many of us jokingly refer to this as "The David Effect." Those emotions that he stirs up in us are so very real.

I had the letter I wrote resting on the stage. It was in an envelope that I printed DAVID on all in capital letters and with little red hearts. My right hand was also resting on the stage next to his letter. He began to move the microphone stand forward towards me and then towards my hand. Once he realized my hand was in the path of it, he quickly moved it to the opposite side. The only problem now was that the letter was in the path of the stand! I thought fast and picked it up to prevent him from accidentally covering it up which would have ruined my chances of having it seen. This time he couldn't help but notice it!

I could tell he was amused and intrigued. He stopped what he was doing, looked at the envelope and then at me, smiled and asked: "Is that for me?" I was in absolute shock and completely elated at the same time. I could not believe that David Cassidy was actually speaking to me. I was shaking inside with delight and most likely outside as well.

Somehow, I managed to muster up a head nod and a "Yes it is!" in response to his question. As he looked over the envelope, he then asked me: "Did you draw these hearts?" referring to the three tiny red hearts I drew on it just for him. I managed yet another head nod and a "Yes I did" with a huge smile from ear to ear. I began to feel that he felt that all I had made him was an envelope with his name on it. I was suddenly feeling very brave from within and wanted to speak up, so I said excitedly: "There's a letter for you inside!" He seemed both surprised and touched at the same time.

He opened the envelope and quickly glanced over the letter. I was really hoping he would have read a little of it to himself, but at the same time he's a sentimental man and also very sweet so I'm guessing he wanted to read it in private in a much more relaxed setting. He put the letter back inside and placed the envelope right in front of the drum kit. That all took place in probably about less than a minute, but to me it felt like a lifetime of happiness in one short burst.

Flowers, photos and record albums were handed to him from adoring fans. He graciously accepted them, could not have been sweeter or any more approachable. It felt like a lifetime of

66 I COULD NEVER REPAY DAVID FOR HOW MUCH HE IMPROVED MY LIFE..... I STILL TALK TO DAVID AND I CAN FEEL HIS PRESENCE 99

To my sweet David,

My name is Cindy, and although I am a very new fan of yours I feel as if I've been passionate about you and your many incredible talents from the moment you began your amazing career. I really want you to know just how special you truly are David. You are so easy to love and admire. The first time I watched The Partridge Family reruns on DVD I was instantly drawn to you. Your charm and natural acting ability were an immediate standout. You without a doubt light up the screen. When I first heard your beautiful singing voice I was in complete awe. I will always be! You are such a talented musician. Your songs never fail to make me happy, and they always brighten my days and nights. You are also one inspiring and unique human being. Always remember that sweetheart. That genuine and beautiful smile of yours melts my heart. You're very special not only to me, but to so many people. You have given and continue to give so much of yourself to everyone. You're a hardworking and determined professional, and I admire that in a person. You are an idol to me. The legacy you have worked hard to build will be forever remembered and cherished. It's important to me that you are aware of this. Always know and feel in your heart that you have my love and support as well as the love and support of millions of others. You are a blessed man, and the world is truly a better place because of you, David. Take comfort in knowing how happy you make people on a daily basis. I also want you to know that just thinking of you, your music and the wonderful soul that you are puts a spring in my step, and a lot of love in my heart. I will always love you. Never forget that. Let that fill your heart with joy and contentment. ♡

Sincerely,
Cindy Davis

Cindy's letter to David

love was in that small venue, and that's because it was. Loving fans of all ages filled the room. David teared up occasionally causing me to as well and I'm sure there was not a dry eye in the room at one point. I particularly recall many tears streaming down my cheeks while David spoke about his life and the love he held for his fans before singing The Beatles classic *In My Life*. I love how real David was. He didn't hide his feelings.

He ended with a final delightful performance of the hugely adored *I Think I Love You*. He told us he greatly loved us, and we returned the sentiment back so very much. He blew us kisses, bowed and exited the stage one final time. It was one of the saddest sights to see him leave, but the euphoria I felt within me from my experiences that night took over and I felt on top of the world.

I didn't want to leave BB Kings. If anything, I just wanted to leave with David. Being near him made me so peaceful and unconditionally happy.

After David left it was a mad rush from many to get to the stage and hand his band members gifts of love and appreciation for him. I wasn't alive to experience how an actual 1970s hysteria enveloped a David concert, but from what I've read and heard about them I felt I was experiencing a mild version of the mania at that point.

David had the unique ability to turn the worst day into the best day just by hearing him sing or gazing at a photo of him. That's a God-given ability I believe, and it's a beautiful thing. I often draw upon his passion and energy to get me through difficult times in my life no matter how big or small. He's a wonderfully positive influence. His naturally sweet nature along with being very humble and gracious helps me to be that way and strive to be a better person each and every day.

The months passed by and I kept thinking of David, hoping and praying he was doing well, working hard on what would become his final studio album titled *Songs My Father Taught Me*. It wasn't easy for David who somehow managed to push forward and finish what he was determined to do. He was constantly in my prayers, but not doing well. I was a mess and in tears often. I wanted nothing but the best for him and pure happiness. I wanted for him what he had given to me. All I could do was remain positive, hopeful and continue to pray. That's all any of us could do. I even looked up information into donating part of my liver for David.

We lost David during the late evening hours on November 21, 2017. I'm sitting here with tears in my eyes. Losing David was one of the most devastating moments of my life so far. I can still remember that night and how I felt. I was numb, completely numb. I couldn't even get myself to cry for the first hour or so. Then reality set in and I sobbed waterfalls of tears. This continued for days and months.

Every 21st of every month is a bitter reminder of losing the most talented, unique, loving and beloved man the world was ever blessed to have known. How do you move on from that? I found out that you really do not. You cannot ever just move on or get over losing someone whom you love dearly in my opinion. You are definitely never the same.

For me having family and friends to lean on helps a great deal, they understand the depth of the hurt, have taught me patience and how to cope. Some days are a little easier than others, but they each carry the same overwhelming sadness. God also helps comfort me so very much. I still talk to David and I can feel his presence. I pray for his peace and that he is finally at rest. I am blessed with many signs and dreams from David.

I've learned through the months that he is with us more than ever now. It has not been an easy journey. It continues to smother my heart with a sadness I've never quite felt before, but in the same breath I wouldn't trade all that I've been through for anything in the world.

David quickly became a huge part of my world and he always will be. To me he is worth all of it and then some. C'mon Get Happy he would always sing. He certainly makes me feel that way every time I think of him, look at him or listen to him. God bless him for that.

David Bruce Cassidy…you will always be loved dearly, and you will always be dearly missed. Rest well sweetheart and Happy Trails to you. Your loving fans will be with you by your side on the bus again one sweet day.

❝ IT FELT LIKE A LIFETIME OF LOVE WAS IN THAT SMALL VENUE. IT WAS ❞

And now there's just an
empty stage where David
sang and David played.......
Photo: Cindy Davis

The legacy lives on

David reaches out for his fans and they are just loving him back
in June 2007. Photo: Kirsten Levisen-Lloyd/Kirstography

66 Every moment I am on the stage, every night, everything I've got in my body, I owe it all to you. I am nothing without you, your support and your love for me. I gave it back to you a thousand times. As long as I've got love in my heart, happiness and kindness I only need to be able to share my heart. Someone recently asked me: what do you want your legacy to be? The fact that everything I have done in my life was to bring light and love into all of the world that I was able to touch. You gave that back to me a hundred thousand times **99**

David speaking to fans at his final show, March 4, 2017

6

★

WE REMEMBER
SUMMER DAYS

INTERVIEW IN LONDON, 1972

I had a letter from a girl who had lost her teenage brother and sister in a road accident and she said playing my records and watching the TV show was the only thing that seemed to help her to forget the horror.

She was so sincere and I was so affected by her feelings that I wanted to help in some way. I wanted to reach out and let her know I cared, even though I'd never known her family.

I sat down and wrote to tell her how I felt about dying. I told her I believe we all go to another spiritual life when our physical life is over in this world. I believe that there is a higher power that decrees how long we spend on this earth and that, if this power has a use for us elsewhere, it is possible for us to leave this world very quickly – whether it's brought about by a road accident, an earthquake or one of the incurable diseases.

That is my explanation for the early deaths of people who have been very special.

Remember James Dean's motor accident, and your British runner Lilian (sic) Board? There is no point in us fighting the power that arranges these things, 'cause if we don't accept them, it brings endless mental anguish to ourselves and those around us.

I've read a lot about spiritualism and I do believe there are people on this earth, called mediums, who have psychic powers and can talk to the spirit world and receive messages from it.

A night out with DAVID CASSIDY

Previous page: David at home. Photo: Roger Morton

CHRISTOPHER JONES – UNITED STATES

David died on my birthday and only minutes from me here in downtown Fort Lauderdale. It was a very dreary day overall. I had other setbacks in my personal life and that 21st day of November 2017 had double the impact. I saw David's passing as something personal; like a friend I never met because I was convinced that if we had actually become acquainted, he would have found me significantly understanding and supportive. I haven't admitted this to anyone before, but when David died, I broke down in private. It was different from all the women who had childhood crushes on him and lost a piece of their past. In my case, I felt like I lost the best friend I never met. It was completely surreal and created great sadness for me. I felt special empathy for David because he was someone whom I could relate to: his giving nature and thereby a longing to meet him and see how we could help each other. Life can be utterly devastating to those programmed with giving hearts.

Though never actually speaking to David, I was near him several times at public or special events in Fort Lauderdale. We exchanged nods, waves and smiles at special events which we both attended. As time went on, David stopped making public appearances altogether. The last I recall was when he was Grand Marshall in Fort Lauderdale's Christmas Boat Parade. I never saw him again after that. I had lost a golden opportunity to meet such a golden person.

David was a significant influence during my formative years as a youth and beyond. I even followed in his footsteps and became a musician. Often, we are introduced to a celebrity and their music at pivotal times in our development and through their art they become a trusted family member and friend. That kind of intimacy and familiarity breeds "friendship", and as we all know, nothing hurts more than the loss of a dear friend or loved one.

On a personal level, not only did we share a love for music, but there were some parallels in our appearances too. It was never meant to be intentional on my part, but we shared such a strong resemblance that people often told me that I looked like him (same hair). Friends and strangers nicknamed me "Keith".

David was also noted for his animal compassion within our community. I was active in the same causes and David would have found a connective interest with me. I will choose to see him at his best of times as he was genuinely a good person at his core. David was a person of love and compassion. He wasn't without his (mostly understandable) setbacks, but his true inner character was pure and sincere. The tragic irony was, David spent the majority of his life truly instrumental towards the "happiness" of everyone else, as memorialized in The Partridge Family song, *C'mon Get Happy*, yet his own happiness largely seemed to escape him.

Perhaps David lacked true inner conviction within his own merit, becoming too accustomed with finding his happiness through aiding the happiness of others and least of all, himself. David seemed to welcome being the source of comfort in others.

For those who truly understood him, his legacy and personage will be forever honored and missed. One of my major regrets in life is not making sure I made contact with David, given my proximity and avenues. If I could just go back in time, nothing could stop me. His loss was resonating.

" LIFE CAN BE UTTERLY DEVASTATING TO THOSE PROGRAMMED WITH GIVING HEARTS "

JILLIAN SAMSON – UNITED STATES

Jillian Samson's tribute to David

I first discovered David Cassidy in the second grade, may seem like a commonplace declaration – and it would be, except I was a second grader in 2004. I lived, loved, and breathed David Cassidy from that day on. I pasted his picture over all my school notebooks and folders, collected his CDs, watched and re-watched *The Partridge Family* till I knew every line of dialogue, etc. I consider myself so blessed to have "grown up" with David Cassidy.

In 2016, I lived the most wonderful day of my life, I had the chance to see David perform live at the Andy Williams Performing Arts Center in Branson, Missouri. My mom and I listened to every David/Partridge Family CD we had as we drove down.

Once we arrived, it was amazing to be able to meet so many other fans and feel the love and appreciation we all shared for David. The show was nothing short of spectacular. Although feeling under the weather, David gave a fantastic performance. With each song, I was reminded of why I fell in love with him and his one-in-a-million voice all those years ago. To quote a song, "man has never found the words…" to describe how magical that night was for me.

Just a year later, our sweet David passed away. When I learned of David's passing, my world stopped. Every happy moment of my life that was filled with him flashed before my eyes: from being gifted membership to his fan club, to sharing his music with my friends, to finally seeing him perform with my mom.

My heart was broken – aching this unimaginable loss, mourning the thought of a world without his immense talent and sweet spirit. At the same time, I felt an enormous sense of joy and gratitude. David was now free from all illness and he had left us with so much. His music, television and movie performances, and giving spirit live on and will continue to be a source of entertainment, enjoyment, inspiration, and nostalgia.

I graduated shortly after David's passing, and wanted to use my cap to remember him. He had such a great impact on me since I came to know him. His music was the soundtrack to my formative years and his life's journey a lesson to me in tenacity, dedication, and love. I always say, "how lucky am I to have lived this life loving you" when thinking of David.

Even though he is no longer physically with us, he's never far away. All we have to do is embrace his spirit of love, listen to one of his songs, or watch an episode of *The Partridge Family*. David, how lucky were we all to have lived this life loving you? Happy trails, friend.

KELLI MCCAIN – ATHENS, GEORGIA, UNITED STATES

I know it's weird, but I'm not ok with moving forward with David Cassidy as a memory. This isn't as hard as Michael Jackson but damnit….. it feels like such a nauseating loss. And now I'm unreasonably fixated on trying to process how people can just end like that. Clearly, I never knew him, but what he symbolized mattered to me. Idolization may be frowned upon and it is undoubtedly a curse to those who find themselves on such pedestals. I hope he and every other larger than life individual who has defined moments and chapters in the lives of so many have at some point found peace, happiness, genuine unconditional love and comfort as the humans they are and not the iconic, decade defining personalities so many of us have selfishly cast them to be.

Thank you, David Cassidy, for sharing that stunning smile, your sexy voice, your timeless charisma, and for giving your fans from the 70s on an escape from real life into a gloriously delusional world of possibility that star-struck teens are exceptionally skilled at losing themselves in.

You were far from perfect, but it's safe to say you left your mark on this society and as long as fanciful, gorgeous, charming characters like you exist, closeted hopeless romantics like me can keep waiting for our own Keith Partridge to steal our hearts.

I hope you're partying in paradise like the rock star you are, and always will be.

Kellie McCain with portrait drawn in 7th Grade

ROBY DI STEFANO – BUENOS AIRES, ARGENTINA

When I was in Elementary School I sang and played guitar in all the music events. It was 1977 when I arrived home for lunch from school and was hooked with a chapter of a series that began to be broadcast, *The Partridge Family*. Here in Argentina it was named *Mamá y sus increíbles hijos*. It was a funny and familiar series. I loved listening to their songs and I liked many of the musical arrangements Wes Farrell introduced to the songs using session musicians from The Wrecking Crew with the chorus of the Ron Hicklin Singers.

But what I really loved was listening to the vocal part of David Cassidy. At that moment I started to see all the chapters listening to those musical arrangements and following David's voice. I was not a fan of a handsome man, as we know he was, I was and still am a fan of his acting talent, audience management on stage, excellent professionalism and performances. That's why he was admired and loved around the world and will be eternally admired because his legacy will never die.

I never had a poster on my wall or David's pics, but he left a trace in my musical career from my beginnings. David was my inspiration in many of my songs, to the point that I included David's songs in my record productions like *Lyin' To Myself* in Spanish *Mintiéndome* and also *Tell Me True* both in my 2011 album that was called SOLO ROBY.

I recorded *I Woke Up In Love This Morning* from my album QUEEN OF LOVE from 2006, even though it is not of his authorship, it was an amazing song because of the way David sang it. When I drive my car, I hear all the songs David sings alone and the songs he recorded with The Partridge Family, that I have in my pen drive.

Today I have many memories of my adolescence with their songs, I really admire the rock pop star that David Cassidy was. God gave me the opportunity to go on tour to Australia and step on places where he performed 39 years before. Obviously, I am not the star he was, but I felt grateful to be there. I was an unconditional fan of the great artist David was and will continue to be. I'm deeply regretting his loss because David Cassidy has inspired hundreds of artists including me and left his amazing musical legacy.

Thanks, David Cassidy, for everything you gave me, I will continue listening to you as I always did in my life. You will be always be in my memories.

David has been a huge influence on Roby Di Stefano's musical career

ROD EDWARDS – MUSICAL DIRECTOR AND SUPERVISOR – UNITED KINGDOM

It is with great sadness that I find myself writing about David after his untimely passing. Having been David's Musical Director in both the USA and in London's West End and UK Touring Companies of *Blood Brothers*, I can recall the time spent with him with great affection.

Firstly, David was a true professional, with all the blessings – and curse, of being a star since childhood. Coming into the world of live theatre afforded him the confidence of his stardom, whilst it also heightened his awareness to learn the ways of full company involvement in a prestigious piece of theatre.

I think some people were probably unaware of his sense of humour and self-deprecation of being a 'star'....... Whenever I good-humouredly pricked this 'star' bubble, his response was always the same, – for instance if we heard a helicopter over the theatre, I would ask if it was there to pick him up to take him to his hotel, with a laugh he would always say – "stop joshing me, Rod....."

At first rehearsals for his featured song – *Long Sunday Afternoon* – we discussed the narrative place of the song in the show, and that it was an extension of the script, seamlessly woven into the character's loneliness and atmosphere of the moment. After many attempts at characterising the Liverpool accent, David said, "please can I sing it as me, my fans want to hear me *sing* the song" – it was a judgement I had to make, and for once, I agreed that we would try this approach as he asked, and the song brought the house down on every occasion.

On a cold, wet and dark night at the Oxford Playhouse, the UK Tour had opened to a rapturous reception. As I left the Stage Door after supervising the music content of the evening, a long queue of bedraggled fans stretched far into the distance..... there was David personally signing and talking to each fan as they stood in the rain. I said, "David, watch you don't get pneumonia out here" – he turned to me and said, "Rod, these fans are why you and I do what we do, without them we would be nothing......" A true assessment of his concern and love for his faithful fans.

On many occasions both in the USA and UK, I would coffee with David in various coffee shops from Dallas to Darlington, and his response to any fan that came up would always be warm and sincere..... he even bought the coffees on occasion!!

Over the years we had a strong professional and personal relationship, musically he was immense, and humble to his fans...... It is sad to have him leave this world, when surely, he could have had much more to give.

In the words of the master, Willy Russell – "Tell Me It's Not True".........

LINDA – UNITED STATES

The one constant presence during most of my years, has been the brown haired, hazel eyed, musician, singer, actor, writer, producer, David Cassidy (hereinafter, DC). He was, to me, pure perfection. Devilishly handsome, charming, and he could act and sing, to boot. For me, DC was that make-believe boyfriend, who I could feel safe and comfortable with, in a non-threatening way.

In October 1971 he came to the Arie Crown Theatre in Chicago. I actually saw him twice that day after agreeing – with hindsight very foolishly – to attend the matinee show free of charge with a ticket scalper. Those tickets were in the nose bleed section, but when DC ran out, and the screaming started, the flashbulbs started popping, my heart lifted, and I was mesmerized by the sight of this tiny ant-sized figure on the stage. He was amazing, and I could not believe I was actually seeing my idol live, with my very own eyes. It was pure Heaven.

At the second show I thought I was going to pass out. My seat was on the main floor. He was beautiful, wearing one of his white jumpsuits. He was truly larger than life, and he did not disappoint. One of the highlights of the night for me, was when David debuted his new single, *Cherish*. I remember crying, and reaching, and wanting desperately to get close enough to DC so he could see that I loved him more than those "other girls". With a classmate we started a small fan club. We would hang pictures in our lockers. DC was the beginning of several close friendships in that first year of high school. I was starting to feel like I fitted in.

When we got word that DC was coming back to Chicago in July 1972, my friends and I got second row seats. We saw DC arrive in a limo his smiling face pressed up against the windows. That memory and his awesome smile has remained with me my whole life.

In 1975 my friend, Kim, whose sister worked at the O'Hare Hilton Hotel, told me DC was in town so knowing his room number we waited outside for hours. It was going on 2–3am when I heard another ding of the elevator. I held my breath. Kim was sound asleep at this point, and I started to jiggle her to attempt to wake her. I heard footsteps coming down the hall, towards us. "OMG….Kim….It's Him! He's here! Kim! Wake up! Wake up!"

As he approached the door, he seemed surprised that we were there waiting for him. We told him we had been there a few hours and he seemed pleased that we would have waited so long. His bodyguard was guiding him out of the conversation with us, and politely excused themselves, after signing a few autographs.

Thirty years later, working at the local Courthouse, I was handed tickets to a show at the Ritz sponsored by the local bank whose president could not go, along with a Meet & Greet where my stomach was in knots and I was sweating profusely. I was so flustered, and had no idea what I said to DC, and the whole meeting is a total blur, but I do remember he was so very gracious and kind. In my flustered state, I had forgotten to give him a small replica of an Irish pub bearing the name "Cassidy's Irish Pub", but his backing singers made sure he got it, and told me he was very touched.

> **❝ AT THE SECOND SHOW I THOUGHT I WAS GOING TO PASS OUT. MY SEAT WAS ON THE MAIN FLOOR. HE WAS BEAUTIFUL, WEARING ONE OF HIS WHITE JUMPSUITS ❞**

I saw DC at the Soaring Eagle Casino in 2006 and four years later at Hemmens Auditorium in Elgin, IL, outside of Chicago when he commented how he was sick, taking medications, and it affected his voice. In the years that followed, DC was clearly facing challenges in his life. I hoped and prayed that he would find a way out of the darkness.

Around the same time, October 2016, my husband, Doug, was diagnosed with prostate cancer. Four months later DC announced he had dementia. I was afraid for him and my husband. My world, as I knew it, was crumbling right before my eyes. The men in my life who had been with me for the last 40–45 years, were facing life threatening diagnosis, and there was not much I could do to stop any of it. Doug passed on October 3, 2017 with a Celebration of Life for him on November 17. David passed four days later.

Doug was my reality in contrast to DC, who was a fantasy. He was never really in my life, although I spent a good chunk of my life devoted to him, loving him, and imagining a world with him and me in it. That fantasy never materialized, but DC certainly brought this old gal a whole lot of light and joy. I am forever grateful that I chose him to be my idol, my fantasy.

The world misses you DC. I hope you realize how much happiness and joy you have brought to those who chose to love you.

Happy Trails.

Linda's ticket stub from the matinee show 10/16/71, balcony seat, $4.50

CHRIS JENKINS – UNITED STATES

*B*eing adopted into a loving family who sang gospel music; they believed that *Love Must Be The Answer* to most problems.

I started *Singing My Song* when I started playing the piano and record player. I was only five years old when I heard *C'mon Get Happy* on TV My family was always close, so it was easy to form an instant bond with The Partridge Family, and thinking – *Together, Having a Ball*.

When I heard *I Think I Love You*, I thought *It's You* in my *Daydream*. This *Daydreamer* thinks *Every Song Is You*.

David Cassidy – my first teen / pop idol. *I Woke Up In Love This Morning*, as most mornings, wishing I could be your *Umbrella Man* while *Walking In The Rain*. *I'm Here,*

You're Here, and *There's No Doubt In My Mind* that *Together, We're Better*.

At the time, I looked up to David more like a brother, not a *Friend & A Lover*. My first Partridge Family album was *Notebook*. It was a birthday present from my mom and aunt when I was around seven years old.

Then *I Heard You Singing Your Song*, as I started learning these new songs. I started taking tap lessons as well as piano lessons and thought, *When I'm A Rock & Roll Star*, I would get to meet my idol, David Cassidy, and say, *I Really Want To Know You*.

I saw similarities in my world and David's world, including parents getting a divorce. Heartbroken and shy, I would cry myself to sleep while

ALICE – UNITED KINGDOM

I was one of David's younger fans in his "hey day" – just 7 years old when I first saw him in 1971 on *The Partridge Family*. He really was my first crush, my first love. In those days, life was simpler and pop stars were much more out of reach. Internet and social media did not exist.

I had pen pals instead of cyber friends; magazines, fan clubs and TV/radio instead of the Internet. We were much less informed. Magazines, scrapbooks and pen pals took up all my spare time.

Somehow, in the mind of a child, it was as if, by writing to my American pen pals I was getting closer to David, and when they stuffed their envelopes with fan pages and posters ripped out of *Tiger Beat, FaVE* and *16*, I was flying high. I made so many friends this way, a handful of which have lasted to the present day. David is responsible for so many friendships, the world over.

Throughout my life, but foremost during my teenage years, if I felt sad, by simply listening to

David's beautiful voice and music, he gave me the lift and boost I needed to snap back into my happy bubbly self, and to leave the sadness behind.

I came from a very musical family and initially I played piano, however after David became a fixture of my childhood, I was inspired to teach myself the guitar. I bought *The David Cassidy Songbook* and the first song I learned to play on the guitar was *Can't Go Home Again*.

I have a photograph of myself aged about 10 years old standing on a platform in my back garden, dressed in a very badly put together Partridge Family costume, holding my guitar with David's Songbook at my feet. In my little head, I was Keith Partridge whilst standing and singing and strumming my guitar on that "stage" in front of an imaginary audience. I was taught to play classical piano, but once I had David's Songbook in my hands, I took more interest in playing pop tunes, including his own.

I ran the only British David Cassidy website for

listening to *I'll Meet You Halfway* on the 8-track player. I also asked myself, *Doesn't Somebody Want To Be Wanted*, like me?

Later I would feel *Something's Wrong. We (I) Got To Get Out of This Place* in my mind. I knew I was loved even though I felt *Lonely Too Long*. The more I looked at David's pictures, I said, *As Long As You're There*, I could accept these new changes in my family.

Then there was a *Brand New Me*. Life improved.

David was more than an idol. When I saw his eyes, it was like *Looking Through The Eyes Of Love*. It felt like *Sunshine*. He seemed to be a real person who loved everyone, including his fans, despite having a celebrity status.

We all have periods in our lives when we get down; walking down a *Boulevard of Broken Dreams*, feeling *Alone Too Long*, including David. I kept wanting to tell him that *Somebody Wants To Love You*. At one time, my crush turned into an innocent *Storybook Love*.

I've always been a fan of David's and his family. I've collected albums, 8-tracks, the Partridge Family books, the game board, lunchbox, etc. My parents and aunt even got me a Partridge football jersey, and my grandmother made me a shirt with a zipper with a circle tab on it, just like David wore.

As popular and talented as David was he never got a star on the Hollywood Walk of Fame or was inducted into the Rock 'n' Roll Hall of Fame. David said his fans' love for him meant more than awards. I can hear David say, *Love Is All That I Ever Needed*.

I'll Never Get Over You, David. I will always *Cherish Every Little Bit Of You*.

All Because Of You, I made it through some rough times. I, like many people, *Wish You Were Here*.

Till We Meet Again, You Are Always On My Mind.

a number of years back in the late 1990s. I met David a handful of times, and in the instances where it was my approach to him, whilst they were great moments, they weren't amazing or particularly significant to me, as they were not instigated by him. However, he did create some other absolutely astonishing and simply incredible moments for me, all of his own doing, when he went to great personal effort several times to contact me. These memories will never leave me – I will hold them dear to my heart until the day I die.

I had seen David heading on a downward spiral for some years before his untimely death. When he died, I was bereft, beyond devastated. I had to take the day off work. My world temporarily stopped turning. My childhood died with him that day. That first day, I spent my waking hours online with many likeminded friends and fans, in a daze... like, what just happened?! I had never felt grief like it. I miss him every single day; I think of him several times a day. Each year, on the anniversary of his death, I will take the day to listen, watch and remember David, turning the anniversary into beautiful new memories.

The impact he had on my life was indescribable, but thankfully, there are plenty of other fans who feel the same way, and we take comfort in each other, knowing there is always someone to share our DC anecdotes and memories with, whenever we need or want to.

David was a "one off" massively underrated talent, the likes of which we will never see again. I am so very blessed to have experienced him in my lifetime and he will always remain one of my most important and joyful influences.

I will cherish my memories for as long as I live.

═══ ═══
EN MIL PEDAZOS (IN A THOUSAND PIECES)

I never thought you left so fast
My heart got broken into a thousand pieces
My adolescence of 13 years
Wanders alone, sad, crying and without direction.

You, my light. You, my angel
You, my innocent and pure love
Wild, insatiable and tender, all in one.

Your strength, your voice, your charisma
They will be engraved on me eternally
Like a Lava river
Leaves its mark of fire
Embraced like this forever
Among the summits of space and time,
Until one day....
We meet again in Heaven.

By Araceli – Spain

DALE CUNNINGHAM – UNITED STATES

My parents separated when I was 7 years old. We had lived in Florida from the time that I was born. Since both were from Iowa, they decided it would be best for my mom to move back here with me, while my father remained in Florida. As a kid it was kind of interesting. A lot of children have this really ugly situation where the parents are playing a sort of tug of war with them. For me it was more like when you have a father who dies. I pretty much went from having a father to not having one overnight. He just totally wasn't in the picture.

The debut of *The Partridge Family* was pretty timely for me. I can't help but think that a part of my obsession with David Cassidy was a result of the separation within our family. Perhaps it filled a hole that needed something at the time.

There were only a handful of times that I ever saw my father again. The most vivid for me was when he flew back to attend my grandfather's funeral. After the services, he took me for a short walk. We talked about very general stuff, like how I was getting along at home and school. At one point he asked me if I still liked David Cassidy. I said, "Yes" which was true. Even though *The Partridge Family* had been off the air for a couple of years by this time, I proceeded to tell him of other things that I liked.

Even at such a young age (12) I remember thinking how out of touch he was with our lives. However, just the fact that he remembered I liked David Cassidy meant the world to me. It was like, even though we weren't a part of his life anymore, he still hadn't forgotten about us completely. I can still remember him trembling when he hugged me goodbye. I maybe saw him twice after that, briefly.

I saw David Cassidy in concert for the first time in 2002. It was like the 9-year old inside of me came alive and brought with it a few special memories. There was one moment that still stands out for me. He had just begun to sing *Summer Days*. I got so excited. I don't know why I didn't expect it, since it has always been one of my favorite recordings. We were opposite sides of the stage when it started, then he worked his way over to our side.

I was standing up by this point. I was the only one in our section so pretty close to the stage and I remember making eye contact. I just gave him a #1 signal with my hand. He made an acknowledging response......
then continued singing......it was a pretty cool moment. I know that 9-year-old kid inside of me was pretty excited. I can only imagine what look he saw coming from this adult man's face.

PAM BYRD – UNITED STATES

My heart still badly aches. I wonder if there will always be an empty spot in my heart for a man I never even met, but loved and admired dearly? I still find myself tearing up over David. I just can't help myself, my heart hurts so bad. I'd almost think I've lost my best friend not a complete stranger I've loved from afar. I've never had this reaction over a celebrity, but I've never felt towards one like I do David. When we get to Heaven, we'll be looking for David. When God gives you a talent, I don't believe He takes it away when you're with Him. David will be singing for eternity, I truly believe that.

JIM SALAMANIS
– AUSTRALIA

I can't even begin to tell you the huge impact that David has had on my life, and I can't believe he's gone, but he will never be forgotten. He shall live in my heart forever more. The day he died I cried in the office and had to be taken out by my colleague. That's how much I love this man. I met David a few times and he gave the greatest hugs.

I couldn't believe one day coming home from work and seeing a postcard from David's beautiful mum, Evelyn, who I had written to. I met her a few times when I travelled to Los Angeles and she took me to lunch. It's something I will never ever forget. I was lucky enough to call her a friend, I would ring her and send her Tim Tams which are Aussie biscuits. She loved them and would always say to me: "you're making me fat!"

Evelyn was full of stories on David but the one that struck out to me the most was when he was young, and she took him to see a palm reader who told him that within the year from now your name is going to be global. David thought she was full of it and laughed it off.

Well a year later David became one of the biggest teen idols in America and by 1973 was the world's biggest pop star. It was such an extraordinary story and I loved hearing this from Evelyn, who always told me how proud she was of David. It was a beautiful unconditional love and he adored his mother. With Evelyn, there were no ifs or buts when it came to David. He meant the world to her and for him she was everything. It was beautiful to see and hear.

If it wasn't for Evelyn I would not have met David at EFX in Las Vegas. She would call him and say "you'd better see Jim, or you'll be in trouble". She would tell me these things and I would laugh.

Seeing David in EFX just blew my mind away. David was standing literally next to me facing the stage. My heart could have literally exploded then and there. He was a tiny man, yet he looked ginormous on television. David's voice was simply extraordinary.

After the show my friend and I were whisked

David and Jim Salamanis in Las Vegas

away by David's PR lady, Robyn, and found ourselves in David's dressing room. When he walked through the door, I almost collapsed on the floor, after all these years to finally meet my idol. His shake of my hand was warm, and he still had that Cassidy smile that could melt butter. I didn't know what to expect and he was so generous with his time for us and we chatted like crazy. He said: "My Mom and I have talked about you on a number of occasions. She thinks you are terrific, and so do I."

He signed many of my photos and posters from the 1970s I had brought with me. I had also filmed some of that on my video camera. The one thing that I had forgotten to do was say a big hello to my friend Philip. That devastated me so the next day I called Robyn and asked her if I could pass on my video camera to her and all she would have to do is press record and make David say a quick hello to Philip…… Robyn said David would like to see you again.

I had given David a framed photo of him live at the Melbourne Cricket Ground with an original ticket stub from the concert. He had put that up on the wall. I was so excited to see this and thought

> ## 66 HE SAID JIM ASK ME ANYTHING YOU WANT. I LET IT RIP AS YOU CAN WELL IMAGINE 99

my heart would have stopped. He remembered that concert as though it was yesterday. David remembered every concert. I put the video camera down for a second and David gave me the biggest hug on this earth. He laughed even harder when I said could you repeat that hug with me on camera this time for all my female friends to see back home. It was fantastic. He was in such good spirits and I certainly made him laugh. I'll never forget those days I met him as long as I live.

The next time we met was when Philip came with me to America to see David live in At The Copa with Sheena Easton. Philip and I ran our Friends of David Cassidy Australia Fan Club with a newsletter three times a year in the 1990s. We did a colour cover to mark the anniversary when he played at the Melbourne Cricket Ground, and had members from all over the world. It was lovely to see David again and he still had the Melbourne Cricket Ground framed photos up on his wall.

When David came back to Australia after almost 38 years absent for concerts, his voice was beyond stunning. I was lucky enough to have seen him in Melbourne as well as Sydney and Newcastle. I was invited to David's Melbourne press conference

where Molly Meldrum was asking him many questions. It was truly such an amazing day which was even better when I got to spend a little over 45 minutes with David at his hotel in South Yarra with two friends of mine who I had invited. He was genuinely warm and wonderful with us and basically, he said Jim ask me anything you want. I let it rip as you can well imagine.

Prior to the concert I had bought almost $10,000 worth of tickets for all my friends. He grabbed my arm and said in a concerned and softly spoken voice: "Jim did everyone pay you for this?" I said they did. He was happy to hear that. I told him I would have had a house by now if it wasn't for all my David Cassidy collecting all these years. He laughed even more.

Till we meet again, David.

RICARDO JEAN – UNITED STATES

I knew nothing about David or *The Partridge Family* until I was 12 years old and ABC debuted the movie *Come On Get Happy: The Partridge Family Story* in 2000. I have always been a fan of happy-go-lucky music and I have always associated *The Partridge Family*, and David Cassidy, with an upbeat feeling. I was sad to hear when he passed and wanted to pay tribute to him with my caricature. When I especially do drawings about music figures, I feel the urge to listen to their music. In a way, I feel like I am channelling their essence when I do that. The David Cassidy caricature was no different. In creating this I played *C'mon Get Happy*, *I Think I Love You*, *I Can Feel Your Heartbeat*, *I Woke Up In Love This Morning* and The Partridge Family rendition of, *Something Tells Me I'm Into Something Good*. All feelgood music to me.

JIM, EVELYN & AL

To Jim,
In remembrance
of his 3rd trip to
America and
finally meeting
David.
Love,
David's mom,
Evelyn

Clockwise from top left: Newsletter; Jim and Evelyn ; Evelyn, cousin Al and Jim plus handwritten note; Jim with cousin Al and Evelyn; some of Jim's massive collection

RUTH POULDING
– NEW ZEALAND

David was, is and always will be my No 1. From the first time I saw him in *16* magazine in 1971 that smile just transformed my life. There will never be another like him, ever. He had the X Factor in bucket loads. He was a SUPERSTAR and a super HUMAN BEING. I knew he was struggling with demons, you only had to "listen" to the lyrics of the songs he wrote. The two s's in Cassidy stand for sincere and sensitive. He hurt inside, smiling on the outside. The world was a bitter place for him.

I saw him twice in concert in February 1974, a double dose because it rained, and they had to move the concerts to the town hall. So instead of hundreds of thousands we had quite an intimate concert compared to others. I was quite close, and he looked at me a few times when he went past. I'll never forget when he came out singing *The Puppy Song*, in a green velvet suit with rhinestones all over the lapels and legs, top hat and tails and cane so dapper. He was a real showman. Then he changed into a cute outfit of denim dungarees with a peacock all up the leg and a puppy on the yellow t-shirt and rocked the roof off. We were in a frenzy.

I was in awe and in Heaven. The second concert was the same except Elton John came and jammed with him for *Rock Me Baby* and *Rocket Man*.

I gave him a small part of me (a book I made) and he wrote to me, so did his Mum. I'm glad he knew who I was. I will treasure those letters forever. David's music makes me cry just now, quite poignant the songs can be and the lyrics of some are heartbreaking: *You Are Always on My Mind*, especially the line, "will I have to go through this old life day after day and find you there always on my mind." His music keeps him alive and that voice of an angel. He's singing with the angels now so happy and out of pain in the biggest gig of his dreams.

I kept my promise that I made all those years ago. "I promise to love, cherish, protect and defend your image to the best of my ability and honour you until the end." I will continue to do so my Smilin' Sam.

I wrote hundreds of poems over the years for ALL his milestones, birthdays, Christmases about the albums, concerts and acting trying to find the words. The words to how I feel for him, and I never did find the right ones because there are none.

> *You'll always be a part of me*
> *That cannot be denied*
> *But when I put it down in words*
> *It can't be simplified.*

≡ THE FIRST ANNIVERSARY ≡

It's been 1 year since
God looked down
Saw your tired body
He put his arms around

It broke my heart to lose you
But I know you weren't alone
Part of me went with you
The day God called you home

Words often fail us
But this we know is true
You live within US
As WE lived in you

You were the best of His work
In feature and form
An angel in disguise
With a heart so big and warm

So on this special day
We remember ALL the joy
The talent the love and the humour
That made our SPECIAL BOY

By Ruth Poulding – New Zealand

★ ★ ★

TRICIA LYDEN-NEWKIRK
– SPOKANE, WA, UNITED STATES

I never thought anyone compared with his talent, intelligence or complexity. I really think he is the best-looking man I have ever seen, mostly because he had such charm and innocence and the most genuine smile I ever saw in my whole life. I really felt he had the best voice I ever heard from a man, a very different voice very soothing and calming. Whenever I heard *Come On Get Happy* I was front and center and nobody touched that dial.

David Cassidy was 17 years older than me, so I was quite young. My mom had his *Rock Me Baby* album and I had it memorized. I played it over and over. I loved his music with *The Partridge Family* and his solo body of work. I always had *The Partridge Family's* Greatest Hits on CD and listened to it quite a bit throughout my life.

I didn't become a huge fan until after he died and that's because when I heard he died I couldn't believe it. I broke down crying and I started looking up things on the internet and I got really obsessed because I could finally find things out about him. I thought he was the most interesting human being I've ever read about.

For three months straight, I cried and read everything I could about him, watched every video and interview I could, then ordered books. David was far more than just a teen idol. He could sing, dance, play the drums, the guitar, the piano, write music and lyrics, and act and do Broadway. There was nothing he couldn't do because his dad was a stroke of genius and that's where he got it from.

My heart went out to him because he deserved a much better life and was owed mass amounts of credibility. To this day I have NEVER seen anyone compare to him.

SOARING EAGLE

He soars to heights
To everyone's delight
We hold him in fond embrace
With loving grace

He opens doors
Into the past
As our dreams soar
Forever it will last

For the Soaring Eagle
Will forever shine
With admiring eyes
And gasping sighs

For the years have been good
To the Soaring Eagle

If we could
Stand as regal

So take flight
To spread your wings
To forever be free
Of all material things
And know that in your heart
We shall never be apart

By Lizbeth McAnary Pierce – United States

BRUCE KIMMEL – UNITED STATES

Back in 1971, I was a young actor. I'd gotten really lucky at the end of 1970 and one day, got a call from my agent about an appointment for the following week, some show called *The Partridge Family*. I don't think I'd actually watched it, so I caught whatever episode was airing on Friday night. I thought the show was charming, and the cast was just great.

I read the scene for director/producer Mel Swope, and the other producers, Bill Bickley and Michael Warren. It was just a quick scene, but it was funny and they laughed at everything I did. I went home and by the time I got there, my agent had already called to tell me they'd loved me and I had the part.

The following Monday, at six in the morning, I drove over to the Columbia Ranch in Toluca Lake. I drove up to the gate and was surprised to see about ten young teenage girls there – of course, I thought, "Why would they be here to see me?" Delusional even then. Of course, they were there to get a glimpse of David. I waved anyway.

We did a rehearsal, and sometimes you just know that something magical has happened, and that magic was so evident – and the magic was that we all bonded instantly. It was like we'd known each other forever. David, especially, was so kind and sweet and we loved playing our little scene together. The only negative was that I was sad when it ended. That episode was Dr. Jekyll and Mr. Partridge.

About two months later, my agent called with some surprising news: They were giving me a guest shot in another episode. I walked on the set for my first day and it was like coming home, I must say. Everyone came up to me and hugged me and said they were so happy I was back.

The director was Jerry London – terrific director who'd go on to do the huge mini-series, *Shogun*. This time, most of my stuff was with Shirley and Susan, but David was around all the time and between takes we all just sat around and laughed. That was

Bruce Kimmel with David on the set

The Partridge Papers. And to show you how kind they all were, they all called me after the show aired. And it kept on like that. They brought me back twice the next season – I seemed to always be Susan's wannabe boyfriend, but I always had a different name. It was such a blast for me, and again everyone treated me like family.

At that time, I'd written a musical about food, called *Feast*, and we were doing it at my alma mater, Los Angeles City College in their small upstairs theater. I invited all of them to come, not ever thinking they would – and yet, they all showed up – David, Susan, Shirley, Mel, Bill, Michael – I couldn't believe it, really. They loved the show, which was thrilling to me. At that point David and I were talking quite often and since he'd really liked the songs that I'd written for the show, he wanted to hear more.

He came to dinner at my apartment. At the time, I was married and had a young daughter – I think she was all of three or four then. She'd watched all the Partridge episodes and loved the show even at that young age (she was VERY smart). So, David arrives, she takes one look at him – David Cassidy, Keith Partridge in the flesh – and runs into her room and shuts the door. Oh, did we laugh.

She finally did come out and the dinner was so much fun. I remember going to his house in Encino and playing him a lot of songs. He really liked them – I pretty much knew they were not the kind of thing he could record, but he was very taken with a song called *I Don't Have to Hide Anymore*, which was more of a pop thing with a really good hook. He had no idea that I'd kind of written it for Susan.

Then we shot what would be my final episode in the show's final season, which all took place on the T.S.S. Fairsea. I'd gotten to cruise to the three ports for a week, along with a couple of the supporting cast, so all the people on the ship pretty much knew me, as I'd been asked to entertain after a couple of the meals, so I played the piano and sang some of my songs. The cast joined us in Acapulco, and we shot on the way back to Long Beach. It was the best time ever. We dined every night together, and laughed and laughed, and Shirley and David were both gracious enough to get up and sing, with me playing for them.

After we wrapped that show, they'd intended to bring that character back, with the idea that Howard

> ## ❝ I ADORED HIM… AT HEART HE WAS A WARM, LOVING, AND HUGELY TALENTED PERSON ❞

would be doing some show in Bakersfield that he'd written (the songs were going to be from that food musical, *Feast*) and the Partridges would come up and save the day by being in it. They wrote it (I still have the script) but the show was cancelled, and it never happened. They all thought I should have become the regular new character, but alas...After that, I saw David a few times, then we all went our separate ways.

Flash forward about 23 years, and David and his brother [Shaun] are doing *Blood Brothers* on Broadway with Petula Clark. I'd had the chance to make an interesting life change in 1993, which I'd grabbed with gusto – I'd become a record producer with my own division at a successful record label, doing musical theater recordings. I'd already been nominated for a Grammy, and I was producing about 19 albums a year, including many Broadway or off-Broadway cast albums. The producer of *Blood Brothers* called me and asked if I'd be interested in recording this cast and of course I said absolutely.

They threw a party for the cast at Tavern on the Green, to which I was invited. I was excited to see David again (who, by the way, was great in the show), but I had no idea if he'd even remember me. So, I was standing there, talking to someone or other, and my eye caught David across a crowded room, his eye lit on me, he came running over, gave me a big hug, and said, "I've thought about you so much over the years". It really was like no time at all had gone by. That was David. Sadly, the deal proved to be too difficult to make work, and we didn't do the album, although they all did it long after they'd finished the Broadway run.

That was the last time I saw him. But I adored him, and I know he really liked me. Yes, he had his demons – who doesn't – but at heart he was a warm, loving, and hugely talented person.

JERRY LONDON – UNITED STATES

Jerry London, who directed episodes of *The Partridge Family*, with David Cassidy and Susan Dey. "David was always a pro, knew his lines and was fun on the set," Jerry recalls. Photo courtesy of Jerry London

BRIGITTE DESRANLEAU – CANADA

One Friday night, in the fall of 1970, we were getting ready to watch a new show on ABC. That's when my dad said that the kid that was in it had the biggest hit of the summer. He looked at me and said: remember *I Think I Love You?* Did I ever! The show started and that was the end of my innocence. I made the connection between the pretty face on *Marcus Welby* a year earlier, and the angel that was right now looking and singing at me as Keith Partridge. He right away stole my heart.

My dad brought the albums and we played them on the 8-tracks player in the car and all sang along. I'm keeping wonderful memories of that time. My time was now spent between school, tennis and David. My mother would buy me *Tiger Beat*, *16* magazines and my room was filled with DC's face. It was all pretty innocent at the beginning.

Then, April 3, 1972, my father had a big surprise for me: tickets to a David Cassidy concert at the Montreal Forum. My first concert ever! I was so excited that I didn't sleep at all the night before. My dad bought me an ocean blue t-shirt with David's face on it. I think I wore it non-stop for three years. We had very good seats and I could watch his every move. The screams resonated in my ears for a month. What I remember the most was his high jumps. In my eyes he had it all, the look, the voice, the smile, the personality, the moves and he was an athlete! I came home with sparkles in my eyes.

It was a special time with the two men of my life: daddy and David. My dad held my hand most of the show. When David passed away, I relived all the moments I spent with my dad, singing his songs and going to the concert. My dad was a music lover. He loved every style. He would always tell that David was one of the few singers who could articulate every word perfectly, you could understand every word he was singing.

I remember buying the first two solo albums with my pocket money. I would spend hours at night listening to them on my little sound system in my bedroom that my grandmother had bought me for my birthday. Those were very busy and happy times for me. I was becoming a teenager and more deeply in love with David. One huge poster hung over my bed. Life-size it was as if David was looking at me all the time, following me around my bedroom. When I would be coming out of the shower or changing clothes I would cover up his eyes with a tissue paper. How crazy can one be!!! I would tell him: please don't look!

My love for him never faded. I always said that he was my first love. Through the years I always kept an eye on what he was doing but from afar. I was busy with my career and getting my parents' succession in order. They both died in 1988, one month apart. After they passed, I traveled and moved a lot.

When David was hospitalized in 2017, my sister who now lives in Mexico, called me to see how I was taking it. I wasn't aware of it, so it was quite a shock. When she called me, I had the satellite radio on and *Cherish* came on. I started crying and told my sister that was a sign that he wouldn't pull through. When the news came on that he had passed, I lost it, cried all week just like when my parents passed. I relived my parents' death all over again. No one understood my despair. Geez, I don't even know how to explain it to myself.

I cry intense tears every now and then. The only music I can listen to is DC's. It is important to me to share with others what David was and still is to us. I know that he brought joy and happiness to many. He probably saved many lives by doing so.

I've been trying to make sense of it all. I have no answer except that it still hurts like hell and that he will forever be with me.

HAL EISENBERG – UNITED STATES

I met David when my band opened for him at The Mable House Amphitheatre in Atlanta, and he was going through a rough time, even back then, July 2003. When we arrived at the open-air venue to do our soundcheck, we were informed that we would have to wait as David had fired his entire band the night before and had flown in a new group of musicians from Las Vegas who were in the process of learning his songs that very day.

This story goes on and on and needless to say, Mr Cassidy was not having a good day. David was indeed trapped in his teen idol stardom, as it was a blessing and curse for him. We could see it in the way he performed his show that day.

He loved the crowd and the admiration, and it appeared that he loved singing the songs that made him famous. This is a rather small venue that seats around 2,500 so everyone got a real treat of being able to be upfront and personable with David that night. He was in a good mood, but made fun of his teen idol image while on stage as well and even seemed somewhat angry about it all.

One of my favorite albums of all time is David's *The Higher They Climb* which has several songs that are obviously autobiographical relating to his rise and fall of teen stardom.

The album was produced by Beach Boy, Bruce Johnston, who also wrote the hit, *I Write The Songs* made famous by Barry Manilow, and recorded on this album by David, which I believe is far superior to Barry's version and included (angelic as usual) background vocals by Beach Boy, Carl Wilson.

The album also had some background vocal sweetening by the brilliant Flo and Eddie of the Turtles fame.

If you're still reading this, and you get the chance, listen to this album and I think you'll get a sense of what David Cassidy was capable of turning out. He had a lot of success, and like a lot of teen idols, a hard time dealing with it, coupled with the fact that he could never get any traction with his attempt to revamp his teen idol image.

I feel David was a tortured soul who never really got the recognition he so richly deserved because of his teen idol type casting. I feel that fame also contributed to his difficulties and frustration for recognition as a legitimate artist, because of the very thing that made him famous in the first place.

I'll always remember him as a great entertainer – I saw his show in Vegas with Sheena Easton – as well as a prolific singer. My hope is that his music, especially the music he was proud he created, will continue to reach a new audience and by doing so, validate the man's immense talent.

> 66 MY HOPE IS THAT HIS MUSIC, ESPECIALLY THE MUSIC HE WAS PROUD HE CREATED, WILL CONTINUE TO REACH A NEW AUDIENCE AND BY DOING SO, VALIDATE THE MAN'S IMMENSE TALENT 99

MICHAEL POMARICO – UNITED STATES

During the 1970s at the height of David's popularity, I had the good fortune to see David perform live three times. On August 14, 1971 I watched David at the Garden State Arts Center in New Jersey, his first concert after his gall bladder surgery and he gave an amazing performance. He said he had lost 18 pounds during his ordeal.

As a guy, I never understood the girls screaming. I guess I got a dose of what it was like to see The Beatles live. The Arts Center is an open amphitheater which at the time seated 5,197 people with space for 5,000 more on the lawn outside the roof area. Hearing most of the teenage girls attending screaming was interesting. But it was nothing like I was going to hear nine months later when I saw David at the greatest arena in the world, Madison Square Garden in New York City, on March 11, 1972.

With my trusty cassette recorder along with my sister, Nancy; cousin, Joy and friend, Janet, we headed into NYC for David's MSG Show. What an experience! If approximately 10,000 screaming humans in an open amphitheater are loud, 21,000 humans in a closed building are even louder!

Now healed from his surgery, this was a whole different David. Such energy, you could tell he was charged up. In fact, he moved around with such force that the lacing on the front of his shirt came undone during the first song. He actually stopped the show to go off stage and attend to the now

Michael Pomarico and David

loose shirt. He was so excited that at times when he spoke, he seemed almost out of breath. David said referring to his concert, "I said when the whole thing started, if I made it here, I wouldn't have to do another show – this is the top and you are."

Over the years I have pulled out my tape and relived that amazing day. I was 16. Now as an adult and with the aid of that tape, I am reminded how great David's performance was that day. His voice was strong and in fine shape. Wes Farrell may have instructed David in the studio as to how to sing on the records but on stage, as a solo artist, David was in control.

David's *Cherish* album had been released a month before the show. The songs he performed from that album were sensational. *My First Night Alone Without You* was powerful and soulful. Also, his performance of *Ricky's Tune* was a standout, strong and sung from the gut, with lots of soul. I actually prefer the way he sung it here than the way he recorded it.

By March 1972 David was at the top of his game. *The Partridge Family* was well into its second year. David had established himself as a good comedic actor, had five albums under his belt, one being a solo album. While all the girls at MSG were screaming their hearts out, I remember thinking, this guy had it all: a career as a working actor on a successful TV show and a recording artist with a voice with endless possibilities. I remember admiring his work ethic during those years, filming a TV show all week, recording at night and flying all over the country to play live every weekend. I never saw David as just another pretty face, rather a talented hard-working entertainer.

I have to admit as a shy 16-year-old I never felt popular in school, I did envy the way he was adored by fans. But I was never one to want to be in front of the camera, my passion was behind the camera. I wanted to direct. I was fortunate to live my dream as a Director on the American daytime drama, *All My Children*, for ABC-TV. My dad worked two jobs to provide a good home for us kids. He seemed to always

be on the go. Aware of David's work schedule, it seemed normal for me during my career to work sometimes seven days a week.

On June 24, 1972 David returned to the Garden State Arts Center. Something happened in the three months since I saw him perform live. Gone were the white stage outfits, instead David wore embroidered jeans, shirt and a jacket. Maybe it was the *Rolling Stone* article that was released in May. Maybe it was the fact that he was on hiatus from the TV show, rested and more confident.

Just as David's soon to be released *Rock Me Baby* LP would have a different "sound" to it, David had a different sound at that show. He had a different swagger to his step. His performance was more mature if you will. His set list was slightly altered. He added a Jeff Beck song *Blues Delux* while some Partridge songs were now done in a medley form.

David played the piano on *Two Time Loser* – a song he said he wrote in a hotel room in Oklahoma City about a relationship he had. Listening back to my recording, it was clearly a different vibe coming from the stage. I was still very much impressed with his performance. He showed growth.

I attended David's last performance on March 4, 2017 at BB Kings. At that show David said out of all the shows he played, two venues meant the most to him: Madison Square Garden and the Garden State Arts Center. The reason he gave was that it was the only time his grandfather saw him perform live [at Madison Square Garden].

Over the years I saw David in *Joseph* on Broadway in 1983 and then in *Blood Brothers* on Broadway with his brother Shaun and Petula Clark in 1993. *Blood Brothers* was amazing. David's performance was amazing, so moving. He had really grown as an actor. When David returned to concert touring in the United States, I attended the first shows at Hershey Park, PA in 1991. They were amazing.

In 1998 David released *Old Trick, New Dog* and clearly David had traveled many miles, grew up as an artist and matured; I guess just as many of his fans from the early 70s had matured.

All My Children was taped in the same building as *The View*, a live American talk show on ABC-TV, and through the studio grapevine, I had heard that David was going to be on there promoting his new CD. I decided to bring my 6-year-old son, Joseph, to work with me that day.

Our studios share a loading dock ramp that all celebrities are brought through. Joseph and I walked out there just as David's limo was pulling up and parking. The door opened, David popped out, saw us and smiled. To our surprise Beau and Sue followed him out. Beau and Joseph locked eyes and Sue made a comment about "another little boy" being here. Joseph and I walked over and introduced Joseph and shook hands with David who signed Joseph's cassette tape of *Old Trick*.

A representative from *The View* escorted David

> ❝ I NEVER SAW DAVID AS JUST ANOTHER PRETTY FACE, RATHER A TALENTED HARD-WORKING ENTERTAINER ❞

to the stage for the sound check. Joseph and I followed and took a seat along the front row. Sue and Beau sat a few seats away. Beau kept coming over and talking with Joseph. It was fun to watch two innocent little boys interact as all kids would. During the rehearsal David walked by the two boys singing to them. It was amazing.

When the sound check was over, Joseph and I headed back to the studios for my directing meeting. As Joseph and I got to the door, I felt a tug at my sleeve I turned around and it was Beau. He said, "my Dad said I could hang out with you guys". I looked toward Sue and she was saying it was ok. Joseph and Beau just did kid talk. I took Beau on a tour of the studio and introduced him to many of our actors including Susan Lucci, the most famous Daytime TV actress. After about 45 minutes Beau wanted to find his parents. I wouldn't let him go by himself, so Joseph and I walked down to *The View* dressing room, found David's door, knocked and Sue answered. I told her I was returning her son. David was sitting by the mirror applying his TV makeup.

Over the years working for ABC-TV, I had many opportunities to meet David, but this experience was most memorable being able to have my son hang out with his son, it was definitely special.

WENDY BRAUN – UNITED STATES

I remember it so well. It was 2001, and I was the spokesperson for a chain of department stores in the US, called Mervyn's. We were gearing up in September to shoot several holiday commercials, when my agent told me the good news. My childhood crush, David Cassidy had been hired to serenade me in a winter wonderland. I almost fell off of my chair. David Cassidy?

And that was exactly the response I gave when he came to my door while filming in the commercial.

The spot opens in my home on Christmas Eve, where I'm busy wrapping presents. I hear the doorbell ring, go to the window and excitedly declare, "Oh look, carollers." It's not until I open the door and see him standing there, that my mouth drops, my eyes blink in amazement and I ask in astonishment, "David Cassidy?"

He smiles, extends his hand and says, "Do you believe in magic?"

Still in shock, I eagerly give him my hand and he twirls me into a winter wonderland filled with beautiful snowflake dancers. I, of course, dance front and center, magically knowing all the moves, while he continues to serenade me with, "Do you believe in magic?"

It was really a childhood dream come true. I grew up watching The Partridge Family and adoring David Cassidy (who didn't?). To think that my own childhood dreams of performing would one day lead me to this very moment. It was magical to say the least.

And in the midst of shooting this beautiful commercial, 9/11 happened. We took the day off shooting as everyone was shocked, saddened and overcome with grief. But shortly thereafter, production resumed, and I experienced a new surreal moment. There I was on the Warner Brothers lot standing in the "Leave It To Beaver" house, holding hands with David Cassidy in a prayer circle for all of the lives lost in 9/11. That is a moment I will never forget.

I was saddened to hear of his passing years later, and happy to add my encounter with him to this book. Ultimately the entire experience reminds me that dreams do come true, life is fragile, and that yes, I do believe in magic. I think David would agree.

MIKE RAGOGNA – UNITED STATES

I wouldn't have had a music career if weren't for David Cassidy, full stop. Because of my childhood obsession with TV's The Partridge Family, I had a music business career that began when I was 15 and lasted until around 2013, it culminating in a recent decade of interviewing musical entertainers as a contributor to The Huffington Post.

Growing up in New York City, I wasn't shy. At some point post-1970 when the show premiered and after having bought every single and LP by the imaginary group, I put together that phoning the record company (Bell) and associated publishing companies (Screen Gems, Colgems) listed on the packaging would immerse me further into the world of the weekly adventures and music of my TV family. That resulted in my becoming friendly with kind people at ASCAP, Screen Gems, Bell Records, and eventually, creative offshoots, such as songwriters Tony Romeo and Terry Cashman (Dennis Minogue) and Tommy West (Tommy Picardo).

Due to my then almost daily calls to Cashman & West's office manager Norma Oshinsky, I met the duo, played them my original songs that were heavily teen pop and somewhat inspired by songs they wrote. Soon afterward, they hired me as the office kid, my having mailroom duties, demo room engineering duties and eventually, being developed as a songwriter and recording artist. That career and variations of it, including as a catalog producer and A&R guy, have been my life for over four decades.

When it comes to David Cassidy's solo music, in March of 1972, about to graduate grammar school in two months, my dad somehow finagled tickets for me and my date, Daria Norton, to the famous Madison Square Garden concert. Although my dad took me to sporting events at the stadium, I never realized it was THAT huge, when Daria and I entered the stadium in search of our seats.

Of course, I remember the overwhelming din of screaming girls but when it began, the music was even louder, if you can picture that volume. "Bette Davis Eyes"' Kim Carnes, then "Kim Ellingson," sang background vocals with others including her husband, Dave, and the music rocked, a cool mix of Partridge and Cherish-era solo material. I remember his version of *My First Night Alone Without You* being awe-inspiring, so beautiful, and *One Night*

Stand was another emotional highlight. And I'll also always remember that concert because it was my very first; you always remember your first.

Decades later, having befriended Tony Romeo early on, when I was living in Massachusetts in the early 90s, he invited me to a concert that, I believe, also had Danny Bonaduce as the opening comedic act. Honestly, I don't remember much about the concert itself though I do recall Tony quickly introducing me to a very harried post-concert David on his way out of the venue.

In the early 2000s, when I was a compilation A&R guy at Universal, Bob Mercer (former EMI and Island honcho who signed acts like Queen, Kate Bush, and The Sex Pistols) and his department needed hosts for a CD/ video retro series that would include a TV advertising campaign. I discovered that both Donny Osmond AND David Cassidy were taking a meeting with some of the higher-ups for the host spots, and I was pretty psyched that I finally might have quality time with David after a lifetime of music that I partly owed to him.

Fate intervened. Nature called and as I was finishing up in the rest room, washing my hands, in walk David and Donny, who saddled up side-by-side to the urinals. I was beyond speechless since this probably was my only opportunity to meet them but under those circumstances, it just wasn't meant to pee…er, be.

David captured on June 16, 2007 at The Desert of the Sun Arena in Primm, Nevada. Photo: Darrell Lloyd/BACKGRID

RANDY FUNG – UNITED STATES

The moment the news came through on the evening of November 21, 2017 that David had died, memories of his youth came back for Randy Fung. A fan of *The Partridge Family* when growing up he wanted to do something to honor David's memory. Creative Director with Lamar Advertising in Seattle, within 24 hours Randy's work depicting a crying partridge on billboards across the United States, had reached a worldwide audience through the Internet. His design won an award for creative excellence. This is his story.

The general rule of thumb when designing a billboard is to try and keep things as simple as possible. People usually don't have much time to take things in, so distilling the message down to its simplest form is always my main objective.

Being a huge music fan, a large portion of the digital billboards I've done have been of musicians who have passed away. Often when someone of celebrity status passes, we as a company will create something to go up across our digital networks around the country. This is usually initiated at the corporate level.

If it is someone I admire or who has inspired me,

I will usually try and put something together on my own. Once I have an idea mocked up, I'll propose it to my branch manager and corporate office for approval. This is what happened with David.

I had just got home from work and the news that David had passed was on the television. Growing up, *The Partridge Family* was one of my favourite shows – my wife and I still enjoy watching the reruns. It was so sad and shocking to hear he had passed away.

Upon hearing the news, I knew I wanted to put something together to honor him, something that other fans could instantly relate to. I gathered my

The award-winning Crying Partridge Billboard. Photo: Randy Fung, Lamar Advertising Company

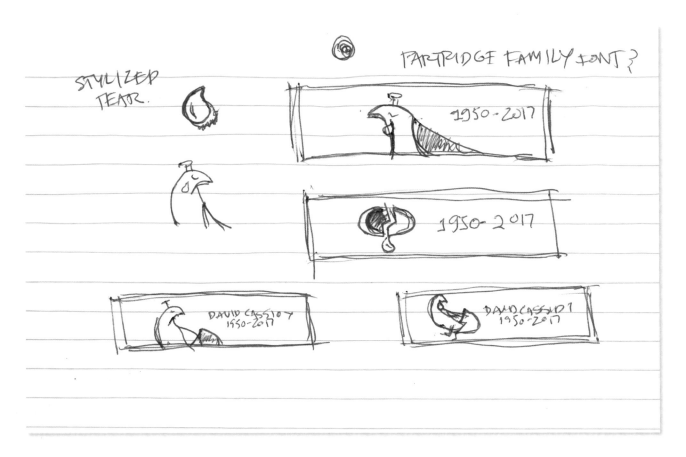

thoughts and put down a few sketches. The iconic mother partridge (from the opening sequence of the show), shedding a tear, seemed like the perfect solution. My initial sketches included his name, but I realized it wasn't really necessary.

I sent it off to my corporate boss and she loved the idea, asking for the digital file to share. It went up the following day nationwide while it was still relevant.

Growing up with the TV show, I've always associated David with Keith Partridge. I knew he was an actual musician and a teen heartthrob with many female fans. What I didn't realise at the time was just how many fans he actually had. Soon after the tribute went up, saddened fans started sharing photos of the boards across social media. One image, posted by Shaun Cassidy, David's half-brother, garnered nearly 2,000 shares and over 10,000 reactions. Based on many of the comments, it was apparent that a good portion of David's fans followed him primarily as a musician, not as Keith Partridge. It was quite a revelation.

I have always loved art. My background is in graphic design and advertising, with degrees in both. Working in the outdoor advertising industry for most of my career has given me the opportunity to utilize both skillsets. In my spare time I also design gig posters for bands I like.

Winning a Bronze OBIE Award for my David Cassidy tribute was a dream come true. The OBIE Awards represent the pinnacle of creative excellence in my industry and I've always wanted to win one. To bring one home, especially for a design that had personal meaning, made it even more special.

The design clearly resonated with many people and summed up what they were feeling in the aftershock of David's death. Seeing the numbers of people commenting on social media, and how devastated they were, I realised just how much he meant to his fans.

David obviously touched a lot of people. It means a great deal to me knowing how much my design clearly touched them as well.

Original sketches by Randy Fung. Photo: Randy Fung, Lamar Advertising Company

MARY POMARICO – UNITED STATES

David Cassidy was so cool, I was a fan from the time *The Partridge Family* started when I was nine years old. I thought driving around in a bus playing music was totally cool. My family had six children. When I was seven years old, my dad bought an old city bus and converted it into a camper and we traveled around the country – of course music was always playing – back then it was an 8-track player. We listened to *The Partridge Family* songs as well as the other artists of the day. I just loved David and thought he'd be the best older brother, willing to trade mine in for him!

I never got to see David when I was a child, it wasn't until I was a grown woman. My first concert of David's was in Hershey Park, PA – this was his first comeback show in September, 1991. Interestingly enough, I was pregnant with my son, Joseph, at the time and during the show, I felt him kick for the first time – making the event even more special.

My husband was lucky enough to see David back at the height of his career in the 1970s. During the *Blood Brothers* shows on Broadway, we attended many. I was pregnant with our daughter,

Above: David engages with Joseph Pomarico at Sam Goody's in 1992, and below, Mary Pomarico catches up with David

Jennifer then. So, there's a feeling of David being part of the fabric of our family. When our son was six months old in 1992, we met David at Sam Goody's in NYC while he was doing an In Store for the *Didn't You Used to Be* CD. We were first in line, David fell in love with Joseph and had a ball with him at his table. We actually held up the line a little bit when David spent so much time playing and posing with him.

We attended many of David's shows in his later years, including many at BB Kings. I find it emotional to think about now and going through my photos of all the concerts, I have to keep stopping and wiping tears from my eyes. David was an amazing performer and I think women just saw him as a sex symbol, but he's so much more than that. I'm not saying I wasn't always in love with him......I was, he's gorgeous. But I also loved his guitar playing and his great voice, the different styles, the blues, the rock, the pop. I will miss seeing him.

As I reflect back, I realize we went to his first "Come Back" show and now we were watching his last show and as he sang his last song of his last concert, *I Think I Love You*, I thought how sad it will be knowing there isn't another show on the horizon. I never thought it would be due to his passing.

My wish after that last concert at BB Kings was that he finds happiness. I just hope he is happy and playing his guitar now up in Heaven and is finally at peace. For someone that gave so much happiness to the world, he deserved to be happy.

KAITY FLOYD
– UNITED STATES

Ever since I was young, I was obsessed with the 70s. Everything from the fashion, to the music, to the television. I always believed that I was raised in the wrong generation because I was born in 1993 yet had such a love for past generations. While kids my age were watching current TV, I was exposed to classic television, because it's what my grandmother would record on tape and send to me. She introduced me to shows like *I Love Lucy*, *The Brady Bunch*, *Gilligan's Island*, *The Partridge Family*, etc. I had an appreciation for the classics pretty early on.

When I saw *The Partridge Family* for the first time, I loved it. I absolutely loved the musical numbers and hearing David sing on the show. The tone of his voice is so recognizable and beautiful, and he had so much charisma. It also didn't hurt that he was incredibly handsome.

Music has been a passion of mine from a young age, and David quickly became an inspiration to me. While my friends were listening to more current music, I was hooked on songs like *Could It Be Forever* and *Daydreamer*. Those are two of my favorite songs to this day. I had shirts with David's face on them and even a birthday cake one year, so you could say that I was a pretty big fan. Sadly because of my age, I rarely come across someone of my generation who shares the love of David and his music like I do, but thanks to the internet, I can connect with fans all around the world who "get it" when it comes to why I think that David is so special.

Like many of his fans, I would play David's songs on a sad day to make me feel better during whatever I was going through. I just can't help but smile when I hear his voice. I would even learn the guitar parts to his songs and sing along to them in my room as I played my guitar.

I've written songs of my own about him and the impact he had on so many people, and plan to record and release them one day. It had always been a dream of mine to sing with David and thank him for all the joy that he brought to me and so many others.

When I heard of his passing I was devastated. It just didn't seem real. I never had the opportunity to hear him sing live or play him my songs. My mom and I would talk about going to his concerts some day and how we'd both sing along to *Daydreamer*, which was a favorite song we shared.

David was loved by so many, and even though the world lost a great musician, his legacy will live on and we will continue to smile when we hear his songs.

Let me close with a line from a song I wrote:

Could it be forever? I think so,
by the way you look at me.
The sparkle in your eyes and the
way you sing Rock me Baby.
You're smile alone can make my day,
that's all you have to do.
People come and people go
but I'll always cherish you.

1973–2008

So excited, so surreal – can't believe it's really me….

14 years old and on my way to Wembley

About to see David Cassidy live on stage

Whose face has adorned every teen magazine page

Soon he appears, there is hysteria and tears

And before we know it the end of the show nears

So many young girls who would never forget

Their first concert and their dreams had been met

But dreams fade….And we all got older

Treasured memories were consigned to the folder

Work, marriage and children took over our lives

We were far too busy being mothers and wives

But with a chance hearing one of his songs on the radio….

We were 14 and young again….where did all those years go?

Now in 2008 we're on our best behaviour and no more screaming

We can go to his concerts and actually hear him sing

For us no more young love, no more tension

It won't be long before we are drawing our pension!

But then….what's this?…An invite?….

A day out with David Cassidy on the Isle of Wight!

That's it, I'm off and booked on the ferry across the sea

….So excited, so surreal – can't believe it's really me.

By Liz Tiley – United Kingdom

SHARRON LIDDLE – UNITED KINGDOM

My story begins like a lot of other young girls at age 11, at a time of unrest and unhappiness in my home. My father left when I was 7 years old and it was only at around 10 to 11 years of age that I started asking why and when was my father coming back home? I never got any answers to my questions and I would make believe stories about my father working abroad and having an important secret job, too embarrassed to tell my friends at school the truth that I had no father at home at all.

The sanctuary of my bedroom and the discovery of David Cassidy was all that made me happy. I'd collect every poster and my bedroom walls had not a single inch of wallpaper spare without David's face lovingly watching me. Even the ceiling was covered in a full-length poster where I'd lie on my bed and stare up at him, and him asking me to marry him.

The very day David got married to Kay Lenz, I was in school and heard it on the radio in my lunch break. I flew to the girls' toilets, cried and locked the door, vowing never to come out ever again until I got a sign that David had changed his mind and wanted to marry me. I spent several hours later in the headmaster's office.

I have been dedicated always to David throughout my life, now happily married travelling to London and wherever I could to see David when he came to the UK.

In 2017 I turned 55, it was November 21. I was rushed into hospital the day before with a retina detachment, surgery followed and I was lying in recovery in hospital when I saw it on my phone.....the thing I was dreading wasn't possible, couldn't be possible, David Cassidy was dead! I cried and it hurt my eye underneath the bandages. I was alone in my grief and no one understood my loneliness and pain, even my husband whom I love deeply, didn't understand and I didn't want him to. It was my David and I didn't want to share him. I'd listen to David's songs on my headphones and cry silently no longer feeling alone.

The love of my life. I honour him and will always be grateful to him for keeping me company when I felt alone, for making me feel happy in times of sadness and showing me the way to spread his love and light forever.

TONY DIGNAM – UNITED KINGDOM

When David Cassidy passed away in 2017 it was a sad loss for the world and, moved by his untimely demise, I felt it was all the more poignant on a personal level because I only came to appreciate his great talent when I reached the age of 32. Discovering the magic of David Cassidy's music was like digging up a buried chest of rare treasure.

In the seventies I had seen odd glimpses of the show, but I admit I wasn't overly interested. An old friend of mine, Dave, asked me one day if I wanted to view some vintage episodes of *The Partridge Family*, attempting to convince me that David Cassidy's talent transcended his pretty boy looks. I was a little dubious as I had always been dismissive of all pop music. Unlike Dave, who had the Cassidy haircut and a teenage sister who devoutly decorated her bedroom wall with large posters of David Cassidy, I was probably the most unfashionable teen on the block. The only single I ever purchased was Frank Sinatra's *My Way*.

I would have had to be living on the moon not to have noticed that David Cassidy was a big part of the music scene at that time and yes, I wished the girls at school would have fancied me as much as they drooled over his boyish fashionably long-haired pin-up looks. For a male to admit to enjoying a Cassidy record would have probably been an invitation to be beaten up. I certainly knew the name and face but that is where my interest ended.

"This will remind you of the old days", Dave reassured me as he placed *The Partridge Family* video into the player. I wasn't convinced. Within a few minutes all my old misgivings were blown away. I was hooked! Seeing the multi-coloured Partridge Family bus as the titles rolled to the theme tune of *Come On Get Happy* a new door suddenly opened to a world of colour, fun, music and bygone fashions. Most of all though the show ended with a great song, *Summer Days* belted out by David Cassidy. I became a fan instantly.

Bursting into my life like a moment of revelation his music and voice took me into a world of brilliant melodies and well-crafted lyrics that I could relate to and in some ways reflected my own life. What's more he seemed to do all this with an aura of charm and friendliness. This was the music and artist that impacted me in a life-changing way. I had finally said goodbye to the square teen who dismissed pop music!

It may have been a long time since my fateful visit to Dave's house but to this day my appreciation of David Cassidy's talent has not faded. He was the epitome of how good 70s music could be. The Gods had given him the gift of an extraordinary singing voice, but they had also given him the ability to express the universal experiences of happiness and sadness in a way that touches the hearts of those listening to his songs.

Nevertheless, to limit David Cassidy to love songs would wrongly overlook his versatility as he could perform raw rock songs like *Rock Me Baby* and was no stranger to trying his hand at writing his own compositions, producing a great song *Ricky's Tune* which made the B side to his number one hit *How Can I Be Sure*. Any of today's singer songwriters would do well to write a song as good.

In the mid-90s at Sheffield City Hall and later in 2005 at Sheffield Arena, I was thrilled to see David on stage. I was awestruck! The irony was that I would never have attended a pop or rock concert in my uncool teens but this time I was there acting like an older person who was a teenager at heart, enjoying something I had missed the first time around.

I count my blessings to have seen David Cassidy before his premature death. The legacy of Cassidy's music has a timeless appeal that resonates with the post-war generation of baby boomers who were brought up with *The Partridge Family*. His voice

was the voice that summed up the heartbreak and joys of those who grew into adults listening to his songs. I am happy to say I am a baby boomer, but I am sure that people in the 21st century will continue to enjoy David Cassidy's records. The 70s album *Cherish* is one of my prized LP's. The personality and talent of David Cassidy has never ceased to hold me in its fascinating spell.

Even though I never met him in person, his vulnerability and openness are perhaps what makes him and his music so appealing and such an influence on my life and yet I could imagine him as the sort of warm person you would buy a drink for in a local pub, as if chatting to a good mate.

In essence these were the qualities that had drawn me to the music, talent and persona of David Cassidy forging a connection that has lasted over many years. There is no doubt I owe a debt to the late great David Cassidy. He opened my door to an exciting new world of popular music and paved the way for me to attend many gigs and concerts. Hence he had a positive life-changing impact on my life with his music. I am no longer the dull untrendy person of my teens for I am now the older person getting nearer to senior years than I care to admit who dances unashamedly at rock venues and concerts.

I give thanks for the songs and talent of David Cassidy and despite the fact I left it a bit late, I can only say, "Better late than never!"

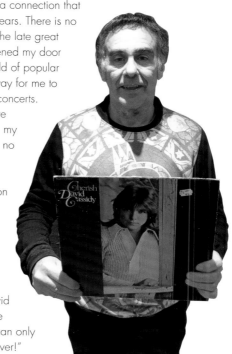

You rocked my little world
1970 I was just 11.
Didn't have to seek you out love,
You crashed into my mind –
The biggest wave upon my shore!

My first love so pure –
So pure, innocent and strong.
Never getting enough,
Always wanting more.
David how could you have known
When you sang those words to us?
I'll sing them back to you my love,
My love, there is no cure for.

The Summer Days of '74
I remember perfectly.
So excited to see you on tour
In London's White City.
The heat, the crush – anticipation
Were almost too much to bear,
But David when you came on stage
We were all walking on air.

Your concerts and your stage shows,
I wanted so much more.
Blood Brothers and *Time*
Thrilled me to the core.

When I finally got to Vegas on hol,
Your shows had sadly ended.
I stayed in the MGM-Grand
To be close to the path you wended.
Determined to find the house you were living in,
Fate dealt me a lucky hand.
I asked all of the cabbies if they knew where you lived,
Across the Las Vegas land.
For the 1st 2 days they all said no,

Then on day 3 my luck was in.
A cabbie said yes he'd given you rides,
And agreed to take us to where you were living.
We went to your house the very next day,
And quickly took some pics.
My young daughter pressed the buzzer on your gate,
Thinking we had come to see you.
Mortified we jumped back in the cab,
Even though I was desperate to meet you.

That familiar face we know so well,
So hauntingly, stunningly beautiful.
Even now when I see it – it grabs my heart.
And so it forever will.

That dreadful day we lost you,
I was meant to be in court.
The horrid, horrid D word,
My tears I couldn't halt.
My best friend Frankie,
Her liver failed – big C.
We lost her on your birthday.
What a strange symmetry!

Today as I wrote these heartfelt words
To you, from me,
Your ashes, were scattered.
What a strange symmetry!

From your Brown Eyes,
I'll never know if you think they are beautiful,
You never saw them.
I can only surmise.

I never touched you once,
Or kissed you once,
But David yes – it is forever.

By Julie Anscombe – Surrey, United Kingdom

Photo: Barry Plummer

DR HALEY GIENOW-MCCONNELL – CANADA

At the age of 14 my life was saved. The cause of my salvation? Officially, recovering from anorexia nervosa. Unofficially, David Cassidy Fever. It was the year 2000, and for this gal, Cassidy Fever was still virulent, some 30 years after its first strains were detected.

At the age of 12, I had begun flirting with an eating disorder, which by the age of 13 had devolved into full-blown anorexia nervosa. By 14, I was so ill and consumed by the disease that I felt poised on the precipice between life and death. Nothing mattered to me as much as my disease, and nothing commanded my attention as much as starving myself. That is, until I discovered David Cassidy.

For reasons that remain elusive to me, in Cassidy I found an outlet to redirect my previous preoccupation with food, and he proved to be a worthy investment of my time. I was surprised to find in Cassidy a level of gravitas that resonated with me.

The irony of Cassidy being irked that his identity was once conflated with Keith Partridge's is that, in retrospect, Cassidy probably would have relished living a life as charmed as Keith's. In his imperfections, and subsequent resilience, I found considerable peace and comfort.

When I discovered Cassidy in the early 2000s, he was experiencing something of a personal and professional high. As a young girl going through the worst period in my life so far, seeing the arc of Cassidy's narrative from international superstar to fallen idol to personally and professionally fulfilled entertainer was significant for me. If my idol could know intimately the depths of despair and come back stronger than ever, maybe I could too. It was with Cassidy posters adorning

> ## " IF MY IDOL COULD KNOW INTIMATELY THE DEPTHS OF DESPAIR AND COME BACK STRONGER THAN EVER, MAYBE I COULD TOO "

my wall, and his 1972 album *Cherish* on my stereo that I began my slow but steady climb from the abyss of anorexia back to health.

Let me be perfectly clear: I am well aware that pop-rock idols do not cure eating disorders. Nor do they liberate oppressed people, eliminate the national debt, or even necessarily create great art. Whatever their caliber, pop-rock idols do entertain us and bring us joy, and that is considerable.

Through joy, pop idols provide a safe outlet for fans, many of them very young, to channel and explore a range of other feelings, such as love, longing, desperation, hope, frustration, passion, self-consciousness, loyalty, mania, maturation, and a host of other feelings for which there are no labels. Pop idols afford a sense of belonging for like-minded fans, in Cassidy's case millions of them.

Today, I am a grown woman whose passion for Cassidy has been replaced by my passion for my work as a historian and disability rights advocate and ally. And the solace I once found in Cassidy's music I now find in my husband and young daughter. I am pleased to report that in the 18 years since fate intervened in the form of a green-eyed, shag-haired guardian angel, I have been free from anorexia.

As someone who long admired Cassidy, my fear is that his legacy will be reduced to that of merely Keith Partridge, a troubled idol. To me, to countless fans, and to his friends and family, he was so much more.

Cassidy may have been known as a darling of the pop scene, but his personal musical affinities tended towards rock and blues. If you had the pleasure of watching Cassidy perform achingly vulnerable and fresh interpretations of Beatles and B.B. King hits live as I did, you'd know this.

One of the great ironies of the coverage of Cassidy's career since his passing has been the attempt to undermine it with a jaded analysis of the pop-industrial-complex. There is no denying that said complex undermined Cassidy's artistic talent, which was considerably greater than the material he was offered as a Partridge and after. The irony resides in the fact that this story is decades old — almost as old as Cassidy's career itself — and Cassidy was the first to tell it.

Cassidy spent a lifetime trying to correct shallow impressions of him, impressions that formed early in his career, and which apparently outlived him, as the rather reductive post-mortem tributes to Cassidy are a testament.

And though he may have turned out to be my guardian angel, neither was he a saint. He had personal demons and shortcomings, and he'd be the first to admit that.

Do I think David Cassidy ought to be lionized as one of the great figures in our cultural pantheon? I'm just objective enough to say no. But do I think he deserves more than the headline "Former Teen Idol Dies at 67"? I do.

He led a fascinating life, made an indelible impression on the pop world, and mattered to people. A whole lot of people. And their numbers are no less because most of his admirers discovered him when they were very young. The significance of their adulation should not be discounted because most of his admirers were female. Perhaps the greatest crime in being dismissive of teen idols is not that it diminishes the idols themselves, but that it diminishes the audiences who idolize them.

I didn't know David Cassidy personally, though I did have the pleasure of meeting him on several occasions.

The first time I met him was thanks to a letter I gave to his tour manager before a concert I attended in 2002. In the letter, I expressed my admiration and gratitude for the effect Cassidy had on my life and the lives of countless others. After reading the letter, Cassidy invited me to meet him after the show. He proved to be every bit the kind, gracious, and charismatic man I'd always imagined him to be.

I will be forever grateful for the positive influence he had on my life. When you hear the name "David Cassidy," I won't fault you if Keith Partridge is the first thing that comes to mind. But please, I beseech you, don't let it be the last.

A longer version of this essay appeared on the website, https://nursingclio.org/ in 2017.

MY LOVE

Dedicated to David Bruce Cassidy with all my love. These lines are dedicated to that wonderful man, who is and will be the love of my life. I have loved him since I was 5 years old and he will always be alive in my mind and my heart. I will always love you my sweet angel.

My love, I come to confess the sorrows of the soul that only you know ...

My love, you who give melodies ...
Accept this sad song of all the people that we crave with the heart, the tenderness of your laughter.

You know the pain and the anguish of tears, but you did not find hands to dry your tears ...

Your being of great sweetness and love, from the sky cleans our tears to be really happy as you are now ...

My sweet angel I come to tell you how much I miss you and the reason why my soul suffers a deep sadness that is accompanied by a strange joy ...

That reason is accompanied by sublime thoughts that spring from the heart, directing the gaze to the sky covered with stars, asking why you are no longer here ...

Honey, you who gave so much love, it was so hard for you to find comfort in this empty world full of nonsense. I ask the stars to give you back the joy that your presence gave to the earthly souls that only caused you pain.

The stars that now cling to you will never allow your happy soul to return to a hostile world ...

For that, my love, my pain becomes an immense joy to know that you are happy surrounded by celestial stars and that is how it must have always been ...

I love you darling

By Mary Gill — Venezuela

66 I do have a hard time coping with the image. I know they think I'm God on that stage. I know it's there and I have to deal with it. I was fortunate too – I burst onto the scene without ever having to play a club. One three-million selling record and I went out and played a 6,000 seat sell-out hall. I just walked on stage and…BANG! In a lot of ways I haven't had to pay my dues 99

Disc, March 1973

David still

DAVID SPEAKING IN 1975 ABOUT HIS ALBUM,
THE HIGHER THEY CLIMB, THE HARDER THEY FALL:

66 Autobiographical in a kind of humorous, sad, bizarre, pathetic way. It was like a therapy album for me, spitting it all out – this is what it was like – wasn't it dumb, wasn't it sad, wasn't it all of that. When I put my name on the new recording contract, I really meant it when I signed next to the space that said Artist. That's what I want to be now. I think I've always been someone who's moved people. They've either loved me or hated me. There's always been a reaction.

When I was analysing myself I knew I could go on playing music in my own living room if I wanted to, but I knew I wanted to reach people. Before, what I was doing was mass misrepresentation of me that I needed to emerge. Mr. Good, Bad or Indifferent, I had to be able to do that. That's what this album is, me emerging on whatever level. It's a first step. A lot of people are saying it's just an image change, but I'm not. I suppose in the final analysis I am, but at long last it's me, and not me being contrived 99

Record Mirror, June 1975

Photo: @RichardImageArtPhotography

BRIGITTE DESRANLEAU – CANADA

When stars go out on earth to reignite in the sky, it always moves something inside us. It puts us in the face of our own finality. As long as our idols are alive, the past, the present, the future, everything is intertwined. Because the past, as long as one is alive, is not a thing of the past. It's part of our present. It's in us.

Then a figure, to which were attached many memories, dies, and all these memories become of the past. They are no longer in color. They become black and white. They are part of a folder. From a complete file. From a classified file.

We mourn our missing idols, but we also cry for a part of us that has just fallen. As the leaves fall from the tree. Because they have done their time. Others will come, but they will not be the same as those of that summer. Those who were in the tree when one hugged below. There are idols that are leaves. And others that are trees.

And when the tree falls, it hurts even more. Because the view is no longer the same. Forever.

There are people who are surprised that when an artist dies, his music, his films, his books take the lead. Nothing more normal. We want to convince ourselves that we are always alive. So, we rush to his works. We listen to his songs to find the emotion they gave birth in us. We want to make sure that emotion is still alive. It is. But there is like a tear hanging after.

Whenever frenzy and posthumous homage breaks out, we find it unfortunate that the principal concerned is not there to see that. He would have been able to appreciate the value of his life. The weight of his soul in our heart. True. But it's impossible. Because gigantic impulses of love can only be triggered by extreme pain. David's passing is a huge loss, a huge hole in our hearts.

66 I never thought about how I want to be remembered. If I gave some thought to it, it would just be as someone who was a really caring, loving human being, a good father and somebody who tried to make the world a little bit brighter, make the world a little bit kinder 99

David speaking in 2015

THE PICTURE

Whenever I have a problem
I rush to my room.
There I find you waiting
To take away my gloom.

I tell you why I'm crying
What is on my mind.
You never think I'm silly
You're much too sweet and kind.

Your eyes seem to listen
In such a gentle way.
As they look right at me
The problems fade away.

Your sweet smile reassures me
As though you've always known.
I'm just a lonely girl
Who feels so all alone.

Though it's just your picture
I'm telling my problems to.
I want to thank you David
For all the good you do.

I know what your picture tells me
Is what you'd really say.
That is why I love you
In a very special way.

By Ruth Poulding
New Zealand, 12/4/73

★ ★ ★

THANKS AND ACKNOWLEDGEMENTS

A number of people provided assistance and encouragement to me in the process of compiling this book and I would like to express my love and gratitude.

Alison Haines, my fellow road warrior and one of the most capable people I know. Thank you for joining me on this journey, for your continued encouragement and the endless lunches we shared at the award-winning Trigger Pond in Bucknell. We knew this was the perfect place to brainstorm ideas when the sign above the entrance was engraved with the title of one of David's finest albums, *Home Is Where The Heart Is*.

Hilary Cook, my best friend since our schooldays. We grew up together sharing a beautiful friendship which has lasted 50 years. You encouraged me to write a book when we were teenagers pouring over our favourite magazines, listening to pop music in poster-decorated bedrooms, sharing dreams and ambitions. You have been urging me for years. I finally got around to it.

To David's friends and colleagues who worked with him in various roles over the years, and everyone who admired him for all he achieved. Thank you for loving him, your heartfelt tributes and generous time with me.

An enormous thanks to the photographers who kindly searched through their archives, thank you for sharing your portfolio of stunning photographs, many of which are unseen and never before published.

Deep gratitude to everyone who shared their personal memories with such emotional honesty, I truly thank you. You have welcomed me into your homes and hearts sharing many personal memories of your families and friends, revealing the role David Cassidy always had in your lives as your idol and, often as a saviour. We have laughed and cried together. This is a compilation of your beautiful memories, a celebration of David's life through your experiences, in your words. I know for many through our private conversations, that being able to relive happy times, talk about them or write down your innermost feelings, has helped with the grieving process around David's passing.

Thank you to Jim Salamanis and Lizbeth McAnary Pierce for opening your vast personal collections to me and acting as research assistants. I truly treasure our friendships, brought together through our shared passion for David and his music.

Special thanks to my dear friends and former newspaper colleagues, Mark Davison and Christine Malthouse, for your proofreading of the manuscript. It was just like the old days back in the newsroom.

A huge thank you to Ian Strathcarron at Unicorn Publishing Group for believing in me and producing this book. I would like to thank all of his team especially Ryan Gearing for your expertise and support; Simon Perks, Lucy Duckworth, Louise Campbell, Lauren Tanner and Felicity Price-Smith for your energy and enthusiasm. A special thanks to Joelle Wheelwright – you took my rough design ideas and sprinkled magic over them.

My deepest love and thanks to my husband, Mark, who means the world to me. I could never have done this without you.

ABOUT THE AUTHOR

Louise Poynton was brought up in Sussex. At the age of 19 she became the first woman to win a nationwide contest for young reporters: the prestigious Sir William Lyons Award, run by the Guild of Motoring Writers. She went on to work on several local, regional and daily newspapers as a news reporter and has more than 40 years' experience with the written word, holding every senior position up to Assistant Editor. For more than 20 years she was a Sports Editor on regional newspapers and has been freelance since 2012. Her work has appeared in lifestyle magazines and national newspapers. Louise has been a David Cassidy fan since 1971.

Louise may be contacted via her website at www.louisepoynton.com

PICTURE CREDITS

I am grateful to the following for their help and assistance to reproduce their photographs in this book.

Iconic Images, Getty Images, Henry Diltz, Richard Sacks @RichardImageArtPhotography, Barry Plummer https://barryplummerphotos.wixsite.com/rock-music-photos, Scott Hicks and special thanks to Master Printer David Hobbs of Atkins Photo Lab in Adelaide; Roger Morton, David Hamilton, Jerry London, Darrell Lloyd, Kirsten Levisen-Lloyd, Gary Stockdale, Mat Gurman, Jim Salamanis, Lizbeth McAnary Pierce.

Original prints from Scott Hicks can be purchased through Hill Smith Gallery via their website www.hillsmithgallery.com.au

Back cover photo courtesy of: ABC Photo Archives/ABC via Getty Images

Special thanks to everyone who contributed images from their personal collection for inclusion.

Page 248: Photos courtesy of Mirrorpix/Getty Images, Richard Sacks, Lizbeth McAnary Pierce.

WE"LL
SEE YOU
IN OUR
DREAMS